Paul E. Griffiths

What Emotions Really Are

The Problem of Psychological Categories

THE UNIVERSITY OF CHICAGO PRESS

Chicago and London

The University of Chicago Press, Chicago 60637
The University of Chicago Press, Ltd., London
© 1997 by The University of Chicago
All rights reserved. Published 1997
Paperback edition 1998
Printed in the United States of America
06 05 04 03 02 01 00 99 98   2 3 4 5
ISBN 0–226–30871–5 (cloth)
ISBN 0–226–30872–3 (paperback)

Library of Congress Cataloging-in-Publication Data

Griffiths, Paul E.
    What emotions really are : the problem of psychological categories
/ Paul E. Griffiths.
        p.   cm. — (Science and its conceptual foundations)
    Includes bibliographical references and index.
    ISBN 0-226-30871-5 (cloth : alk. paper).
    1. Emotions.   I. Title.   II. Series.
BF511.G75   1997
128'.37—dc21   96-48993
                                                              CIP

∞ The paper used in this publication meets the minimum requirements of the American National Standard for Information Sciences—Permanence of Paper for Printed Library Materials, ANSI Z39.48-1992.

To Hilary

He who admits on general grounds that the structure and habits of all animals have been gradually evolved, will look at the whole subject of Expression in a new and interesting light.

CHARLES DARWIN, *The Expression of the Emotions in Man and Animals* (1872).

Contents

Acknowledgments

I began writing about emotion as a graduate student at the Research School of Social Sciences, Australian National University. I owe a debt to all the staff and students in the department of philosophy, but especially to Kim Sterelny, to whom I owe my conception of philosophy. The present book took shape during a graduate course I taught at the University of Maryland at College Park in 1992. It was substantially reworked during a semester as a visiting scholar at Northwestern University in 1994. Both of these departments provided a stimulating environment for an academic visitor. So many individuals have contributed to the project in seminars and informal discussions over the years that I could not list them all even if I could be sure of recalling them! I would, however, like to offer particular thanks to Elliott Sober for a series of discussions of the first draft, to Bill Lycan for continuing encouragement of this project over many years, and to Alan Musgrave for the supportive research environment in the world's southernmost department of philosophy. Most of all, David Hull, Susan Abrams, and the manuscript readers for the University of Chicago Press have helped me to write a far better book than I could ever have written alone.

1

Introduction

1.1 Emotions as Psychological Kinds

The aim of this book is to bring to the philosophy of emotion the insights of the last thirty years in the philosophy of mind and philosophy of language—insights that have been studiously ignored by specialists in the field. Emotions are postulated kinds of psychological event. The term "emotion" and the names of individual emotions are kind terms that figure in our everyday understanding of ourselves. This everyday understanding is commonly called "folk psychology." This simple fact implies a great deal about the theory of emotion. It implies that questions about the nature of emotions cannot be answered in the armchair alone but must be sought in part by empirical investigation of emotional phenomena. We can no more investigate the nature of emotion without the life sciences than we can investigate the nature of the planets without the physical sciences. But while the relevance of scientific data has been accepted in the rest of the philosophy of mind, emotion theory has remained deep in the armchair and has used science only as a source of anecdote.

The fact that emotions are putative kinds of psychological state also draws attention to what should be a central question for the philosophy of emotion. Does our best current science have any role for these postulated psychological kinds? If it does not, then there is an important sense in which the emotions do not really exist. This does not mean that nothing is going on in people who are said to be experiencing emotion. It means that the emotion category does nothing to illuminate what is going on in those people. The category of superlunary objects, or objects outside the orbit of the moon, had an important role in Aristotelian science. There really are objects outside the orbit of the moon, but the category of the "superlunary" is as arbitrary a way of grouping objects together as it is possible to devise. There is no such thing in nature as a distinction between the superlunary and the sublunary realms. The search for a theory of super-lunary objects and their characteristics was a mistake. Similarly, the idea that we need a theory of the emotions, or a theory of some specific emotion, may be a mistake. The failure of the philosophy of emotion to look to the science of emotion and ask these questions puts it seriously out of step with the rest of philosophy. The question of whether the apparatus of folk psychology is the best way to understand the mind has been a central question in the philosophy of mind for decades. It has hardly been raised in the philosophy of emotion.

For the last thirty years the philosophy of emotion has been dominated by a single program of research, albeit one that has had a number of variant forms (Griffiths 1989; Deigh 1994). At the core of this program is the belief that emotional phenomena can be dealt with by a psychology whose main theoretical entities are the beliefs and desires that feature in everyday explanations of people's actions. These theoretical entities are the "propositional attitudes" of folk psychology. I call the accounts that have issued from this program "propositional attitude theories." Propositional attitude theories are primarily concerned to combat the "feeling theory" of emotion. The feeling theory holds that emotions are introspective experiences character-ized by a quality and intensity of sensation. The identity of the emotion depends on this quality. The inherent pleasantness or unpleasantness of the quality causes people to act in ways characteristic of the emotion. The propositional attitude theorist thinks this picture pernicious as well as false. It protects emotions from rational criticism and bolsters false views in ethics and aesthetics that depend on the contrast between thought and emotion (e.g., Greenspan 1988). In recent years, however, the hostility to feeling theories has lessened and some propositional attitude theorists have attempted a compromise, allowing emotions a number of elements, one of which may be introspective sensations (Clarke 1986; Ben-Zeev, 1987).

Because propositional attitude theorists see an account in terms of feel-ings as the only other option, they often refer to their view as the "cognitive theory" of emotion. In previous work I have gone along with this (Griffiths 1989, 1990), but the label "cognitive" suggests a concern with the findings of cognitive psychology and with the study of emotions as part of human information processing and nothing could be more misleading. The mainstream philosophy of emotion has little interest in empirical research and has systematically ignored the ways in which our understanding of the mind/brain has been enriched during the last thirty years. The alternative views that I shall canvass have at least as much claim to be called "cognitive," since they derive directly from the study of human information processing. But these views find themselves at odds with most of the commonplaces of the propositional attitude program.

The opposition between propositional attitude theories and the feeling theory, and the derivative debates on the rationality and moral status of emotions, have dominated the philosophical literature. Well-known alternative approaches like the "affect program" theory discussed in chapters 3 and 4 have been largely ignored by philosophers. The publication since 1985 of articles on the social construction of emotion (e.g., Armon-Jones 1986a, 1986b) has rather broadened the debate, but even here the old concern with the dichotomy of thought and feeling has been apparent. Philosophical constructionism, rather than challenging the orthodox view, sees itself as an ally against the evils of the feeling theory. In consequence, the issues between the profoundly individualistic propositional attitude theory of emotions and a theory which stresses the place of emotion within the social system remain almost unexplored.

In this book, I reject propositional attitude theories in two ways. First, I reject them on a substantive level. I show in chapter 2 that all major variants of the program face substantial objections and that the research program as a whole has a range of standing problems on which it has made little progress. Second, and more important, I reject them methodologically. The adherents of propositional attitude theories have relied almost entirely on conceptual analysis to derive their account of emotion. I suggest that these epistemological foundations will no longer bear the weight. The use of conceptual analysis to study emotions seems to rest on the following argument. Conceptual analysis can reveal to us the conditions for the application of various emotion terms. Understanding these application conditions will allow us to frame "definitions" of these various emotions, and, by abstraction, a general definition of emotion. This approach is nicely exemplified in Wayne C. Davis's dismissal of empirical findings about fear: "Such facts are not generally known, and so could not be part of the meaning of 'fear,' which is my concern in this paper" (1988, 465–66). This sort of thinking is why so much of the existing literature consists of "definitions" of emotion concepts using necessary and sufficient conditions or prototype analyses.

But this approach to emotion presupposes a view of the semantics of kind terms. It presupposes that the meaning of kind terms is given by the rules which competent speakers use to apply those terms. We can investigate emotion by conceptual analysis because everyday beliefs about the referents of kind terms are true by definition. This is a view which has been very broadly rejected in the philosophy of language.

The initial impetus for this rejection came from the causal theories of meaning of the 1970s (Kripke 1980; Putnam 1975). These theories proposed a new kind of semantics for "natural kind terms." This is the philosopher's sense of 'natural kind' rather than the social scientist's sense. The philosopher's natural kinds are categories that correspond to real distinctions in nature, like chordata or chlorine. The social scientist's natural kinds are categories that all human societies tend to use, such as tree and bird. Causal theories claimed that the meaning of a natural kind term is in part a schema, to be filled in after further empirical investigation. The term "water" has as part of its meaning a schema such as "whatever is of the same kind as the samples of wet, potable stuff which we call 'water.' " Wetness and potability constitute a "stereotype" of water. The stereotype is used to pick out the putative natural kind, but it may turn out later that the stereotype is unrepresentative of the kind as a whole. In the case of water, it turns out that the natural kind is HOH and that the stereotype is not bad. However, causal theories also allows the possibility that our original samples do not constitute a scientifically interesting kind. If this occurs, two responses are possible. First, speakers can accept that some of the samples aren't really instances of the kind or that some things which were rejected as samples really are instances of the kind. In this case the kind term is retained with a revised extension and stereotype. For example, barnacles turned out to be crustaceans, like crabs and lobsters, although those who introduced the kind "crustacean" thought the opposite. Second, speakers can respond by deciding that the kind is not really a kind. The superlunary and "hysteroid depression" have disappeared from our ontology, although their instances remain.

If fear is a putative natural kind like water or crustacean then a causal theory would say that "fear" has as part of its meaning a schema awaiting the results of future research. Fear is "whatever is happening to people in these paradigm cases." This implies that conceptual analysis alone cannot determine the real nature or the extension of fear. Linguistic intuitions about the extension of a natural kind term may simply be mistaken (Stich 1983). All conceptual analysis will reveal is the current stereotype of fear. To insist that all and only the things that fit this stereotype are examples of the kind is simply to stand in the way of clarifying the concept. It is exactly akin to insisting that whales are fish because people called them so. Current science, rather than conceptual analysis, must be used to fill in the schematic element of the meaning of "fear." If science can find no interesting kind corresponding to all the paradigm cases of fear, then we must either reclassify some of the paradigm cases or replace fear and its companions with some more adequate categories.

Although the semantics of natural kind terms is a complex and changing field, there is broad agreement that revision of stereotype and revision of extension, sometimes to the point of elimination, are characteristic of the development of natural kind terms over time. Any adequate semantic theory of kind terms must explain these facts. This is enough to overthrow the methodology that has supported the propositional attitude approach to emotion. Analyzing the current understanding of a term does not reveal the nature of its referent, only what people believe about that referent. These beliefs, and hence the understanding of the term, can change in the light of empirical discoveries about the referent.

The causal theory of reference has become increasingly controversial in recent years, particularly because of its association with a strong form of metaphysical realism. Another area of controversy has been the category of natural kinds itself. In their classic modern incarnation, natural kinds are envisaged as the objects of spatiotemporally unrestricted laws of nature (Quine 1977). They are the nodes around which theories in the fundamental sciences are structured. But in recent decades philosophers have gained more respect for the biological and social sciences. Projects for the reduction of special sciences to more "fundamental" sciences have been abandoned, and the "unity of science" has dwindled to a minimal commitment to a single reality studied in many different theoretical frameworks. This has led to what Richard Boyd has called "the enthusiasm for natural kinds" (Boyd 1991). Categories from any special science that enter into the generalizations of that science are now commonly regarded as natural kinds.

Inflation, schizophrenia, and allopatric speciation events take their place alongside electrons and stars. In this more liberal perspective, natural kinds are not the most fundamental categories of nature, to be contrasted with categories which are useful but superficial. Instead they are nonarbitrary categories, to be contrasted with arbitrary, nominalistic schemes of classification. They are ways of classifying the world that correspond to some structure inherent in the subject matter being classified. The "naturalness" of such schemes of classification is not undermined by the fact that there are many of them.

In part two of the book I draw on recent work in cognitive psychology to construct a semantics of kind terms which takes account of these developments. Children do not create concepts simply by grouping particulars on the basis of overall similarity. Instead, they create causal explanatory theories of particular domains and cluster instances according to their possession of theoretically significant properties in these schemes of explanation (Keil 1989). In childhood these theories are relatively simple and are similar across many cultures. In later development, however, theories become more complex and diverge between cultures and individuals. A key finding of these studies is that children make periodic intellectual breakthroughs in which they form new beliefs about how categories in a particular domain are to be explained. In response to these breakthroughs they revise both the extension (range of application) and intension (associated descriptions) of each concept in order to bring extension and intension into line with their new beliefs. These findings suggest that concepts have something like the schematic structure ascribed to them by causal theorists. Concepts presume that there is some reason why properties are clustered in similarity space. This presupposition underlies people's everyday inductive practices. It is assumed that the property correlations marked by concepts will hold up in future instances. In children, the extension and intension of concepts are refined as the child becomes acquainted with its culture's best explanation of why those concepts are useful in explanation and induction. This psychology of concepts informs the account of natural kinds and theoretical categories in the life sciences which I develop in part two of the book. I argue that the phenomenon of conceptual change due to scientific discovery is a continuation of this pattern of human conceptual development. The theory of natural kinds finds its real home as part of the psychology of concepts and can be made independent of issues concerning metaphysical realism.

The implications of the "theory view of concepts" for the practice of conceptual analysis are similar to those of the older, causal theories of meaning. The theory view implies that conceptual analysis can reveal only a community's current beliefs about the referent of a concept. Concepts are answerable to future findings about the referent, as well as to the way that referent is currently understood. Analysis can reveal the epistemic project in which a community is engaged with a concept, but the way that project develops will depend on what the community finds out through empirical investigation. If philosophers want to know about emotion, rather than about what is currently believed of emotion, analysis must proceed hand in hand with the relevant empirical sciences.

There is one ray of hope for someone hostile to the assimilation of psychological discourse to scientific discourse. This is the view, forcefully argued by Ian Hacking (1991a,b, 1995), that in everyday life concepts are not used exclusively for explanation or induction. They are used to structure social systems, to further the interests of individuals or groups, and to promote programs of political action. This suggests that the way in which the world is conceptualized by ordinary speakers will not simply conform itself to the most powerful explanatory and predictive taxonomy suggested by current science. These views form an important addition to the theory view of concepts, and one that I try to take account of when considering the implications of the science of emotion. They do not, however, provide any grounds for a complacent return to the traditional practice of conceptual analysis. A delicate analysis of the concept of child abuse in 1970 would not have explained why the concept had changed in the last decade and could not have predicted how it would change in the next (Hacking 1991c). The social and political context in which this concept was enmeshed could not be reconstructed from the concept itself. In approaching this sort of politically and socially involved concept, traditional analysis can only be part of a wider historical and sociological investigation.

1.2 Current Theories of Emotion

In chapter 2 I look at the origins of the propositional attitude research program and at some of the theories it has produced. The next five chapters look at the scientific literature on emotion from diverse disciplines including ethology, evolutionary theory, neuroscience, cognitive psychology, and anthropology. In chapters 3 through 5 I consider two theories of emotion based on evolutionary theory and human ethology. The first of these evolutionary approaches is the "affect program" theory associated with Paul Ekman and inspired by Darwin's work on emotion (Ekman 1972; Darwin 1872). I describe both Darwin's and Ekman's research and compare the conclusions at which they arrive concerning particular emotions. In its modern form, the affect program theory deals with a range of emotions corresponding very roughly to the occurrent instances of the English terms "surprise," "fear," "anger," "disgust," "contempt," "sadness," and "joy." The affect programs are short-term, stereotypical responses involving facial expression, autonomic nervous system arousal, and other elements. The same patterns of response occur in all cultures and homologues are found in related species. These patterns are triggered by a cognitive system which is "modular" in the sense that it does not freely exchange information with other cognitive processes. This system learns when to produce emotions by associating stimuli with broad, functional categories such as danger or loss. To do this it uses the organism's past experience and some specialized learning algorithms which depart substantially from the norms of traditional learning theory. It is not possible to do justice to Ekman's views using the common opposition between "naturalistic" and "social constructionist" views of emotion so often applied to scientific research on emotion. The "naturalist" is normally described as someone who believes that all or some emotional responses are the same in all cultures (Armon-Jones 1986b). But at the very least a distinction must be drawn between the input and output sides of emotional responses. Ekman claims that the output of the affect programs is stereotyped and pan-cultural, but he makes no such claims about the eliciting conditions of affect programs.

I interpret the affect program research in the light of several recent debates in the philosophy of biology. I argue that both Darwin and Ekman make a good case for the view that the pan-cultural facial expressions call for evolutionary explanations and show that this does not lead to the usual conclusion that emotional responses are innate. The notion of innateness is multiply ambiguous and does not form a useful framework for thinking about evolved traits (Bateson 1991; Gray 1992). I show how to tease apart the question of whether a trait has evolved from the question of how it is built in ontogeny, using the developmental systems approach pioneered by Susan Oyama (1985). I also distinguish two radically different things that are meant by calling a trait "universal." Ekman believes that many aspects of emotion are *pan-cultural*—they are found in all or most human populations. But this is a very different thesis from the claim that these aspects of emotion are part of a universal "human nature." Brown eyes are found in all or most human populations, and are a product of human evolution, but they are not part of a universal "human nature." The affect-program theory is quite consistent with the idea that human emotions are *polymorphic*—they display heritable variation within populations. Finally, I consider Darwin's and Ekman's work in the light of the debate over adaptationism. I interpret this debate as a methodological one concerning the adequate confirmation of evolutionary hypotheses. I argue that Darwin and Ekman employ adequate methodologies to guard against the charge of adaptationist "storytelling" and contrast their success in this regard with the failures of some other authors who have adopted an evolutionary perspective on emotion.

While there is considerable evidence to support the affect program theory, it is of limited application. A quite different account is needed of higher cognitive emotions such as envy, guilt, jealousy, and love. In chapter 5 I look at some current attempts to extend evolutionary thinking to these sorts of psychological states. The general framework of these attempts is the "evolutionary psychology" of Jerome H. Barkow, Leda Cosmides, and John Tooby (1992). Their program stresses the evolutionary explanation of underlying mental mechanisms. Robert Frank (1988) offers some specific proposals about emotion. He argues for the existence of various motivational states designed to facilitate social interaction and identifies these with some familiar emotions. These emotions produce apparently irrational behaviors, but Frank argues that these behaviors result from following globally rational strategies for social interaction. The general conception of an emotion in this theory is an irruptive pattern of motivation that affects the higher cognitive processes which control long-term, planned action. This vision of emotion is similar to that offered by some theorists from the propositional attitude school.

The evolutionary psychology program has many shortcomings. First, in common with much evolutionary biology, it overestimates the heuristic value of evolutionary theory. Darwinian psychologists are inclined to think that psychology can be done a priori. They do not make enough effort to test the existence of the phenomena which they set out to explain. More work in psychology is needed before the evolutionary theorists set to work.

Second, despite some serious attempts to come to terms with the complexities of development, the evolutionary psychologists do not succeed in escaping the confusions surrounding the nature-nurture debate and the distinction between "biological" and "cultural" traits. Finally, some evolutionary psychologists make a strong and in my view misguided commitment to the thesis that there is no variation among individual humans in their evolved psychological traits (the "monomorphic mind"). Nevertheless, evolutionary psychology has important insights concerning emotion and in the last part of chapter 5 I show how the program can be improved. I use a developmental systems approach to show how psychological phenotypes are constructed through the interaction of biological resources, cultural resources, and resources which are hard to classify in terms of that dichotomy. This interaction allows the psychology of emotion to diverge in different human lineages as a result of the extragenetic inheritance of cultural resources. But these diverse emotions retain patterns of resemblance which reflect their common origins. The construction of emotion from a set of heterogeneous resources, some paradigmatically "biological," some paradigmatically "cultural," and some neither, explains both the similarities and differences in human emotions across the world.

Chapter 6 outlines the popular social constructionist approach to emotion. I evaluate a number of different conceptions of "social construction." The most interesting insights of constructionism are embodied in the view that there are emotional responses whose existence depends on the existence of cultural models of normal emotional response. These responses are interpreted by the subject and their society as natural and involuntary when they are in fact produced in conformity to local cultural norms. In some cases the production of an emotional response may involve subconscious planning to conform to a cultural model. These responses are distinguished from simple pretenses by the subject's lack of conscious access to their causes. In other cases, the role of the cultural model may be more distant. Cultural norms form an environment which reinforces certain behaviors. This results in conformity to the norms without an explicit representation of conformity as a goal. While the imperialistic claims of social constructionists to explain the whole domain of emotional phenomena are unjustified, their theories are important for a number of reasons. First, the constructionists have drawn attention to the fact that the everyday "folk psychology" of emotion is not purely descriptive. It contains prescriptions of how people should behave, and collective pretenses about how people do behave. These mythical aspects of emotion cannot be smoothly integrated into a developing scientific understanding of human psychology. Common beliefs about emotion must be understood as social products rather than the simple results of introspection. The function of such beliefs is often to misrepresent rather than to illuminate underlying cognitive processes. The socially active nature of folk psychology points once again to the shortcomings of traditional philosophical work on emotion. Philosophers have only analyzed the current stereotypes of emotion concepts. Studies of the social role of a concept can reveal why a stereotype takes its current form and how it may respond to changing social conditions. I argue that many emotion concepts will be epistemically unstable. Like traditional concepts of gender, they cannot serve their social functions once those functions are publicly acknowledged. Social constructionist research can therefore contribute to a fuller understanding of the dynamics of kind concepts.

There is another reason why social constructionist research is important. Cultural models of emotion play a major role in the construction of the psychological phenotype. Social constructionist ideas can make an important contribution to the research program into the higher cognitive emotions described in chapter 5.

1.3. Homology, Analogy, and Psychological Categories

Chapter 7 outlines a general approach to kinds and kind concepts. Chapter 8 applies this approach to the life sciences. One major theme which emerges is the previously unnoticed relevance of the principles of biological classification to psychology. One aspect of the Darwinian transformation of biology has been the realization that many biological categories must be historically defined and that historically defined categories can play roles in science for which they were once thought to be unsuitable. It has become generally accepted that biological species and other taxonomic groupings of organisms are defined not in terms of their intrinsic properties, but in terms of their evolutionary origins (Ghiselin 1974; Hull 1976). Birds do not belong to the order Aves because they are feathered bipeds, but because they are all descended from a single ancestral species. Any member of a species descended from that ancestral species would be a bird, no matter what its intrinsic properties.

A similar account can be given of biological traits. Phenotypic and molecular traits can be classified by *evolutionary homology*. My arm is a vertebrate limb not because of the organization of the bones it contains, but because it is united in a pattern of ancestry and descent with all the other vertebrate limbs. A structural gene like *Hoxd-4* in a modern mouse is the same gene as one which occurs in a modern lizard not because of its similar sequence but because both are modified copies of a *Hox* gene in an ancient species ancestral to them both. The alternative to a classification by evolutionary homology is a classification by what was traditionally called *analogy* and is now often called *homoplasy*. Analogous characteristics resemble one another, but are not descended from a common ancestral form. The flight feathers of birds and the wing membranes of bats are analogous. Although many formal definitions of analogy would encompass purely accidental resemblances it is usually assumed that analogies reflect similar adaptive forces. The advantages of flight drove birds and bats in the same direction. Classifications by analogy are *functional* classifications, placing together things which serve the same evolutionary purpose. Classifications by homology and classifications by analogy are normally viewed as complementary to one another. Two complementary mechanisms explain the patterns of resemblance among living forms. The mechanism of descent acts as a general, inertial force ensuring that organisms resemble their ancestors (and hence frequently resemble their relatives). Natural selection acts in the context of this general inertial force to produce new forms. These new forms reflect the nature of the adaptive process at each place and time. Similar adaptive processes produce similar forms. These two processes create two patterns of resemblance that overlay one another.

Although biologists routinely apply these principles of classification to behavioral and neurological traits, these principles have rarely been explicitly applied in psychology. Psychologists and philosophers of psychology have become used to the idea that psychological states and mechanisms should be classified by their function—by what they do. This reflects the dominant research programs in the philosophy of mind and in artificial intelligence. These aim to model, and perhaps reproduce, human cognition by constructing information processors that can perform the same functions. Psychologists and philosophers have therefore assumed that if evolution illuminates the mind it will throw light on mental states and processes classified in terms of their function and will do so by describing the adaptive purpose for which they evolved. In the light of these presuppositions it is surprising that the most successful detailed work on the evolution of emotions—the affect program theory—classifies emotions as evolutionary homologies. The affect programs are identified with certain emotional states in primates and more broadly with emotional states in other vertebrates. The objects the theory describes, like the fear affect program, are the products of a particular sequence of evolutionary events. The research leading to the affect program theory assumes that human emotions will resemble those of animals roughly in proportion to the degree of relationship between humans and other species. Octopuses have psychological mechanisms which serve the same function as fear—avoiding dangers— but no one expects to find the fear affect program in octopuses.

The nature of the affect program research will be less surprising to biologists and philosophers of biology.[1] Systems of genealogical classification are well developed compared to any system of classification by adaptive origins. A classification by analogy of organisms or their traits presumes a highly developed science of ecology. Such an ecology would identify the adaptive forces in an environment in such a way as to allow the reidentification of the same adaptive role in different ecosystems. We do not have such a general ecological theory at our disposal. Claims about similarity of function are informal, "commonsense" observations, not the results of a well-articulated theory of adaptation. Biology's primary classifications are still classifications by homology. An ecological classification that could provide objects of study for psychology would have to meet an even more stringent demand. The traits that arise whenever the same adaptive forces are present would have to share a rich cluster of properties. The ecological theory need not be able to predict these properties, but it must predict that there is some such rich cluster of properties to be investigated. This is necessary for the kinds produced by the ecological classification to be productive objects of study. No such rich ecological classification is currently available, and some biologists are skeptical that such a classification exists. The role of historical contingency in evolution may be so great that the ecological role of a trait places only the broadest constraints on

---

1. In the philosophy of science it is the philosopher of *biology* David L. Hull who is found advocating grouping scientists by sociological descent, rather by the similarity of their ideas (Hull 1988).

what other properties it will have. This point can be expressed in terms more familiar to philosophers of psychology. It amounts to the claim that the task description of a psychological trait can be realized by many different kinds of psychological mechanism.

My most original thesis in chapters 7 and 8 is that the historical kinds that current biology offers are closer to the traditional ideal of natural kinds than is commonly supposed. Classifying biological traits by evolutionary homology creates categories that share a huge number of properties. These kinds are rich objects of study for other sciences. The success of the affect program theory is an object lesson in the scientific interest of historical categories. It is possible to discover a mass of scientific detail about homologous fear responses in vertebrates, from the behavioral sciences right through to neurochemistry. Only a few platitudes have been discovered about responses to danger in general and it is unclear how many more will be forthcoming. I suggest that psychology and other human sciences could benefit from the realization that homologies are legitimate objects of study, and that these studies may be as profitable as or more profitable than studies of functional or analogous categories.

1.4 Eliminating "Emotion"

My central conclusion is that the general concept of emotion is unlikely to be a useful concept in psychological theory. It is meant to be a kind of psychological process that underlies a certain range of human behaviors. But there is no one kind of process that underlies enough of this behavior to be identified with emotion. Emotion is like the category of "superlunary" objects in ancient astronomy. There is a well-defined category of "everything outside the orbit of the moon" but it turns out that superlunary objects do not have something specially in common that distinguishes them from other arbitrary collections of objects. In the same way, a social and historical account can be given of why various aspects of human psychology and physiology have been brought together under the single heading of "emotion." However, what we know about these phenomena suggests that there is no rich collection of generalizations about this range of phenomena that distinguishes them from other psychological phenomena. They do not constitute a single object of knowledge. Current knowledge suggests that the domain of emotion fractures into three parts.

The best understood emotional responses are the short-term, salient cases of anger, fear, disgust, sadness, joy, and surprise. The affect program approach gives a reasonable account of these states.

The social constructionist approach also gives a good account of a limited range of emotions. These emotional responses are socially sustained pretenses, akin to socially constructed illnesses like ghost possession or "the vapors." They have no more in common with other emotions than a piece of playacting has in common with the behavior it imitates. Many of these pretenses are instances of types like anger which have other, more substantial instances, but there may be emotion types all of whose instances are social pretenses.

In addition to these pretenses, social constructionist literature discusses a much larger range of emotions which are at least somewhat variable across cultures. This variation suggests that cultural factors play some role in the construction of these emotional responses in each person. But these are the very same emotions—guilt, vengefulness, moral outrage—about which evolutionary psychologists have speculated. Furthermore, while these emotions vary across cultures, they also display patterns of resemblance. As I have suggested above, the perception of conflict between these two bodies of theory is the result of an inadequate picture of psychological development. An adequate theory of the construction of the psychological phenotype will describe how a wide range of resources interact to produce the adult emotional repertoire. The developmental resources common to all human groups explain the resemblances among emotions across cultures. Those that vary explain their differentiation. The biology/culture divide plays no role in this "heterogeneous construction" of emotion. A rare allele is "biological" but may help explain some culture-specific features. Play is a "cultural" input to the development of emotion, but it almost certainly has an evolutionary history. With this sort of theoretical framework I can glean illumination from both social constructionist and evolutionary psychologist work on higher cognitive emotions. I suggest that there is at least some reason to suppose that there exists a group of irruptive motivational states that contrast in interesting ways to other forms of motivation.

The argument from these findings to the conclusion that "emotion" should be eliminated from our psychological vocabulary depends on the account of theoretical categories in the life sciences developed in part two and can be only very inadequately sketched here. There are some obvious lines of thought that lead to the opposite conclusion. It is possible to argue that the socially sustained pretense emotions are "not really emotions." The emotions that this leaves behind all have something in common. They can all be described in some sense or other as "irruptive motivational states." A person who was concerned to minimize the disruption of our existing conceptual scheme could propose that there really is a category of psychological states corresponding to "emotion." The emotions are the irruptive motivational states. I strongly reject this move for two reasons, both argued in part two. First, the purpose of categorization in the sciences is to group together things which resemble one another in many different ways because of some underlying, similarity-generating mechanism. Instances of the same chemical element resemble one another because of shared microstructure. Homologous traits resemble one another because of a common inheritance. Grouping instances in this way produces concepts useful for explanation and induction and also facilitates research into the postulated underlying causal processes. But instances of the proposed new category of irruptive motivational states are of two very different kinds. The affect program states are phylogenetically ancient, informationally encapsulated, reflexlike responses which seem to be insensitive to culture. The other emotions are aspects of higher cognition which differ across cultures due to the roles of culture in psychological development. The two kinds of emotion have different phylogenies, different adaptive functions, different neuroscience, and different roles in human psychology. The concept that groups them together has no discernible theoretical utility. The proper response to current knowledge is that there is no object of scientific knowledge which corresponds to "emotion."

Second, the nature of categorization in science is an extension of an important aspect of category formation in everyday human cognition. The idea that concepts in everyday use can be isolated from scientific advance presumes an unrealistic discontinuity between the scientific project and the projects of everyday life. Explanation and induction are goals of everyday life as well as goals of science. It is part of normal human development to modify concepts to accommodate new beliefs about the underlying nature of the referents of those concepts. The aim of this modification is to have concepts of greater epistemic utility. I do not suggest, however, that everyday thought about emotion will simply accommodate itself to the best explanatory taxonomy suggested by science. The projects in which emotion is involved include such things as excusing socially disruptive behavior and maintaining gender roles, as well as explanation and induction. Scientific claims about the nature of emotion have a social significance that will make them a focus of considerable conflict. The models of emotion that become socially prevalent will be the outcomes of this social process.

The three-way fracturing of the emotion category into socially sustained pretenses, affect program responses and higher cognitive states extends to many specific emotion categories, such as anger. Some instances of anger fall into each of these three categories. How this fracturing will show up conceptually is hard to predict. Although the concept of emotion is part of our everyday self-understanding, it is utterly vague in the same way as concepts like "spirituality." It is relatively easy to imagine it falling into disuse. Many specific emotion concepts, however, have a central role in everyday explanations of human and animal behavior. One possibility is that the current range of states will continue to be called, say, "anger" for the purposes of everyday life, but with an increasing recognition that different kinds of anger are merely homonymously the same. Within psychology, attention may focus on those instances of the category that have been most adequately explained.

I

Emotion

2

Philosophy and Emotion— The Poverty of Conceptual Analysis

2.1 The Propositional Attitude School

In its thirty-year history the propositional attitude school has produced many variants. This section describes the main thrust of the program and looks at its origins in the work of Anthony Kenny. Section 2.2 looks at the relationship between the propositional attitude theory and "cognitive" approaches to emotion in psychology. In section 2.3 I outline both a very simple propositional attitude theory and the problems that its sophisticated descendants try to solve. Remaining sections examine some of the proposed solutions and conclude with a set of deeper problems that have rarely been addressed. Even if propositional attitude accounts succeeded in their own terms, they would not explain most of what should be explained by a theory of emotion.

Propositional attitude theories are often presented as if they were a simple consequence of the idea that emotions involve the occurrence of mental states which represent states of affairs in the world (states with "content"). William Lyons introduces his "cognitive" account of emotion in this way: "In general a cognitivist theory of emotion is one that makes some aspect of thought, usually a belief, central to the concept of emotion and, at least in some cognitive theories, essential to distinguishing different emotions from one another" (1980, 33). This presentation of the propositional attitude theory makes it seem relatively uncontentious. Most theories of emotion accept that the occurrence of an emotion involves the occurrence and manipulation of mental representations. What is distinctive about the propositional attitude theory is the interpretation it gives to the words *thought* and *belief*. The mainstream philosophical tradition in which Lyons is located assumes that our everyday understanding of these notions is adequate for a theory of emotion. The second half of Lyons's definition is also important. An emotion type is distinguished from other types by the particular propositional attitude, or attitudes, which it involves. A token emotion is an instance of fear, for example, because it involves the belief that danger is present. Some more sophisticated theories allow that the occurrence of these propositional attitudes is not *sufficient* for the occurrence of emotion. But the additional factors—Lyons requires "abnormal physiological disturbance"—are general requirements for emotion. The details of these other factors are of no importance in distinguishing one emotion type from another. This strongly distinguishes the propositional attitude theory from many scientific approaches to emotion.

Propositional attitude theories are established by conceptual analysis. The early exponents of such theories were aware that people might expect a theory of emotion to be informed by empirical findings. In *Action, Emotion, and Will* (1963) Anthony Kenny devotes an entire chapter to establishing that empirical psychology can tell us nothing about emotion. His task is made somewhat easier by the number of early empirical workers who subscribed in some measure to the feeling theory of emotion. Kenny is able to catch them in various inconsistencies as they struggle to combine a belief in Cartesian private events with the experimental method. But the main thrust of Kenny's argument depends on certain alleged conceptual links between emotion, propositional attitude ascription, and rational action. According to Kenny a physiological state without a suitable intentional object, or which does not lead to appropriate intentional behavior, cannot count as an emotion. It just doesn't make sense to suppose that people can be afraid without believing they are in danger or exhibiting avoidance behavior. Whereas these links between emotion, mental contents, and rational action are conceptual and criterial, the links between emotion and physiological states are merely contingent and empirical. The contingent, empirical attributes of emotion cannot be part of a definition, because there is no contradiction in supposing an emotion to lack these features. Only the links to belief and desire are logical links and can form part of a definition. It follows for Kenny that "the investigation of [physiological] processes may well lead to results of the highest interest, but it cannot have the status of an experimental examination of the nature of the emotions" (Kenny 1963, 51).

Kenny's apriorism is important, as the rise of the propositional attitude school is in no small part the result of his work. Propositional attitude theorists think conceptual analysis is the only tool they need to investigate emotions because they accept, explicitly or implicitly, a Wittgensteinian distinction between the "criteria" which logically define a mental state and the inessential "symptoms" that can be studied empirically. Mental states are *defined* by the rules which ordinary speakers use when applying mental state terms. Thus two decades later we find Robert Solomon echoing Kenny's sentiments almost word for word: "That anger also has biological backing and includes sensation is inessential to understanding the emotion, though no doubt significant in certain measurements, which only *contingently* correlate with the intensity of the emotion or its significance" (Solomon 1984, 249; italics in original).

The seminal nature of Kenny's work can easily be overlooked because where later authors talk of propositional attitudes, Kenny talks of the "formal objects" of emotion. Kenny argues that emotions are intentional states directed onto objects of some particular class. The defining property of that class is what makes the state a particular kind of emotion. The formal object of envy, for example, is another's good and that of gratitude a good done to oneself. The equivalence of these views to propositional attitude analyses of emotion is fairly clear. Kenny himself is certainly aware of it. He cites Aristotle as saying that anger is a *desire* to avenge what is *believed* to be an insult (Kenny 1963, 193) and accepts this as equivalent to his own analysis in terms of formal objects. We can state the equivalence as follows: when an emotion has the class of A's as its formal object, one must believe or desire that something is an A if one is to have that emotion.

Applying this translation scheme to Kenny's theory yields the claim that certain propositional attitudes are necessary for certain emotions. If a person does not believe something is dangerous, then they do not have a state which has danger as its formal object. Therefore, according to Kenny, they cannot be afraid. Most propositional attitude theorists are satisfied with this claim. The propositional component is a necessary, but not a sufficient, component of the emotion. They admit that emotions may require additional elements such as physiological arousal. But a few theorists do claim that the propositional component of an emotion is sufficient. The propositional component does not need to be accompanied by any other component to make up a full-fledged emotion. Solomon's (1977) theory lends itself to such an interpretation, as does Nash's (1989) "pure" cognitive theory.

My objections to this set of foundations for philosophical research into emotion were summarized in my introductory chapter and are developed at more length in part 2. Kenny and his followers assume that a concept is entirely constituted by what is currently believed about its referent. In fact, a concept can embody an ongoing project of discovery. The referent towards which this project is directed is picked out by the use of concrete examples and by the goal of forging an epistemically useful concept, as well as by current beliefs about the referent. These other factors allow a concept to change as discoveries are made about its referent. It is not surprising that Kenny did not allow for this possibility. The philosophy of language of his day did not have the capacity to describe and explain the conceptual changes that have marked the history of science. What is surprising is that this philosophy of language should have remained unreflectively entrenched in the study of emotion while being controverted and widely rejected in the general philosophy of mind.

2.2 Links to Cognitive Psychology

The rise of the propositional attitude school was roughly contemporary with the decline of behaviorism in psychology. In the psychology of emotion, this meant a shift away from physiological approaches to emotion and towards approaches stressing the role of cognition. This shift was accompanied by the rise of "cognitive therapy" for emotional disorders. This interest in the relationship between cognition and emotion seems to have reassured propositional attitude theorists that, insofar as psychology had any relevance to their project, it supported the view that the main component of an emotion is a cluster of mental representations. Propositional attitude theorists normally cite the classic Schachter and Singer experiments (1962) in support of this view. Schachter and Singer injected subjects with adrenaline to produce physiological arousal. The subjects were subjected to a range of conditions designed to provide appropriate settings for different emotions. The subjects' reports of emotion reflected these settings. The conclusion drawn by Schachter and Singer, whose experiments are discussed at greater length in chapter 4, was that emotions are labeled on the basis of environmental cues, not the particular quality of physiological arousal which accompanies them. Propositional attitude theorists have taken this result to support their view that the identity of an emotion depends solely on the beliefs and desires that it involves.

Despite the wide citation of the Schachter and Singer result, the support for the propositional attitude view from cognitive psychology is equivocal. Mainstream cognitive psychology contains "noncognitive" as well as "cognitive" theorists. These labels are somewhat misleading. The dispute is over the type of information processing involved in the production of emotional responses, not over whether information processing takes place. The debate between the so-called cognitive and noncognitive approaches in psychology was started by R. B. Zajonc's paper "Feeling and Thinking: Preferences Need No Inferences" (1980). In the course of this debate it became clear that the central tenets of Zajonc's "cognitivist" opponents, particularly R. S. Lazarus (1982), were twofold. First, they claimed that an emotional response must be preceded by processing of information concerning the stimulus. This is relatively uncontroversial. Even a response as simple as surprise at a sudden noise requires some processing of the sensory input. The triggering of fear, rage, and so forth undoubtedly requires it too. Second, however, the cognitivist claims that this processing must be of a kind sufficiently sophisticated to be called cognition. Zajonc opposed this claim, citing a large number of empirical findings which suggest that there are very direct pathways leading from the perceptual system to responses that would usually be regarded as emotional. He argued that the intervening processes do not deserve to be regarded as cognitive.

The dispute between Zajonc and his opponents is not over the correct use of the term "cognition," although it sometimes seems that way. The substantive issue is the sort of information processing involved in the production of emotional responses. Although "cognition" is used very loosely in contemporary psychology, there are certain traditional paradigms of "cognitive" processes, such as problem solving, and certain traditional paradigms of "noncognitive" processes, such as reflexes. Zajonc claims that the triggering of emotions sometimes resembles the latter sort of processes. His opponents claim that they always resemble the former. Thus, the psychological doctrine of "cognitivism" has at its core something very similar to the propositional attitude theory in philosophy. The cognitions involved in emotion are the ones we are familiar with from our everyday explanations of people's actions in terms of their "thoughts."

Zajonc does himself and his allies a considerable disservice by allowing Lazarus to call his theory cognitive. Many psychologists have come to think of all neural activity as cognition in some sense or another. So many casual observers of the debate do not see what Zajonc can mean by denying that emotions are cognitive. A psychology professor once remarked to a student of mine that the only alternative to emotions' being cognitively mediated was that they happened by magic! Zajonc is not proposing anything quite that radical. At most he sometimes claims that the processes that trigger emotions can be adequately understood at a mechanical, neurophysiological level and thus that any computational or information processing analysis is unnecessary.

Another interesting parallel between cognitivists in psychology and propositional attitude theorists in philosophy is a tendency to use a priori arguments for their view. Lazarus is prone to stipulate that cases that don't involve his preferred form of cognition can't count as emotion: "Those who are less sanguine than I about the causal role of cognition in emotion often point to the startle response, since cognition is obviously absent or negligible in this reaction. I do not consider startle an emotion. Emotion results from an evaluative perception . . . Startle is best regarded as a primitive neural reflex process" (Lazarus 1982, 1023). This tendency to argue for "cognitivism by definition" may reflect the same linguistic intuitions that drove conceptual analysts to the propositional attitude view.

Once these definitional disputes have been put to one side the real issue in psychology is the degree to which the information processing responsible for emotional response is subserved by the same mechanisms as those which lead to longer-term, planned action. Do we react with disgust because we think something is disgusting, or are the processes that lead to this thought (and thus to voluntary action) distinct from the processes which lead to the emotional response? Among the results Zajonc cites are those of Garcia and Rusiniak (1980), who found that a disgust response to a food can be elicited in rats by giving them food while they are conscious, rendering them unconscious and inducing nausea in them while unconscious. On awakening, the rats reject the food in the same way that they reject any food whose ingestion is associated with nausea. Zajonc's point is that it seems perverse to insist that these rats exhibit the disgust response *because* they believe that the food is unhealthy. It would be more natural to say that they believe the food is unhealthy because it disgusts them. This is roughly what Zajonc means by the "primacy" of affect over cognition. In cases of affective primacy, affective responses to stimuli are not the effects of beliefs about the stimuli. The beliefs are produced in parallel with the response or even as a result of the response.

The whole idea of discussing what rats believe about the food they eat is somewhat problematic. It would be much more satisfactory to have similar data on humans. Zajonc is able to cite experiments showing that differential affective responses can be conditioned using subliminal stimuli. W. R. Wilson (1975, 1979) employed dichotic listening to present a selection of melodies to one ear of subjects while presenting a story to the other ear. By encouraging subjects to track the story against a written test he was able to reduce recognition memory of the melodies to chance levels. But despite this he obtained the well-known exposure effect for the melodies. Those that had been heard before were preferred to new melodies. This suggests that information is reaching systems involved in emotion, or at least in preference formation, without reaching those involved in paradigm "cognitive" processes such as recognition. In a follow-up study Kunst-Wilson and Zajonc (1980) presented visual stimuli for very short intervals (1 millisecond). When the stimuli were presented again along with novel stimuli, recognition was at chance level but preference was linked to previous exposure. Once again information seems to be available for affective processes that is not available to paradigm "cognitive" processes.

The phenomena of affective primacy are a matter of concern to the propositional attitude theorist in philosophy as well as to the cognitivist psychologist. Zajonc's data suggest that people can have an emotional response to something they have no thoughts about in the everyday sense of "thoughts." The data suggest the need to postulate information-processing mechanisms that operate parallel to the formation of reportable beliefs.

2.3 The Simple Theory and Its Problems

The simplest form of propositional attitude theory is exemplified by Robert Solomon in the first edition of *The Passions* (1977). Solomon straightforwardly identifies emotions with evaluative beliefs:

> My anger *is* that set of judgments . . . an emotion is an evaluative (or a normative) judgment. (1977, 185; emphasis in original.)

Solomon is concerned to show that his account is more complex than this and hints at a social constructionist element:

Chapter Two

An emotion is a basic judgment about ourselves and our place in the world, the projection of the values and ideals, structures and mythologies. (1977, 185–86)

But this element, which is important in Solomon's later work (Solomon 1984), plays little role in this presentation. It does not cause him to qualify or modify the basic reductive claim:

> My embarrassment is my judgment to the effect that I am in an exceedingly awkward situation . . . my sadness, my sorrow and my grief are judgments of various severity to the effect that I have suffered a loss. (1977, 186)

Solomon's theory is an excellent starting point for a critique of the propositional attitude approach. It has been taken seriously enough to be no mere straw man and yet is simple enough to be open to almost all the criticisms that more subtle propositional attitude theories have tried to avoid. It gives us a chance to display the persistent, underlying problems with a propositional attitude approach. These may be listed under six heads:

1. *Objectless emotions.* States such as depression, elation, and anxiety are generally thought to be capable of clinical instances where they have no (intentional) object and thus involve no propositional attitudes. The generalized feeling of being "down" does not involve being down about anything and so cannot consist of a set of beliefs about anything. The typical cognitivist reply to this objection is to deny that there are such states. William Lyons claims that clinical depression requires the judgment that things are pretty bad (Lyons 1980). The object of this state is things generally.

2. *Reflex emotions.* The judgments which cognitivists take to be at the heart of emotions are often very different from ordinary judgments. The fear of earthworms and the conviction that earthworms are harmless commonly co-occur. The judgment supposedly underlying the fear is one we would hotly deny making. Some research on disgust (Logue, Ophir, and Strauss 1986) shows that humans can be disgusted by foods whose ingestion was followed by nausea even though they are convinced that there was no causal connection between the two events. Solomon, following Sartre, argues that all such cases are examples of self-deceit, but this is desperate. I discussed some other difficult cases in the previous section. If emotional

responses can be triggered by subliminal stimuli (Zajonc 1980, 1984b), then they can be triggered without the subject's making any judgments in the conventional sense.

3. *Unemotional evaluations.* Identifying emotions with evaluative judgments gives us far too many emotions. Many smokers believe smoking to be dangerous but smoke without fear. There are whole classes of evaluative judgments that are never likely to be the contents of emotions. A bored worker in the quality control unit makes such judgments thousands of times every day. An account is needed of why only some evaluative judgments are emotions.

4. *Judgments underdetermine emotions.* Lyons (1980) gives as an example the judgment that Ashkenazy is a fine pianist. This might give rise to envy or admiration or several other emotions, or perhaps to no emotion at all. The occurrence of these various emotions need not prima facie involve the judging subject holding any further beliefs about Ashkenazy. Such cases suggest either that the evaluative beliefs associated with an emotion do not exhaust its content or that emotions are not individuated by their contents.

5. *Emotional responses to imagination.* Several philosophers (e.g., Stocker 1987; Greenspan 1988) have argued that people can have full-blown emotions by imagining suitable objects. Here the beliefs and desires of the propositional attitude analysis are ones the subject explicitly does not possess! The obvious reply for the propositional attitude theorist is that in such cases people don't actually have emotions, but only imagine they have them. It might also be argued that if people do become genuinely emotional they must have confused their imaginings with reality. This defense can be sustained quite convincingly against most anecdotal evidence. But the original interpretation of these anecdotes is very plausible and the fact that it has to deny that interpretation is one more point against a simple propositional attitude approach.

6. *Physiological responses.* The propositional attitude school neglects the physiological aspects of emotion. Emotional responses are characterized by at least four classes of physiological changes: facial expressions, musculoskeletal changes such as flinching, expressive vocal changes, and autonomic nervous system changes such as adrenaline release and change of

heart rate. Chapters 3 and 4 outline the empirical evidence that some of these responses form syndromes associated with particular emotions. It can also be shown that the recognition of emotion in others utilizes these factors. Propositional attitude theories do nothing to explain these connections.

2.4 Adding Desires to the Theory

Some theorists believe that the problems just outlined can be avoided by including desires in the propositional attitude cluster that constitutes an emotion. Joel Marks (1982) argues that emotions are simply belief-desire complexes which include strong desires. Desires have two properties that make them a useful resource for the propositional attitude theorist. First, desires often persist when the beliefs that originally caused them have been revised. Second, there can be stable combinations of desires that conflict with one another (Robinson 1983). Marks uses these two features of desires to solve problem 2, the reflex emotions. For example, people frequently experience fears of things they believe to be harmless. Marks claims that such an "irrational" fear of, say, earthworms, consists of a strong desire to avoid earthworms and the belief that an earthworm is present. The fear is robust in the face of information about the harmlessness of earthworms because the desire to avoid them persists, as desires typically do. The fear persists in the face of a desire not to be so silly, because desires typically tolerate contradictions of this sort.

Marks hopes to solve problems 3 and 4, those of the underdetermination of emotion by judgments and of unemotional judgments, by simply adding appropriate desires to the conditions for the possession of the various emotions. In answer to problem 6, the problem of physiological response, he argues that we already know that strong desires are accompanied by physiological disturbance, and the disturbance which accompanies emotion is just an instance of this. He has nothing to say about problem 1, the objectless emotions. Like any propositional attitude theorist, he must simply deny that there are any. Similarly, I think he would have to give the usual replies to objection 5—emotional responses to imagination.

Marks's main worry about his theory is that it is too "liberal." It counts as emotions things we would not usually count as such. He considers the case of a person who has a strong desire to go to Paris in August. He suggests that this would not normally be called an emotion and worries that his theory makes it an emotion. Intuitions like this would not cause me to lose sleep if I were Marks. Simply changing the word "desire" to "yearning" in the story might produce the opposite intuition. Marks should be more concerned to defend himself against the accusation of "chauvinism." Some emotions do not involve strong desires. The positive emotions resulting from the satisfaction of desire are a good example. At least some instances of happiness are cases where a person has no strong unfulfilled desires left, since they have just been satisfied. It is possible to cook up some connected desires for these cases, such as the desire that what has been attained not be lost, but it seems back to front to suggest that the strength of someone's satisfaction depends on the strength of their wish not to have that satisfaction taken away. Furthermore, there are achievements which cannot be reversed and these seem as likely to give rise to positive emotions as any others.

Taylor (1984) confronts this problem by suggesting that there are two fundamentally different kinds of emotion, both analyzable in terms of beliefs and desires. "Appetitive" emotions like Miss Muffett's fear are just combinations of beliefs and desires and fit Marks's model. "Possessive" emotions include the counterexamples to Marks just proposed. According to Taylor, possessive emotions consist of the belief that some antecedently existing desire has been satisfied. The physiological arousal associated with possessive emotions is the result of the *satisfaction* of a strong desire. There are some cases which fit neither model, but Taylor certainly succeeds in associating desires of some sort with a great many emotions, and this must be of some help to Marks. As long as there are some desires about during the onset of an emotion, he can ascribe the physiological arousal associated with the emotion to those desires.

The most serious problem with Marks's account is a fundamental ambiguity in the notion of desire. The states referred to as "desires" in philosophical psychology are states which interact with beliefs to produce rational action and which are attributed on the basis of their efficacy in explaining behavior. But this notion will not serve Marks's purpose. Marks wants to use the desires to account for the physiological and phenomenological effects of emotions. He argues that we know that strong desires are accompanied by physiological effects and distinctive phenomenology and should therefore expect emotions to be accompanied by such effects if they are composed in part of strong desires. To get this argument to go through

Marks needs to use "desire" in the sense in which it denotes urgent, phenomenologically salient states—"yearnings," "longings," and "burning desires." Despite the problems of the famous James-Lange theory it seems reasonable to ascribe this phenomenology to the perception of the physiological effects, such as adrenaline release, raised heart rate, etc., which accompany these states. When we use "desire" in this sense, the strength of a desire is taken to mean its degree of phenomenological salience—just how "burning" or "painful" it is. But in the more usual philosophical use of "desire" the strength of a desire is taken to be its motivational effect, as revealed in actual or counterfactual behavior. It is a commonplace that these two kinds of strength do not correlate at all well. Sexual desires are generally far more salient phenomenologically than moral desires, yet many people follow their moral desires when the two conflict.

The fact that there exist these two senses of "strong desire" leaves Marks facing a fairly unpalatable dilemma. Suppose he opts to use the behavioral concept of desire. He will have an attractive concept with which to reduce the phenomena of emotion—a concept which seems suitably independent of the emotions and suitably central to at least some philosophies of mind. But his account will do little to explain the physiological and phenomenological effects of emotions. Suppose that he uses the phenomenological concept of desire. His explanatory project will be more likely to succeed but the notion used to explain the emotions seems as problematic as the emotions themselves. We have no clear taxonomy of these phenomenological desires, and in understanding their relationships to qualia and to physiological changes we encounter the same problems found in relating these things to emotions. In fact, these desires seem to be a variety of affect, along with moods, emotions and the rest. Marks's account will (almost) be one which analyzes emotions into beliefs and emotions! Marks (1984) recognizes the distinction between these two different senses of desire, albeit in a slightly different philosophical context. He gives the impression in this later paper that he thinks that "genuine" desires (e.g., phenomenologically salient states) are what are involved in emotion. It seems likely, therefore, that Marks would choose the second horn of the dilemma and hope to solve the various problems about "genuine" desire so as to establish a firm basis for an analysis of emotion.

None of these points constitutes a decisive refutation of Marks's theory. However, when taken together they make it far more programmatic than it first appeared. My own rejection of the program rests on rather broader considerations. First, as suggested below (section 2.7), even if a propositional attitude theory of emotion were entirely successful on its own terms, it would not yield a satisfactory theory of emotion. Second, as is made clear in chapters 3 and 4, much information is available about the physiological and expressive aspects of emotion. In light of this, it will seem very strange to suppose that these data can be adequately accounted for as the undifferentiated effects of "strong desire." The data will also compel us to take seriously the possibilities of objectless emotions and emotion via imagination, objections to which Marks's theory has no reply.

2.5 "Hybrid" Theories

One of the underlying problems with cognitivism is that it ignores the physiological dimension of emotion. This problem appears explicitly as the sixth of the objections to the simple propositional attitude theory. It is also at the root of several of the other objections. When a counterexample is proposed to a propositional attitude theory, it is usually the physiological aspects of emotion that support the claim that an emotion has or has not occurred. One popular response to these problems has been to propose hybrid theories, where both propositional attitudes and physiological responses are required for emotion. Classic examples are the "causal-evaluative" theory of William Lyons (1980) and the "causal" theory of Wayne C. Davis (1988).

According to Lyons, emotions are that class of evaluations which cause physiological disturbances. The addition of this causal requirement leaves the central doctrine of the propositional attitude theory intact. The identity of an emotion is determined by the evaluative attitude that it involves. To fear something is to evaluate it as dangerous, to love something is to evaluate it as lovable. There are two strands to Lyons's account of "evaluation." The first is represented in remarks such as "to evaluate is not to gain knowledge, but to relate something . . . to some rating scale" (1980, 5). It seems reasonable to accept Joel Marks's interpretation of these remarks (Marks 1982). To evaluate something as dangerous is to believe it capable of harming you and to desire that it not do so. The evaluative component of Lyons's causal-evaluative theory thus seems almost identical to Marks's belief-desire theory. The other strand in Lyons's account of evaluation is his talk of "seeing as." Suppose a climber sees a rock face and judges it to be dangerous. Lyons claims that they would then go on to evaluate the rock face by seeing it as either exciting or frightening. This process decides whether they feel excitement or fear. This sounds suspiciously like the substitution of metaphor for theory. The phrase "seeing as" and others like it occur at several points but there is no sustained attempt to explicate them.

So far Lyons's account of emotion seems close to that of the belief-desire theorists. It remains close despite its supposedly new "causal" element, because Lyons insists that emotions are attributed and classified purely on the basis of the evaluations that they involve. An emotion must upset a person but it is not possible to discover the emotion's identity from the nature of that upset. Emotions can be identified only by inferring the person's beliefs and desires by the usual behavioral/explanatory means. This view of emotion attribution and taxonomy turns out to be straightforwardly, empirically false. In chapters 3 and 4 I discuss a large body of results on the cross-cultural recognition of emotions from facial displays. The ability to attribute emotions on the basis of physiological effects turns out to be an important feature of human psychology. Lyons's introduction of physiological effects of emotion comes to very little, because he makes so little use of his new resource. In all essential respects Lyons remains a belief/desire theorist.

Wayne C. Davis (1988) offers a hybrid theory that departs slightly further from the belief-desire theory. In place of "evaluations" he offers "propositional fear," defined by: "S is afraid that p iff S desires that not-p and is uncertain whether p, where S's uncertainty is not based solely on his indecision about a course of action" (Davis 1988, 460). This is similar to the belief-desire theorist's analysis of fear, but Davis does not offer it as an analysis of fear itself. Fear itself—which Davis calls "occurrent fear"— happens when propositional fear causes both involuntary physiological arousal and "unhappiness." The addition of unhappiness is supposed to distinguish fear from a separate emotion called "anxiety." Propositional fear causes unhappiness if the addition of the propositional fear and certain ancillary beliefs to the subject's occurrent intentional states decreases the subject's happiness. Obviously, some account of how to measure happiness is in order, and Davis cites his own (Davis 1981). A person's current degree of happiness is the sum of the products of the degree to which each currently entertained proposition is believed and the degree to which it is desired. This in turn seems to call for an account of how to measure the strength of desire on a ratio scale, as opposed to the ordinal scales we actually possess and which would make Davis's calculations incoherent. Davis does not address this problem. He does not even appear to notice it!

The work of Davis, and of other authors considered in this chapter, is straightforward conceptual analysis. These theories can be criticized in two quite different ways. First, one may doubt the quality of the analyses on offer. In the course of his paper Davis claims that people cannot be afraid of events which have already occurred. A man who has heard conflicting reports about an air crash involving his wife can be *anxious* about her safety, but not *afraid* for her (1988, 471). Davis's concept of fear is obviously different from mine, as I don't share his intuition. Davis's belief that fear requires uncertainty also leads him to say that nobody can be afraid of the bare fact that they must, at some stage, die (1988, 482). He suggests various other things that people may have in mind when they say they are afraid of death. They may be afraid of hell, of future suffering, or of dying at some particular time. Once again, I just don't share Davis's intuition. I see no reason why the certainty that their consciousness must sooner or later be utterly destroyed cannot fill someone with terror.

Doubting the particulars of the analysis, however, does little damage to the overall project. There is a second and more important way in which Davis's account and others like it may be criticized. This is to question the appropriateness of conceptual analysis as a way of finding out about the emotions. The poverty of conceptual analysis can be seen from Davis's discussion of data suggesting that some emotions can distinguished from one another by the fact that they involve different patterns of autonomic nervous system activity and are typically accompanied by different facial expressions. He argues that these facts should not be incorporated into his account of the identity of these emotions for two reasons. First, there is a logical possibility that these physiological measures might have been different. Like Kenny, Davis thinks that a definition of emotion must involve only things logically connected to the emotion. Second, most ordinary speakers don't know these facts, and so they "could not be part of the meaning of 'fear', which is my concern in this paper" (Davis 1988, 466). Both these arguments fail, and they fail by ignoring the last twenty years of the philosophy of language. The counterexamples to Davis's two arguments are well known. Our best definition of water is the formula HOH, but this could not have been established by conceptual analysis! Ordinary English speakers in the past did not know that water was HOH, but this is still an important part of what "water" means. Davis's arguments assume that the meaning of an emotion term is a cluster of descriptions known to every competent speaker. But pure description theories of this sort have been very widely abandoned. In the second half of this book I develop a particular version of the sort of account of category terms which has replaced pure description theories. According to this account a key component of the meaning of "fear" is something like "whatever is going on in people in the paradigm cases of being afraid." Like many other concepts, the concept of fear has built into it the possibility of elaboration and improvement as the underlying causes of the phenomena that led people to introduce the concept are uncovered. So the scientific facts unknown to most speakers are entirely relevant to "the meaning of fear."

2.6 "Emotional Thoughts"

The final sort of propositional attitude theory to be considered here realizes that emotions cannot be analyzed in terms of beliefs and desires, but tries to provide the additional machinery required without looking to the natural sciences. These theorists use conceptual analysis to discover additional kinds of propositional attitudes which do the work that belief and desire could not perform. Michael Stocker (1987) presents a powerful case against conventional propositional attitude theories, relying largely on objections 4 and 5 of my list (emotions are underdetermined by beliefs, and one can have real emotions as the result of imagining things). Stocker wants to show that while emotions do involve entertaining propositions, the attitude we have to those propositions need not be one of belief, or indeed of any evidential or truth-aiming kind. To support his thesis, he describes some interesting examples of the underdetermination of emotion by belief. Stocker claims that when he is in an aircraft he can oscillate between fear and confidence, without changing his beliefs about air safety. He takes this to show that having the emotion is a matter of having some attitude other than belief toward propositions about the aircraft's crashing. He tries to make the same point with cases of imagining oneself into an emotion. Suppose Stocker is in a dark room. He knows that snakes are not often found in suburban Melbourne, but imagining that one is coiling away silently in that dark corner, he finds himself becoming afraid. He takes this to show that the way in which a proposition activates an emotion need not be by becoming more probable or better grounded. A parallel argument applies to desires. Stocker sums up his position in the following way: "the claim that emotions have cognitive content is not usefully put by holding they involve beliefs. Often, they involve only *emotionally held thoughts*. Similarly, emotions need not involve *values* and *desires* which the agent *really has*. They, too, can be held only emotionally" (1987, 59; emphasis in original). This raises the question of what it is to "emotionally hold" a belief or desire. At various points Stocker talks of "attending to," "entering into," "living," and "taking seriously" these propositional contents, but little illumination is to be had from this proliferation of tired metaphors. Stocker himself admits that "I find the notions of *entering into* and *living* a thought very difficult to characterise. But, as I trust the cases presented here have shown, they are not so difficult to illustrate" (1987, 64).

The burden of this last remark is that Stocker takes his examples to be a conclusive refutation of the belief-desire theory and supposes that a new propositional attitude is the only conceivable solution. He is not too worried about his inability to characterize that attitude, since he is sure it must exist and that his examples capture it. But, as I shall show in the next two chapters, the introduction of notions such as modularity and informational encapsulation will allow us to handle these examples without positing this mysterious new attitude and in a way that meshes in well with the general program of modern philosophy of mind. Stocker has correctly appreciated both the shortcomings of the propositional attitude school and that the problems can be solved only by introducing into the analysis something unique to emotions and quite separate from our usual stock of action-rationalizing beliefs and desires. Unfortunately, he chooses to go for the notion of a qualitatively different kind of mental content, a notion which seems irremediably mysterious. In the next two chapters we shall see how to elucidate the idea of specifically emotional mental contents without using any such problematic notion as an emotional attitude toward propositions.

Another late propositional attitude theory, calling itself the "New (Pure) Cognitive Theory" (Nash 1989) shows many of the same tendencies as Stocker. It introduces a special, emotional mode of having an intentional state. Unlike Stocker, however, Nash does not allow that a thought can be purely "emotionally held." He limits himself to claiming that emotional thoughts are believed or desired more intensely than normally. A particular intentional content or contents becomes subject to "an *obsessive overevaluation:* a focus of attention on particular aspects of the situation resulting in a disproportionate weighting of the facts" (1989, 495; italics in original). The main problem with Nash's account, as with Stocker's, is that it is undeveloped. Nash illustrates his central theoretical concepts—"focus of attention" and "overevaluation"—with anecdotes. Focus of attention seems to concern the degree to which the subject loses consciousness of other facts and events, but no attention is given to fitting this idea into any theory of human information processing. Overevaluation is the degree to which the "agent's evaluation of the situation is more extreme than it would be in the absence of the emotion" (1989, 497). It seems that an emotional evaluation must be irrationally strong since it is supposed to contrast to a "dispassionate norm."

What is promising in Nash's account is that he sees emotions as characteristic irruptions of motivation that interfere with the achievement of an agent's stable goals. He notes that such patterns of irruptive motivation may be adaptive for the agent and suggests that they may have an evolutionary explanation. This brings the propositional attitude tradition into contact with work in ethology and evolutionary theory on deviations from rationality in higher cognition. Robert H. Frank (1988) has shown that systematic deviations from rational decision making can be effective strategies in many of the game-theoretic situations used to model the evolution of social cooperation. He suggests that emotions may be just such systematic deviations. Frank's work and the more impressionistic discussions by certain evolutionary theorists constitute an interesting, if speculative, branch of the current science of emotion. They offer some prospect of constructing a theory along the lines proposed by Nash. Theories of this kind are discussed at greater length in chapter 5.

2.7 What Would a Successful Propositional Attitude Theory Achieve?

The prospects for a successful propositional attitude theory seem bleak. I have suggested (Griffiths 1989) that the research program was still grappling with the same set of problems twenty-seven years after Kenny's book set the agenda. This seemed a good reason to think it fundamentally flawed. Nothing has happened since then to change my mind. A recent, relatively friendly assessment of the program by John Deigh (1994) also concluded that the apparatus of propositional attitude psychology is inadequate to the task. I have suggested above that the problem is methodological. Conceptual analysis can tell us only what people currently believe about emotion. There are many puzzles about emotion that cannot be resolved by mere analysis of what people currently believe. To answer these questions it is necessary to look at the referent of the concept as well as the concept itself. It may even be necessary to revise the concept in order to better accommodate its referent. But the proponents of the propositional attitude approach seem quite undaunted by its bleak history and are so firmly committed to the methodology of conceptual analysis that they may regard my cure as worse than the disease. In this section, therefore, I offer some reasons to suppose that the propositional attitude program is hopeless which are general rather than particular but do not depend on my rejection of conceptual analysis.

A successful propositional attitude theory would yield analyses of emotion types like love, fear, hope, and anger. Each analysis would specify what content a set of propositional attitudes must have if it is to be a particular emotion (or the cognitive component of such an emotion). The aim is to produce analyses that are extensionally adequate, that is, which capture all and only the instances of a particular emotion. In this section I show that even if this enterprise were entirely successful, it would not produce a satisfactory theory of emotion.

Emotion types, in the propositional attitude view, are content schemata. But the analyses of emotion found in the literature are content schemata of a very special sort. This is because these analyses try to preserve the existing categories of folk psychology. An analysis of the vernacular concept of fear must not be so fine grained as to differentiate the state of thinking something is a man eater and wanting to run from the state of thinking it is poisonous and wanting to cycle away. This need for rough-grainedness becomes even more apparent when different environments and cultures are considered. People may face an utterly different range of stimuli with an utterly different set of background beliefs, and still be afraid. An emotion schema must be able to be filled in with a wide range of particular beliefs and desires.

This fact has perhaps been overlooked because a sentence like "P believes that x is dangerous" can be read as implying that P believes of x precisely that it has the general property of being dangerous. But it is both implausible and unnecessary to insist that a person explicitly tokens this belief every time they are afraid. A person can be afraid because they believe that they are about to be torn limb from limb by a lion without forming a further explicit representation of the fact that being torn limb from limb is dangerous. On a propositional attitude analysis of fear, if someone is afraid, then it follows logically from what they believe that they are in danger. But they need not actually draw this conclusion. One can, of course, define a sense of "belief" so weak that a person believes the deductive closure of their beliefs (everything that can be logically deduced from something else that they believe). But this is not the sense of "belief" relevant to propositional attitude analyses of emotions. The correct way to read "P believes x is dangerous" in a propositional attitude analysis is as a *vague* schema. It doesn't say precisely what P believes about x, but merely tells us that whatever P believes amounts, among other things, to believing x to be dangerous. It is left open whether P believes that x is a vicious political opponent, or that x is the spirit of his ancestor inhabiting a tribal mask. If either of these is enough to make something dangerous against the background of the person's other beliefs, then they can be a component of the person's fear. It is this second reading of the schema that will allow the analysis to specify all the various combinations of propositional attitudes that could, in some situation, constitute fear.

There is nothing special about fear in this regard. Consider these purported analyses of other emotions. Hope is the state of believing a situation to be possible and strongly desiring that situation. Envy is "wishing to have what someone else has and which is important for the subject's self-definition" (Ben-Zeev 1990, 489). Hate requires some of the following beliefs: that the object has some fundamentally negative traits, is a threat to something of fundamental value to the subject, is opposed to the subject's basic standards, or deserves to be avoided or eliminated. It also requires some of these desires: to reduce its influence or eliminate it, or to reject the current situation (Ben-Zeev 1992). Clearly, there are innumerable different sets of propositional attitudes which could fulfill the requirements of these analyses in different times, places, and cultures. So each analysis specifies a range of different sets of attitudes. Having something in this range is a necessary condition of having the emotion. On a "pure" propositional attitude theory it is also a sufficient condition for having the emotion.

If an analysis of an emotion specifies a whole range of sets of propositional attitudes, then two questions immediately suggest themselves. First, it can be asked what the sets of propositional attitudes that constitute one type of emotion have in common. What makes them all the same emotion? Second, it can be asked why some sets of attitudes constitute an emotion, while innumerable other sets do not. The answer to the first question may be relatively straightforward in some cases, such as fear. The propositional attitude theorist links fear to the perception of danger, and it may be possible to give an independent account of what it is for something to be dangerous. If so, the theorist can say that the proposed analysis of fear captures just those sets of propositional attitudes which are proper responses to danger. But this strategy will not work for most emotions. It is not generally true that there is some cognisable property that all the objects of a particular emotion have in common. The objects of love are not lovable, or the objects of hate hateful, except in the sense that they are objects liable to provoke those emotions in some people. Lovableness, hatefulness and infuriatingness, enviableness, and so forth are response-dependent properties. They are defined in terms of the emotion they elicit. Words referring to response-dependent properties can be used in two ways. They can be used "rigidly," to refer to whatever property characteristically causes the response. This is usually a highly disjunctive property. Something is infuriating if it is either A or B or C or . . . The second way to use these words is "dispositionally," to refer to the property of being such as to cause the response. An infuriating thing is something with the property "apt to infuriate people." If lovableness, hatefulness, and so forth are used in the dispositional sense, it will not be true that the occurrence of the emotion is normally the result of perceiving the property. People do not typically hate someone as a result of noticing that they are a sort of person apt to produce hatred! If, on the other hand, we use the words in the rigid sense, it will be true (by definition) that people typically have the emotion as a result of perceiving this property. However, the property will be a disjunctive one, and the question I started out with occurs in another form. What is it that holds together this disjunction of properties? Why do A, B, C, and so forth all count as infuriating? Neither the response nor the elicitor has any source of coherence. The propositional attitude approach has no answer to this problem. In most cases there is no rationale for a propositional attitude analysis other than that it is extensionally adequate to an existing folk category of emotion. The distinctions between one emotion and another are drawn in terms of their content, but content distinctions are taken notice of only when they happen to coincide with distinctions already present in the folk theory. In the case of fear there are obvious distinctions between instances in which the feared event has not yet occurred, instances in which it has already occurred, and instances in which it is currently occurring. These are interestingly distinct types of propositional content, but they do not form different emotions. A theory of emotion should throw some light on this.

The second question I posed for the propositional attitude theory was why some range of sets of attitudes constitutes an emotion, while innumerable other ranges that could be defined do not. What makes a cluster of propositional attitudes an emotion? The obvious way for the cognitivist to draw the distinction between emotions and nonemotions is to point to the physiological disturbance that accompanies emotion. The cognitivist can say that certain collections of propositional attitudes are emotions because as well as playing the usual role of propositional attitudes in our mental economy, they lead directly to physiological disturbances. Lyons, Marks, and Davis all adopt such a strategy. But there are two problems with this reply. The first is that it may well not be true. It is not obvious that all emotions cause physiological disturbance. The second and more important is that it still leaves a lot unexplained. It remains a brute fact that the occurrence of these propositional attitude sets lead to physiological disturbance, while others do not. It also remains a mystery that particular emotions cause certain kinds of physiological disturbance and not others. The fact that the propositional attitude school cannot address these questions is made worse by the fact that other, rival approaches can.

Another thing which the propositional attitude school cannot explain is why we classify the emotions as we do. We could use more content distinctions, and so group the sets of propositional attitudes that constitute token emotions into smaller emotion types. Conversely, we could ignore some of the content distinctions and form larger emotion types. Social constructionists argue that different societies really do group emotions differently. One society considers certain emotions to be of the same type while another would distinguish between them. If such variation actually occurs, then the grouping of emotions is even more in need of explanation. Once again, other approaches to emotion have explanations where the propositional attitude theorist does not.[1]

So it seems that even if the propositional attitude theory could provide an extensionally adequate taxonomy of emotions, it would have no way of addressing many fundamental questions about emotion. Not only is the program unlikely to achieve its goals, those goals are deeply unsatisfying.

1. A theorist at least very loosely in the propositional attitude tradition but who has a more adequate approach to these issues is Ronald De Sousa (1991). His treatment has affinities with the social constructionist treatments of eliciting conditions for emotions described in chapter 6.

3

The Psychoevolutionary
Approach to Emotion

3.1 Darwin's Work on Emotional Expression

The psychoevolutionary approach to emotion has its roots in Darwin's
The Expression of the Emotions in Man and Animals ([1872] 1965). One
of Darwin's explicit aims in this book was to refute Sir Charles Bell, who
had argued in the tradition of the British natural theologians that the human face contained muscles provided by God for the purpose of expressing
emotion. Some commentators have argued that Darwin countered Bell by
showing that emotional expressions are vestiges and therefore not constructed for the purpose of expressing emotion (Richards 1987). Darwin
saw the baring of the teeth in angry humans, for example, as a vestige of
a more primitive agonistic response:

> with mankind some expressions, such as the bristling of the hair under
> the influence of extreme terror, or the uncovering of the teeth under
> that of furious rage, can hardly be understood, except in the belief that
> man once existed in a much lower and animal-like condition. The com-
> munity of certain expressions in distinct though allied species as in the
> movements of the same facial muscles during laughter by man and by
> various monkeys, is rendered somewhat more intelligible, if we believe
> in their descent from a common progenitor. ([1872] 1965, 12)

But the psychologists and biologists who have been inspired by Darwin's
book have read it rather differently. They accept that human expressions
of emotion are to a large extent vestiges of responses in ancestral species
which served functions that are no longer significant. But these scientists
have mostly taken Darwin to say that these expressions were retained after
their original significance had declined because they had acquired a second-

ary function in intraspecific communication. Their current function is largely communicative. I have agreed with this interpretation elsewhere and have argued that Darwin pioneered a powerful pattern of "adaptive-historical" explanation (Griffiths 1992). Emotional expressions take their current form because they were adapted first for one purpose and then for another. This pattern of explanation made it possible for ethologists like Konrad Lorenz (1965, 1966) to assimilate Darwin's treatment of emotion to the ethological concepts of "derived activity" and "ritualization," in which the fact that a movement is reliably associated with some behavioral disposition becomes the basis for the evolution of a communication system. This reading of Darwin's theory has inspired modern psychoevolutionary theorists.

While the functionalist interpretation of Darwin is defensible, and I believe correct, another aspect of the modern reading of Darwin is clearly not what Darwin himself intended. Darwin did not conceive of his work as explaining the evolution of the emotions or as giving an account of what emotions are. His aims were relatively limited when compared to modern psychoevolutionary theories. He claimed to explain only why emotions are *expressed* in the ways that they are. This is because Darwin, like most of his contemporaries, accepted a version of the feeling theory of emotion. He thought of an emotion as a sensation expressed by the physiological manifestations he studied. Modern theorists treat emotions as syndromes, meaning that they have many elements and that no one isolated element constitutes the essence of the emotion. Emotions often involve qualitative states of consciousness, but these are no more central to the emotion's identity than is its characteristic facial expression. An emotion feeling isolated from all other cognitive and physiological elements is not an emotion, any more than a facial expression produced by direct electrical stimulation of the muscles is an emotion. Viewed from this perspective, Darwin's theory becomes a theory of the evolution of emotions themselves, conceived as patterns of response involving the activity of several bodily and cognitive systems.

The starting point for Darwin's theory was an anatomical account of human facial expressions. Some of Darwin's most valuable data came from the work of the French anatomist Duchenne, who had photographed electrically induced facial muscle movements. In his use of Duchenne's and others' photographs, Darwin anticipated the two most common forms of research on emotion used by later theorists, the *component analysis* and the *judgment test.*

A component analysis is an account of the role of the various facial muscles in the expression of the emotions. Darwin used Duchenne's work and other evidence to form such an analysis. He then tried to test it using the judgment test—perhaps Darwin's most original methodological contribution. In a judgment test, subjects are shown still photographs, films, or drawings of what are thought to be clear emotional expressions and are asked to state which emotion they think is expressed in the picture. Darwin used Duchenne's photographs for the first such test ever administered (figure 3.1). He was able to show that certain of the photographs elicited very general agreement and took these to be reliable expressions of their* associated emotions. Regrettably, Darwin used the judgment test only in England. Its main use in more recent work has been to demonstrate the cross-cultural recognition of emotional expressions.

Darwin used a rather less satisfactory technique to obtain information about the expression of emotion by members of other cultures. He dispatched questionnaires to missionaries, traders, and others, asking them about the facial components used to express emotion in the areas they worked in. He obtained results from an impressive range of sources, including Australia, the Pacific, India, the Americas, and Africa. Unfortunately, Darwin's questionnaire suggested which facial components he expected to represent which emotions. He thus made it very likely that his observers would read the desired results into their observations.

Darwin also placed some weight on the expressions of children and the mentally ill. He hoped to find in these two groups expressions of emotion relatively unmodified by culture. Darwin treated this data in a typical nineteenth-century recapitulationist framework. The stages of a child's development correspond to earlier stages of human evolution. They can therefore be used to uncover the evolutionary origins of human traits. Mental illnesses can be used in the same way if it is assumed that they represent regression to some of these early phases of development-evolution. Ontogeny is no longer regarded as a simple recapitulation of phylogeny, although it remains a rich source of information. The idea that mental illnesses are atavistic in nature has been long abandoned. Some of Darwin's arguments which rely on these premises must therefore be rejected. For example, Darwin's observation that there is an increased tendency to bite

3.1. Some of the heliotypes used by Darwin to test recognition of emotion from facial expressions. 1–3: degrees of mild amusement; 4: impassiveness; 5: true smile; 6: false smile (note electrodes used to stimulate the muscles). From Darwin ([1872] 1965).

in rage among children and the mentally ill does not support his proposal that the baring of the teeth in rage is the vestige of an agonistic response.

Although the theoretical grounds that led Darwin to study children and the mentally ill were mistaken, it may well have been productive for him to do so. It may have helped him to avoid becoming confused by the prevalence of "display rules" among fully enculturated subjects. Although pancultural expressions of emotion exist, their display is often affected by cultural norms. I discuss the classic experimental demonstration of this in the next section. Japanese subjects were shown to cut short expressions of negative emotions in response to stressful stimuli if they experienced the stimuli in the presence of an authority figure. A failure to allow for display rules is at least partly responsible for the idea that the Japanese have radically different facial expressions of emotion.

Darwin's investigations produced detailed accounts of the facial and musculoskeletal expression of various emotions. These descriptions make up the main body of his book and are very similar to those accepted today. While describing the expressions, Darwin suggests homologies to responses in other species and suggests possible functions of the expressions both now and in the evolutionary past. I outline here those of Darwin's findings that have been of central interest to later theorists.

1. *Fear.* In fear, the eyes and mouth are wide open. The body freezes. Heart rate is elevated. Blood is drawn away from the periphery, causing pallor. Other effects include trembling and piloerection. Darwin is struck by the homology between piloerection in humans and in other animals. Humans utilize the same muscles as a dog or a cat. He suggests that as well as contracting the tiny muscles associated with each hair follicle, humans contract the scalp muscles so as to raise the front- and back-sloping hairs on the front and back of the head. He argues that these muscles are homologous with the muscles which raise the hairs along the spines of other animals. Darwin is also particularly exercised by the contraction of the platysma myoides, which draws the corners of the mouth back and down and creates longitudinal neck ridges. Although this is highly characteristic of fear, Darwin can make no functional sense of it. Eventually he suggests that it is a side effect of the trembling associated with fear (which he regards as an outlet for "excess nerve energy," an element of his theory which I discuss in section 3.4 below).

2. *Surprise.* Modern theorists regard surprise as a separate emotion. Darwin regards it as a mild grade of fear in which the platysma contraction is absent. His concern with function is particularly evident in his discussion of surprise. He argues that the elevation of the brows is required to fully open the eyes and thus maximize the visual field. He notes that in surprised monkeys the open eyes are present but not the open mouth and suggests that this is because, unlike monkeys, humans must open their mouths if they are to breath as hard as possible in fleeing from danger. This is a good example of Darwin ascribing a current function to an emotional expression, not merely a function in an ancestral state.

3. *Anger.* In humans Darwin notices a tightly compressed mouth, a frown (vertical brow ridges caused by the brows being drawn together), redness of the face, a fixed stare at the object of anger, and a body posture ready for attack. However, he suggests that the particular body posture adopted varies by culture. He suggests that extreme rage is a distinct state, in which the mouth is open to expose the teeth. In monkeys he notices the same stare, the redness of face, and the prevalence of tooth baring but is struck by the total absence of the frown.

In these descriptions Darwin combines elements of what ethologists now call Anger 1 and Anger 2 (Chevalier-Skolnikoff 1973). Anger 1 is marked by closed jaws and lips. In chimpanzees this signifies a confident, dominant threat. Anger 2 is marked by a square open mouth which reveals the teeth. In chimpanzees this signifies a subordinate threat, or a mixture of fear and anger. Homologues of both expressions are found in humans, both apparently signifying anger.

4. *Disgust.* In disgust, the human frown is accompanied by an open mouth and retching. Darwin suggests that retching is a relic of voluntary vomiting and offers anecdotal evidence for voluntary vomiting in monkeys. His discussion of the distinction between disgust and contempt is also of interest. He says that the manifestations of these two emotions are almost identical. Modern theorists are divided over whether or not two distinct responses exist (Ekman and Friesen 1986; Izard and Haynes 1988)

5. *Sadness/grief.* In sadness, Darwin notes a general relaxation of the facial muscles, leading to the "long" or "fallen face." Active elements include the pulling down of the corners of the mouth and "oblique eyebrows"—

brows drawn together with inner corners raised and outer corners lowered. Darwin notes the difference between the muscle movements involved in this form of brow elevation and the usual voluntary form. In sadness the brows create a lump or fold above their meeting point, whereas in the voluntary movement furrows extend all across the brow.

6. *Happiness/joy.* Darwin makes the usual observation that laughter is a universal expression of joy. The corners of the mouth are drawn up and the upper lip is raised, causing wrinkles under the eyes.

3.2 Modern Work on Emotional Expression

In the first half of the twentieth century it was customary to dismiss Darwin's work on emotional expression on the grounds that his evidence was mostly anecdotal or gathered in methodologically flawed experiments. The favored research programs were those of the anthropologists and students of kinesics, most notably W. La Barre (1947) and R. L. Birdwhistell (1963), who hoped to give an account of expression as a culturally specific, learned code. But with the revival of interest in evolutionary accounts in the second half of the century many of Darwin's results have been confirmed and extended.

The recent experiments on facial expression can be divided into four classes: judgment tests between literate cultures; judgment tests between literate and preliterate cultures; component analyses of spontaneous facial expressions; and component analyses of the expressions of blind-born infants. The aim of most of this research is to show that the facial expressions Darwin discussed are reliably associated with certain emotions in all human cultures.

Izard (1969) developed a set of thirty-two photographs and presented them to observers in eight different cultures. His observers made judgments using a selection of emotion category labels which had been translated into their own language. Izard obtained very high levels of mutual recognition of his photographs, but there were certain discrepancies. His results were weaker for Africans and Japanese than for other culture groups. Izard's African subjects were people from many parts of Africa all presently living in France and Izard believed that there were severe translation problems. Izard's Japanese translations have also been criticized by other translators and this may well account for his deviant results in that case. A similar experiment was conducted by Ekman and Friesen (1971) on observers in five literate cultures and they obtained no deviant results. But data from cultures subject to Western influence may merely show that cultural contact allows members of different cultures to learn each other's conventions for facial expression. In order to really demonstrate the pan-cultural nature of emotional expressions it is necessary to conduct studies on visually isolated cultures.

Ekman, Sorensen, and Friesen (1969) conducted studies on the recognition of emotion in two visually isolated, preliterate cultures in Borneo and New Guinea. They used the same stimuli from which positive results were obtained in five literate cultures. While the results were similar to the results from literate cultures, the data were weaker and difficulties were encountered with the judgment test. It is hard to show an observer a photograph and ask him to choose a label from a list when, being illiterate, he is forced to memorize the list on each occasion. Their results were also criticized because the visual isolation of the tribes with which they worked was arguably incomplete.

In their next experiment, Ekman and Friesen (1971) utilized a judgment task designed for working with children. The observer was given three photographs at once, each showing a face, and told a story which was designed to involve only one emotion. This method also has the advantage of avoiding the necessity of translating delicate emotion terms. The observers were from the Fore language group in New Guinea. They had seen no movies or magazines, they neither spoke nor understood English or pidgin English, they had not lived in any Western settlement or government town, and they had never worked for a white. Forty photographs were used in experiments with 189 adult and 130 child subjects. High degrees of agreement were observed between the categories which the pictures were intended to represent by the Western experimenters and the categories which they were chosen as representing by the Fore. In one experiment, photographs intended by the Western experimenters to represent sadness, anger, and surprise were shown to the New Guineans, who were asked to select the picture representing the face of a man whose child has died. The face intended to represent sadness was selected by 79 percent of adults and 81 percent of children. These results strongly suggest that for a certain range of emotions, similar facial behavior is selected for the same emotion concept in visually isolated preliterate cultures.

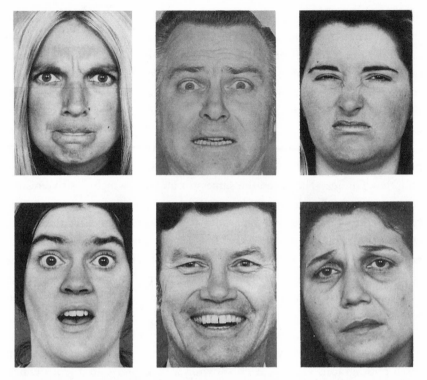

3.2. Some photographs used in Ekman and his collaborators' cross-cultural research. From top left: anger (closed-mouth type), fear, disgust, surprise, happiness, sadness. From Ekman and Friesen (1975).

Ekman and Friesen also conducted a reverse test using their New Guinean subjects. They asked visually isolated members of this culture to show how their face would appear if they were the person described in one of the emotion stories that had been used in the judgment test. Videotapes of nine New Guineans were shown to thirty-four U.S. college students. Except for the poses of fear and surprise, which the New Guineans had difficulty in discriminating, the students accurately judged the emotion intended by their poses. The New Guinean end of the experiment was repeated by another team at a later date, with similar results.

The New Guinean experiments concentrated on six facial expressions, which Ekman labeled surprise, joy, sadness, fear, anger, and disgust (figure 3.2). In recent work he has argued for a seventh, previously confounded with disgust, and has called this contempt (Ekman and Friesen 1986; but see Izard and Haynes 1988). These seven expressions have become the core of Ekman's revival of the Darwinian approach to emotion. They have been the subject of later studies which have elaborated the New Guinean studies (Ekman 1971), of studies of other elements of emotional response (Ekman, Levenson, and Friesen 1983), and of studies using the other Darwinian experimental paradigm which Ekman has revived, the component analysis. Modern findings about the pan-cultural expressions of emotion are summarized in table 3.1.

A component analysis of spontaneous facial expression was conducted by Ekman and a large group of collaborators (Ekman 1971). Previous research had established that certain stress-inducing films elicited similar self-reports of emotion from both Japanese and American subjects (Lazarus et al 1966; Averill, Opton, and Lazarus 1969). In the experiment by Ekman and his collaborators twenty-five subjects from the University of California at Berkeley and twenty-five subjects from the Waseda University in Tokyo were shown a neutral and a stress-inducing film while alone in a room. Each subject was aware that skin conductance and heart-rate measures were being taken but unaware that a videotape of their facial behavior was being made. When the repertoire of facial behaviors shown during the stress phase by the two sets of subjects was compared it was discovered to be very similar. Correlations between the facial behavior shown by Japanese and American subjects in relation to the stress film ranged from .72 to .96, depending upon whether a particular facial area was compared or the movement of the entire face.

Perhaps the most interesting result from the experiment was that when an experimenter was introduced into the room and allowed to ask questions about the subject's emotions as the stress film was shown again, the facial behavior of the Japanese differed radically from that of the Americans. The characteristic difference was that the Japanese showed more positive emotion than the Americans and less negative emotion. The Japanese appeared to have masked their negative feelings by politely smiling. Slow motion video tape analysis showed the micromomentary occurrence of characteristic negative emotional expressions, and then showed them being replaced with a polite smile. This behavior appears to have been unconscious and relatively automatic on the part of the Japanese. It is presumably

Table 3.1. Modern Descriptions of Emotional Expressions

	Brows-Forehead	Eyes-Lids	Lower Face
Surprise	Raised curved eyebrows; long horizontal forehead wrinkles	Wide-open eyes with schlera showing above and often below the iris; signs of skin stretched above the eyelids and to a lesser extent below	Dropped-open mouth; no stretch or tension in the corners of the lips, but lips parted; opening of the mouth may vary
Fear	Raised and drawn-together brows; flattened, raised appearance rather than curved; short horizontal and/or short vertical forehead wrinkles	Eyes opened, tension apparent in lower lids, which are raised more than in surprise; schlera may show above but not below iris; hard stare quality	Mouth corners drawn back, but not up or down; lips stretched; mouth may or may not be open
Anger	Brows pulled down and inward, appear to thrust forward; strong vertical, sometimes curved forehead wrinkles centered above the eyes	No schlera shows in eyes; upper lids appear lowered, tense, and squared; lower lids also tensed and raised, may produce an arched appearance under eye; lid tightening may be sufficient to appear squinting	Either the lips tightly pressed together, or an open, squared mouth with lips raised and/or forward; teeth may or may not show
Disgust	Brows drawn down but not together; short vertical creases may show in forehead and nose; horizontal and/or vertical wrinkles on bridge of nose and sides of upper nose	Lower eyelids pushed up and raised, but not tensed	Deep nasolabial folds and raising of cheeks; mouth either open with upper lip raised and lower lip forward and/or out, or closed with upper lip pushed up by raised lower lip; tongue may be visible forward in mouth near the lips, or closed with outer corners pulled slightly down
Sadness	Brows drawn together with inner corners raised and outer corners lowered or level, or brows drawn down in the middle and slightly raised at inner corners; forehead shows small horizontal or lateral curved and short vertical wrinkles in center area, or shows bulge of muscular contraction above center of brow area	Eyes either glazed with drooping upper lids and lax lower lids, or upper lids are tensed and pulled up at inner corner, down at outer corner with or without lower lids tensed; eyes may be looking downward or eyes may show tears	Mouth either open with partially stretched, trembling lips, or closed with outer corners pulled slightly down
Happiness	No distinctive brows-forehead appearance	Eyes may be relaxed or neutral in appearance, or lower lids may be pushed up by lower face action, bagging the lower lids and causing eyes to be narrowed; with the latter, crow's feet apparent, reaching from outer corner of eyes toward the hairline	Outer corners of lips raised, usually also drawn back; may or may not have pronounced nasolabial fold; may or may not have opening of lips and appearance of teeth

Source: From Ekman (1971).

inculcated in childhood. The convention that negative emotions are to be masked by smiling in certain social settings represents what Ekman has called a "display rule."

Other researchers have carried out component analyses of expression in the deaf and blind born. Eibl-Eibesfeldt (1973) examined the facial movements of infants born deaf and blind. He discovered that the same patterns of muscular activity were used to display the same kinds of emotions as in other children. Even the outré possibility of children learning the expressions by touch was excluded in some cases, as some of the thalidomide-affected children lacked suitable limb structures. Eibl-Eibesfeldt's findings confirm earlier findings (Thompson 1941; Fulcher 1942) that the same patterns of muscular activity are displayed by the blind and the sighted for each type of emotional behavior. This result seems to have been fairly well confirmed and has extremely important implications for the developmental theory of these emotions.

3.3 Why Evolved Emotions Are Neither "Innate" nor "Universal"

The experiments just cited are normally used to support the view that certain facial expressions of emotion have evolutionary explanations. They are also used to support the view that emotions are, in one of several senses, innate and the view that they are part of a universal human nature. In this section I want to sort out just what we can infer from the fact that certain emotional expressions occur in a wide range of cultures and develop without anything that would normally be called learning.

Discussions of these results are often hopelessly confused about the distinction between the "input side" and the "output side" of emotional response. The input side of a response is the stimuli that cause it. The output side is the response itself—the organism's behavior. All the experiments I have discussed deal with the output side of emotion. The experiments of Ekman and others show that people in all cultures respond in a similar way to things that frighten them. They do not show that people in all cultures are frightened of the same things. It is an entirely separate question whether the input side of emotion can be explained in evolutionary terms. This is an important distinction, as many attacks on "naturalistic" theories of emotion use data suggesting that emotions have different causes in different cultures to rebut the view that the same emotional responses occur in different cultures (e.g., Armon-Jones 1986b). Considerable confusion can be avoided if these two issues are kept separate. I discuss the "input side" of emotion in the next chapter.

The experiments I have reviewed strongly suggest that the output sides of the affect programs have evolutionary explanations. There are two aspects to the claim that a trait has an evolutionary explanation. First, the possession of an evolved trait by individuals is explained by the process of inheritance. I have the capacity to produce affect program responses because I am descended from ancestors who had this capacity. Second, the form of an evolved trait can be illuminated by considering the historical process which produced it. The fact that I bare my teeth in extreme rage reflects historical facts such as the ecological conditions under which my ancestors lived and the range of alternative forms in the population at that time (which in turn depends on earlier historical episodes). In addition to evolutionary explanations there are two other kinds of explanation that might be brought to bear on the affect program responses. These are developmental explanations and "competing" explanations. Developmental explanations describe the process by which traits are constructed in the growth of an individual. Evolutionary explanation can go badly wrong by ignoring facts about development (for example, by trying to find functions for traits which are inevitable developmental concomitants of something already fully explained). Despite this, developmental and evolutionary explanations are essentially complementary. Evolutionary explanations aim to explain why developmental resources are arranged so as to produce one trait rather than another (Griffiths and Gray 1994). I use the term "competing" explanations for those explanations which do seem to drive out, rather than complement, evolutionary explanations. Norman Ellstrand (1980) presents a spoof evolutionary explanation of why juveniles are smaller (and younger) than their parents. His point is that giving birth to younger offspring is logically necessary and giving birth to smaller offspring is usually developmentally necessary. These facts drive out any evolutionary explanation of these traits. In general, competing explanations aim to show that a trait would be expected as a consequence of other conditions already known to obtain. This affects both aspects of the claim that the trait has an evolutionary explanation. It may be true that my ancestors had the trait, but the competing explanation suggests that I would have it even if they had not, as a consequence of other traits I inherited.

The competing explanation also suggests that the form of the trait can be adequately understood without thinking about the historical conditions under which it previously existed.

Competing explanations are typically offered when evolutionary psychology lines up against more traditional psychological research. The evolutionary psychologist takes a phenomenon like a common but "irrational" pattern of reasoning and argues that this behavior was selected for some advantage that it confers. A neuropsychologist might reply that any computational method that solves this general class of problems will be very prone to errors of the sort identified in human reasoning. This would be a competing explanation and would drive out the evolutionary explanation. A social psychologist might reply to the evolutionary psychologist that an established theory, perhaps a theory of group identity, will adequately explain this particular pattern of reasoning (they might also endorse an evolutionary explanation of why people represent in-group/out-group relationships in this way). This would also be a competing explanation. The general aim of such competing explanations is to show that the trait would exist whether or not it conferred any selective advantage. One problem with competing explanations which is not often remarked upon is that they require a highly atomistic approach to the organism. They suppose that we can break the organism down into discrete traits and make sense of the claim that a range of other traits would have evolved whether or not the trait currently being studied was present. Hence we can explain the one trait as a side effect of these others. While this is clearly correct for Ellstrand's explanation of small offspring, it is far less obvious in many of the psychological cases. It is often objected that evolutionary explanations are atomistic in this way (Gould and Lewontin 1979), but the objection is equally applicable to many competing explanations.

The experiments reviewed in this chapter suggest a role for evolutionary explanation, rather than competing explanations, because the affect program responses are pancultural and because they are apparently homologous with responses in related species. I will leave aside the evidence from homology for a moment. The fact that affect programs are pancultural requires some additional argument to turn it into evidence of evolution. There are obvious competing explanations that can be offered for the fact that a trait is pancultural. Some systems of communication may have developed separately in many human societies because of their utility. For example, all human societies have names for the tools they use. Nevertheless, it is unnecessary to suppose that the trait of naming one's tools exists so widely because it is inherited from a common ancestor who had the brilliant notion of naming tools. The general cognitive abilities of humans and the fact that it is useful to have these words suffices to explain why all societies have them. Opponents of evolutionary accounts of emotion have argued in a similar vein that humans have used their general cognitive abilities to come up with facial expressions for anger, fear, and so forth because it is useful to be able to communicate these emotions via facial expressions (Birdwhistell 1963). This possibility is ruled out, however, by the fact that many facial expressions of emotion are not only pancultural but *arbitrary*. The way the eyebrows move in anger is no more specially suitable for expressing anger than the word *cat* is specially suitable for talking about cats. The fact that an *arbitrary* feature is found throughout the species stands in need of evolutionary explanation. Darwin himself was well aware of this:

> Whenever the same movements of the features or body express the same emotions in the several distinct races of man, we may infer with much probability that such expressions are true ones—that is, are innate or instinctive. Conventional expressions, or gestures, acquired by the individual during early life, would probably have differed in the different races, in the same manner as do their languages. (Darwin [1872] 1965, 15)

The principle of inference being employed here is a common one in evolutionary theory. Independent origination of the same features is to be expected only if the features are adaptive. If traits resemble one another in arbitrary, nonadaptive respects, then this suggests a common ancestry. The possession of these traits by individuals is probably best explained by descent, and the form of the traits can probably be illuminated by considering their history. In other words, such traits probably have evolutionary explanations. The same principle is used in historical linguistics. The fact that words with the same meaning have arbitrary syntactic or phonetic features in common is good evidence for their descent from a common ancestral language. The same principle also explains why the apparent homology between affect program responses of humans and those of related species is good evidence for the evolution of these expressions. Nonfunctional resemblances are the key to diagnosing homology. The fact that emotional responses emerge in very early infancy also supports an evolutionary explanation against competing explanations. Early emergence militates against the idea that emotional responses are acquired from the local cultural milieu, because the infant has had insufficient exposure to that milieu. The facial expressions of infants must be either the results of evolution or brute facts about physiology: all infants smile in response to pleasurable stimuli because that's just what happens when you stimulate that mechanism in that way. An explanation in terms of brute physiology is an interesting possibility when the response in question is entirely arbitrary. I discuss below how Darwin used this idea as part of his theory of the origins of emotional communication. He thought that the brute physiological side effects of emotion were important elements of expression. When an infant's expression is functional, however, as is the case with the surprise response, then a purely physiological account leaves something unexplained. Only evolution can explain why the infant should be born producing *functional* responses to stimuli. The explanatory advantages of the evolutionary approach are even greater in light of Darwin's idea that the arbitrary responses are vestiges of responses that were once functional (and whose homologues in other species are still functional). This renders the brute physiological explanation unsatisfying even for these arbitrary responses.

The experiments I have reviewed might be thought to show not only that emotional expressions can be given evolutionary explanations, but also that they are innate. Indeed, it might be thought that if the expressions have evolutionary explanations, then they *must* be innate. Both these implications should be rejected. The psychoevolutionary theory of emotion (and evolutionary theory in general) need not be committed to any particular view of the developmental mechanisms which create emotional expressions. Innateness is a fundamentally confused concept. It confounds under one term several independent properties. These include the properties of having an evolutionary explanation, being insensitive to variation in "extrinsic" factors in development, being present at birth, and being, in various senses "universal" (Bateson 1991; Gray 1992). Traits are often said to be innate because they have one sort of property, and then assumed without sufficient warrant to possess the other properties associated with innateness. The classic example of this sort of elision is found in the early work of Konrad Lorenz. Daniel S. Lehrmann's classic critique (Lehrmann 1953) points out that Lorenz typically moves back and forth between the idea that a trait can be given an evolutionary explanation and the idea that its emergence is unaffected by the removal of the environmental inputs which might be thought to provide information for its construction. Lehrmann argues that there is no conceptual link between the evolutionary and the developmental elements of Lorenz's innateness concept; between the fact that a trait is an evolutionary adaptation and the fact that it is insensitive to environmental variation. It is of no evolutionary consequence whether a trait is sensitive to environmental variation, as long as the actual historical environment regularly provides the required input. "Nature selects for outcomes" and is indifferent to how they are achieved (Lehrmann 1970, 28).

Lehrmann supplemented this conceptual point with a host of examples of the role of environmental input in the production of evolved traits. The female rat's abstention from eating her young, for example, depends on her licking of her genitalia during pregnancy. Many later examples make the same point. Under normal developmental conditions, young ducklings show a preference for the maternal call of their own species. Gilbert Gottlieb showed that exposure to their own prenatal vocalizations is required for the development of their preference for the quite different maternal call (Gottlieb 1981). Parasitic bird species are adapted to their particular host species, but the association between parasite and host is often maintained by imprinting on the foster parent (Immelmann 1975). The social and hunting behaviors of the European barn owl have been shown to be a function of environmental variables. Birds of the same species that are moved to Malaysia produce a totally different behavioral phenotype (Lenton 1983). In an exciting recent study on an ant species the body size of queens and the social structure of the nests they create were shown to be functions of the pheromonal environment of the parent nest (Keller and Ross 1993). Lehrmann was at pains to point out that these sorts of facts do not show that traits are learned as opposed to innate. They show that evolution achieves stable outcomes by exploiting reliable interactions between the developing organism and its environment to create reliable developmental outcomes. The fact that a trait has an evolutionary history has no implications about the nature of the process by which it develops, except that the outcome is sufficiently reliable to allow selection.

There are some common arguments for a link between evolutionary explanation and developmental fixity. One argument runs as follows. Evolution operates by changing gene frequencies. Therefore, if emotional expressions have evolved, they must be "coded for" by certain genes. This argument goes on to infer from the fact that there is a gene for a certain expression that environmental inputs must be relatively unimportant for the emergence of this expression. Another argument suggests that if evolution is to favor a trait, the trait must be present over many generations. It is then argued that only if the emergence of the expression is strongly linked to genetic factors, and relatively insensitive to environmental inputs, will this stability be possible. In fact, however, evolution can operate on traits whose emergence is highly sensitive to environmental inputs. It is also possible for a trait to be pancultural and stable over many generations, like the emotional expressions, while being sensitive to environmental inputs. These things are possible because organisms inherit an environment along with their genes. This does not just mean that they are thrown into the same portion of the world as their ancestors. Rather, their parents create very specific conditions for them and the adult is the product, not of its genes, but of the interaction of its genes with this structured developmental context. It is this "developmental system" that is the real source of stability across generations (Oyama 1985; Gray 1992; Griffiths and Gray 1994). The role of the environment in the stability of developmental systems is particularly evident in the development of mental capacities. An infant primate inherits a social context without which it will not develop a normal adult mind. Even short periods of deprivation of the usual social stimuli may throw its development permanently off course. Social deprivation in the infancy of rhesus monkeys can entirely eliminate normal play and maternal care from its behavioral phenotype and create inability to successfully complete copulation.[1] It would be absurd to deny that maternal care and copulation behavior are the result of evolution, and yet their development requires a richly structured environment. These results have been extended to emotion with the finding that although fear expressions develop in socially deprived monkeys, they are less easily understood by other monkeys than the fear expressions of monkeys with a normal infancy

1. Harlow 1961, 1963; Harlow, Dodsworth, and Harlow 1965; Harlow and Harlow 1962, 1969; Harlow, Harlow, and Hansen 1963; Harlow and Zimmermann 1959; Mason 1960, 1961, 1963, 1965.

(Miller, Caul, and Mirsky 1967). The lesson of such examples is that the transgenerational stability of form required for evolution can be produced in many different ways. All that can be inferred from the fact that a trait is widespread in a species is that it is a candidate for evolutionary explanation. The source of its developmental stability is a matter for the developmental biologist and should not be prejudged.

Breaking the link between the claim that an expression has an evolutionary explanation and the claim that it is "innate" adds to the credibility of the psychoevolutionary approach. It allows Ekman and his followers to dismiss objections which assume that evolved features are innate in the various other senses of that word. Carl Ratner, for example, argues that the discovery of classic facial expressions in infants does not show that the corresponding adult expressions are an evolved feature, because environmental inputs are needed to maintain such performances to adulthood (Ratner 1989). Once the role of the environment in the normal development of evolved features is recognized, such arguments come to nothing.

The multifaceted nature of the concept of the innate also contributes to confusion over the "universality" of some biological traits. It is often inferred that if a trait is a product of evolution it must be "innate" (part of "human nature") and therefore "universal." But not only is this inference unreliable, its conclusion—universality—can mean two quite separate things. "Universal" sometimes means that a trait occurs in all (or most) cultures. It is much clearer to call these traits "pancultural." Much of Ekman's work is clearly intended to show that the affect programs are pancultural. Another sense in which a trait might be "universal" is that every human being has the trait. It is much clearer to call these traits "monomorphic." The contrast between polymorphic and monomorphic traits is familiar to all working biologists. Polymorphic traits exist in several different forms in the same species. Eye color is polymorphic in humans. Monomorphic traits exist in the same form in every individual.[2] Leg number is mono-

2. Or every "normal" individual. There are major unsolved problems here. Hull (1986) describes the inadequacy of most common notions of normality, but most biologists will still want some way to exclude thalidomide-affected children from the official taxonomic description of *Homo sapiens*. Millikan (1984) and others have grounded notions of normality in notions of adaptive purpose. Abnormal features are those which do not result from an adaptive process. It may be simpler to accept a position in the spirit of Darwin himself. Variation is ubiquitous, but there is a rough distinction between significant and insignificant variation. Polymorphism is significant where the evolutionary process maintains several types at

morphic in humans. None of the experiments described above was designed to show that affect programs are monomorphic.

Distinguishing these two senses of "universal" makes it possible to assess whether the fact that a trait has evolved implies that it will be universal in either sense.[3] The first question is whether the fact that a trait has evolved implies that it is monomorphic. Obviously it does not. Eye pigmentation in humans is a result of evolution! Human behavioral traits may be just like eye color. Many models of behavioral evolution strongly predict polymorphic outcomes. An evolving population will be in equilibrium when some of its members are built to behave in one way and others are built to behave in another way (Maynard Smith 1982). This is because the evolutionary advantages of one behavior often depend on the presence of a different behavior in other individuals. Aggression pays best when other people are passive. It has recently become fashionable among evolutionary psychologists to argue that human cognitive mechanisms will be monomorphic. I return to this claim in chapter 5 and show that there is little reason to accept it.

The second question is whether the fact that a trait has evolved implies that it is pancultural. It might be thought that it does, because all humans are members of a single evolutionary species. This suggests that all human populations share a single evolutionary history, which in turn suggests that they will all display any evolved character. There are two important caveats to this argument. First, like many other species, humans are divided into different populations. Until recently there was far more interbreeding within these populations than between them. These populations descend from small samples of an ancestral population. Since many traits are polymorphic there was room for sampling error to yield a descendant population that lacks some of the traits found in the ancestral population. It is obvious from gene maps that this has occurred. Some very ancient alleles are nevertheless rare or absent in some human populations (Cavalli-Sforza et al. 1994). In consequence some diseases linked to particular alleles are

---

substantial levels in a population or where the existence of a rare type has had some effect on which other types are common. This variation should be noted in a description of the species. Rare polymorphisms with no noticeable evolutionary impact are just expressions of the ubiquity of natural variation and need not be included in a description of the species.

3. I have already discussed the two reverse inferences. In some circumstances the fact that a trait is pancultural can be used to infer that it has evolved. Monomorphicity implies evolution in exactly the same circumstances.

more common in one human population than another. It cannot therefore be absolutely ruled out that some human populations may lack an evolved trait or possess it in different proportions from that in which it is normally found. Second, we must beware of the definition of evolutionary homology. Homologies are traits possessed by all and only the descendants of the ancestral species in which those traits originate. The groups defined by a homology include those species descended from an ancestor which had the trait, but in which the trait has been deleted by reverse evolution. Thus, snakes and cetaceans are tetrapods—a group of creatures with a characteristic four-limbed body plan. They are regarded as tetrapods either because they have vestiges of their tetrapod limbs, as most snakes and cetaceans do, or because their other characteristics can be satisfactorily explained only by supposing them to be descended from creatures which had tetrapod limbs. Despite an initial sense of perversity, it is easy to see why defining traits in this way is useful when thinking about evolution. Homologies also include examples of a trait which have been radically transformed in form and function. Human arms, the wings of birds, and the flippers of dolphins are all tetrapod forelimbs. It is worth bearing in mind that the fact that humans have a homologue of some response in another species does not mean that it serves the same function in the two species or even that it is present in a substantial form.

3.4 Darwin's Theory of the Evolution of Emotion

Darwin believed that the facts he had discovered about the expression of emotions could be explained by three general principles: the principle of serviceable associated habits, the principle of antithesis, and the principle of direct action. In this section I consider how Darwin's three principles hold up in the light of modern research and how they might be amended to provide a plausible theory of the evolution of the pancultural emotional expressions.

The Principle of Serviceable Associated Habits

The principle of serviceable associated habits is the most important of the three principles. But in Darwin's own work it is often unclear whether he is discussing the acquisition of a habit by an individual or the acquisition and inheritance of a habit by a species! This is apparent when he introduces the principle:

Certain complex actions are of indirect service under certain states of the mind, in order to relieve or gratify certain sensations, desires, etc.; and whenever the same state of mind is induced, however feebly, there is a tendency through the force of habit and association for the same movements to be performed, though they may not then be of the least use. ([1872] 1965, 28)

The basic idea is that the apparently arbitrary elements in an emotional response are vestiges of previously functional responses. Some work is needed to separate this insight from Darwin's idea that the functional responses started as learned habits and then became incorporated into the hereditary material as instinctive behaviors. Consider the baring of the teeth as part of the primate anger response. It is plausible to suggest that this behavior was originally a preparation for attack. As such it may have had a direct survival value. The baring of the teeth in humans, however, is no longer a preparation to use them for fighting. At some stage during the development of the species this behavior has lost its original function. But this is not to say that it is now useless. It has acquired an alternative role, namely that of signaling aggression to other members of the species. Its survival value in this new role may be at least as great as that which it originally possessed. In other places (Griffiths 1992, 1993) I have called these cases where the function which explains the continued prevalence of a trait is not that which originally caused it to spread in the population "secondary adaptation" or "exadaptation." The idea of secondary adaptation provides a non-Lamarckian version of Darwin's principle of serviceable associated habits. A behavior originally associated with an emotion because it fulfills some function will not cease to be associated with the emotion simply because it has ceased to serve that function. If it has a signal value because of its past association with that emotion, then it may remain part of the species's behavioral repertoire. The exact nature of the response, however, will only be explicable as a vestige of its original, utilitarian function.

In this reconstructed version, the principle of serviceable associated habits is of great service in explaining the evolution of emotional behaviors which would otherwise seem quite arbitrary. The secondary adaptation pattern seems to be quite common in the evolution of expressions of emotion and received a great deal of attention from the classical ethologists under the name of "ritualization" (Tinbergen 1952). The concept of ritualization, however, differs slightly from the concept of secondary adaptation. It "refers primarily to the evolutionary changes which such movements have undergone in adaptation to their function in communication" (Hinde 1966). The more general concept of secondary adaptation applies to all derived signal movements, whether or not they have been modified for their new role. This is an advantage because, as Hinde notes in the article just cited, many interesting derived behaviors have not undergone any significant modification.

The Principle of Antithesis

Darwin's second general explanatory principle seems to have been proposed for purely empirical reasons. He noted, for example, that:

> When a dog approaches a strange dog or a man in a savage or hostile frame of mind he walks upright and very stiffly; his head is lightly raised, or not much lowered; the tail is held erect and quite rigid; the hairs bristle, especially along the neck and back; the pricked ears are directed forwards, and the eyes have a fixed stare . . . These actions . . . follow from the dog's intention to attack his enemy. ([1872] 1965, 50–51)

Darwin then considers the dog's response when he recognizes the "stranger" as his master:

> Let it be observed how completely and instantaneously his whole bearing is reversed. Instead of walking upright, the body sinks downwards or even crouches, and is thrown into flexuous movements; his tail, instead of being held stiff and upright is lowered and wagged from side to side; his hair instantly becomes smooth; his ears are depressed and drawn backwards, but not closely to the head. From the drawing back of the ears, the eyelids become elongated, and the eyes no longer appear round and staring . . . Not one of the movements, so clearly expressive of affection, are of the least direct service to the animal. They are explicable, as far as I can see, solely from their being in complete opposition or antithesis to the attitude expressive of anger. ([1872] 1965, 51)

Darwin's idea is that emotions can be seen as standing in relations of opposition and that an animal disposed to act in one fashion under the influence of one emotion will act in the opposite fashion when under the influence of an opposite emotion. But it is not at all clear what is meant by saying that two emotions are "opposite," although this description has an obvious intuitive force, and some modern theorists have been attracted by it (Plutchik 1970; Russell and Fehr 1987).

A sound evolutionary rationale for the principle of antithesis can be derived from Darwin's own comments. He remarks that:

> As the power of intercommunication is certainly of high service to many animals, there is no a priori improbability in the suggestion, that gestures manifestly of an opposite nature to those by which certain feelings are already expressed, should at first have been voluntarily employed under the influence of an opposite state of feeling. ([1872] 1965, 61)

Darwin goes on to reject this proposal because he is unwilling to attribute such communicative intentions to animals. But we can strip his insight of the suggestion of communicative intent and merely note the survival value of clearly communicating emotional states and their opposites among animals of the same species. For a social animal, the display of an absence of aggression is as important as the display of aggression itself. It may, for example, placate more powerful individuals. An animal which clearly displays passivity by reversing normal signs of aggression is sending an important signal. The principle of antithesis in this version is not committed to any very precise version of the idea that emotions can be opposite to one another. All it requires is that an organism can be in two different emotional states and that it is important for it to communicate the fact that it is one rather than the other (Tinbergen 1952, 29). If one emotion has clear behavioral consequences then displaying the opposite behaviors may be an effective way to do this. This view of the principle of antithesis will allow it to retain a place in the psychoevolutionary explanation of emotional expression.

The Principle of Direct Action

Darwin's third principle is the principle of the direct action of the nervous system. Darwin shares the famous nineteenth-century "hydraulic" conception of the mind. The mind is powered by "nerve force" or "nerve energy." Once a certain amount of nerve force has been released, it is like pressurized hydraulic fluid and must find an escape valve somewhere—a means of expression in action. He suggests that this has been

> highly influential in determining many expressions. Good instances are afforded by the trembling of the muscles, the sweating of the skin, the modified secretions of the alimentary canal and glands, under various emotions and sensations. ([1872] 1965, 81)

The classical ethologists took much the same view of the origins of many signal movements. According to Niko Tinbergen (1952) some signals are derived from "displacement activities" in which the internal drives of one "instinctive" behavior are unable to produce that behavior and spill over into another instinctive behavior system. Like Darwin, he sees this as a mechanism by which the central nervous system is protected from damage: "I think it is probable that displacements do serve a function as outlets, through a safety valve, of dangerous surplus impulses" (1952, 23). Unlike Darwin, however, Tinbergen emphasizes the fact that these mechanical side effects have acquired a secondary function as signals, or "social releasers," which affect the behavior of other animals. Darwin accepted that "direct action" effects of emotion might be used in communication but does not seem to have considered the possibility that these effects had been modified for this purpose. Tinbergen argues that "this new function must have started a new evolutionary development during which the displacement activities became increasingly better adapted to it. This evolutionary development I have called 'ritualization,' following Huxley" (1952, 23).

The principle of direct action is probably the most questionable of Darwin's three principles. His central examples of useless direct actions are now interpreted as highly functional. Trembling and sweating function to control body temperature. The secretions of the various glands have important functions in preparing the body for action. In a modern psychoevolutionary account physiological responses take their place alongside facial behavior, action tendencies, and subjective feelings as aspects of an integrated emotional response. In fact, the adaptive role of autonomic nervous system effects in emotion has been a major focus of investigation since the 1920s (Cannon 1927, 1931). The extent of the adaptation of autonomic nervous system responses to the purposes of the various emotions is a vexing question which I address at some length in chapter 4.

The rejection of the principle of direct action does not imply that every element of the emotional response has an adaptive explanation. Emotional response will very likely have nonadaptive features, either because of the presence of vestiges of past phases of evolution or because of the presence of side effects of adaptive elements. But these side effects are not the consequence of the mechanical overflow of nervous energy! The "hydraulic model" of the mind has no basis in current neuroscience. The classical ethologists' treatment of displacement activities is outdated for exactly the same reason. Their phylogenetic interpretations of displacement activities are of the first interest, but their hydraulic explanation of these behaviors is a mere historical curiosity.

It is now possible to summarize the role that Darwin's three principles are likely to play in a modern psychoevolutionary theory of emotion. The principle of the retention of serviceable habits (secondary adaptation for communication) is likely to retain a central position in any theory. A modern version of the principle of antithesis will also lay more stress on the value of communication. It is the importance of clearly communicating emotions to conspecifics that gives a genuine evolutionary rationale to antithesis. The principle of the direct action of the nervous system appears to be largely superseded.

3.5 Modern Theories of the Evolution of Emotion

Darwin was mainly concerned with the detailed morphology of emotional expressions. Modern theories have had a very different emphasis and have taken less interest in the actual details of emotional response. Instead, they have concentrated on the broad ecological functions that emotions might be thought to fulfill. One of the longest running research programs has been that of Robert Plutchik (1962, 1970, 1980a, 1980b, 1984). Plutchik's ecological theory claims that animal behaviors will fit into four pairs of adaptive categories. They must be to designed to protect/destroy, reproduce/deprive, incorporate/reject, or explore/orient. He then claims that there will be four pairs of emotions corresponding to these four adaptive functions.

Another ecological theory of emotions is presented in Robert H. Frank's *Passions within Reason: The Strategic Role of the Emotions*

(1988). Frank's work is a version of a theory of emotion often hinted at by sociobiologists. The best known of these sketches is the discussion of the moral emotions in Robert L. Trivers's classic article "The Evolution of Reciprocal Altruism" (1971), but similar ideas can be found in the works of most leading sociobiologists (Weinrich 1980). Frank notes that emotions often lead people to behave in ways which conflict with calculative rationality. Loyalty leads someone to keep an agreement, although there is no advantage to them in doing so and no possibility of retribution for betrayal. Resentful or vengeful people often cause further harm to their own interests in order to hurt the person who harmed them initially. A strong emotional response to perceived exploitation (the "sense of fairness") may lead people to refuse to participate in an arrangement because they believe that the other party is exploiting their bargaining position to ensure an uneven distribution of the spoils. This is irrational, because however uneven the distribution of the economic product of the transaction there is still an absolute gain to be made by participating.

The key to Frank's explanation of emotional behaviors is that although each behavior is locally irrational, being disposed to produce those irrational behaviors can be globally rational. It can be rational to adopt the strategy "when in this situation, act irrationally." For example, the fact that someone may get angry can deter a more powerful party from harming or exploiting them. If the weaker party were perfectly rational at all times, the stronger party could harm them while using the threat of still greater harm to prevent any response. But the irrationality of anger can block this strategy. In the same way, the fact that a person has a sense of fairness can compel someone to offer them a fair bargain, rather than offering them the worst bargain which it would be rational to accept.

Frank is able to relate his theory of the evolutionary function of emotions to Darwin's theory of the actual emotional response. Frank's theory depends on the ability of individuals to communicate their emotions, and hence their behavioral dispositions, to one another. Verbal threats and promises are insufficient, as they are not strong guarantors of future behavior. Information about other times when an individual has faced the same situation is not usually available. The intrinsic connection between facial behavior and emotion might sometimes function as a solution to this problem. Frank and his associates conducted a series of experiments in which subjects were able to predict to a significant extent who they could trust to keep agreements on the basis of unrelated social interactions with their "partners" before the game commenced. Presumably, each party communicated aspects of their personality to the other individual, and it is at least plausible that Darwin's facial behaviors played a role here.

These are ingenious ideas, and I return to them in chapter 5. Unfortunately, they are only ingenious ideas. It would take a lot more work to turn them into established explanations. In the next section I show how this might be done.

3.6 Adaptationism and the Study of Emotion

The widely discussed problem of adaptationism in evolutionary biology is a problem of *confirmation*. Adaptive hypotheses are too easy to form and too difficult to test. This is what Stephen Jay Gould meant when he called adaptive explanations "just-so stories" (Gould 1978). Adaptive theorizing has "no constraints but the inventiveness of the author and the gullibility of the audience" (Rosen 1982). The sociobiological literature of the seventies and eighties helped to highlight this problem with such absurdities as the adaptive origins of the correlation between resource predictability (a.k.a. high income) and frequency of oral sex (Weinrich 1977). This gives rise to two related problems. First, because adaptive explanations are always available, alternative forms of evolutionary explanation are not considered. Second, because several equally compelling adaptive explanations can be constructed, evolutionary theory threatens never to rise above the provision of "how-possibly" explanations.

Adaptationist stories are not compelling because of the nature of the generalizations they appeal to. These generalizations state that any trait which can perform some function F will enhance an organism's fitness. The existence of traits apt for performing F is explained as the result of selection. But a trait's relative fitness value depends on the environment and on the range of competing alternative traits. Furthermore, the outcomes of selection processes are subject to purely stochastic factors. So adaptationist theorizing can be genuinely explanatory only if there are generalizations about the superiority of certain traits that hold across a wide range of environments and alternative traits and are robust in the face of stochasticity. There are unlikely to be many of these generalizations. Evolutionary theory is a historical science. Its outcomes are continuously affected by historical accidents. If we could replay the tape of life it would play out differently every time (Gould 1989). George C. Williams elevates this to one of the three guiding insights of modern biology (Williams 1992; see also Hull 1987; O'Hara 1988; Griffiths 1994).

The historicity of evolution means that adaptive forces are insufficient to predict what will occur or explain what has occurred. They will yield predictions (or explanations) only in conjunction with a rich set of historical assumptions. The traditional adaptationist approach is to point to how neatly the adaptive generalizations *would* explain the observed trait *if* the assumptions were true. The neatness of fit is supposed to confirm the historical assumptions. But this kind of "argument to the best explanation" fails if there are many good explanations, as there typically are. The traditional savanna theory of human brain expansion, the aquatic ape theory, the thermoregulation hypothesis, and the machiavellian intelligence hypothesis all give excellent explanations of the growth in human brain size if their historical assumptions are granted. The only way to tell them apart is to test those assumptions directly. Biologists today are increasingly doing just that. These tests eliminate many of the candidate explanations. This makes it possible to legitimately justify a surviving hypothesis by argument to the best explanation. It may also be possible to recognize alternative forms of evolutionary explanation when no adaptive explanation passes the available tests.

Many recent studies of adaptation take the form of mapping competing adaptive stories onto independently established phylogenetic trees so as to discriminate between the stories, a procedure whose potential has been widely acknowledged.[4] This technique has been made possible by advances in cladistic methods for establishing evolutionary relationships and the ease with which modern molecular techniques generate data sets for those methods. Jonathan Coddington provides a simple example (1988, 10–11). Living species of rhinoceros have either one or two horns. As both horn numbers are "strategies" demonstrably available to the evolving rhinoceros, it is natural to invent an adaptive scenario in which both horn conditions are evolutionarily stable strategies, or ESSs (e.g., Lewontin 1978). Once a population contains a large proportion of individuals with

---

4. Brooks and MacLennan 1991; Coddington 1988; Felsenstein 1985; Harvey and Pagel 1991; Lauder 1981, 1982, 1990; Lauder, Armand, and Rose 1993; Miles and Dunham 1993; Taylor 1987. A brief outline of cladistic methods can be found in section 8.2.

one number of horns it cannot be invaded by a mutant with the other number of horns. Victory goes to whichever strategy gets in first in a particular population. Various sexual selection scenarios would fit these requirements. However, a cladistic analysis of the rhinoceratid group shows that the two-horned condition preceded the one-horned in the phylogenetic tree. This suggests that at some point or other, in some environment, the one-horned form was adaptively superior. To sustain the existing proposal it would be necessary to add an auxiliary hypotheses such as the claim that a small population containing one-horned mutants was isolated and the one-horned form drifted to a frequency from which it could become an ESS. This claim could also be tested using cladistic biogeographic methods which associate taxa with habitats and allow inferences about ancestral habitat associations.

It is possible to distinguish three general ways in which adaptive explanations are constrained by their association with the phylogenetic tree. First, because the adaptive stories for all the characters are related to the same tree, they must be coherent with one another. Many adaptive stories describe a suite of characters that are supposed to be adaptations to a postulated evolutionary scenario. The ability of the scenario to explain so many characters is often urged as its main explanatory strength. Thirty or so characters of humans are meant to be explained by the single "aquatic ape" story (Morgan 1982). But stories of this kind can be rejected if the supposed "adaptive character suite" is a collage of traits acquired at different points on the tree. Still finer discriminations of this kind can be made using the sequence in which the traits appear on the tree, since the supposed adaptive advantage of one trait is often contingent on the existence of some of the others.

The second way in which the tree constrains adaptive explanation is by allowing rigorous uses of the "comparative method." Traditional, narrative presentations of adaptive scenarios are particularly prone to invalid comparative tests. One common method is to choose one or more species as "living ancestors" and to argue from the utility of the trait in those species to its adaptive origins in the species under study. This form of argument is particularly prominent in the study of human evolution, with other primates playing the roles of ancestors. Many such stories can be tested rigorously if a phylogenetic tree is available. If a "living ancestor" is supposed to demonstrate the ancestral function of a similar trait in humans then the trait or its vestiges should be observed in other species descended from the common ancestor of ourselves and the comparison species. If it is claimed that a trait is correlated with certain adaptive conditions, then we can use a phylogenetic tree and biogeographic techniques to see if the trait originated in those conditions, not merely if it occurs in them today.

A third way in which the tree constrains adaptive explanation is through its relationship to habitat factors. Coevolutionary studies offer relatively direct tests of postulated interactions between one species and another. If a suite of characters in one group of species is the result of an "arms race" with another group, then there should be congruence between the trees for the evolution of the characters in the two groups. Such congruences have been widely observed in the case of parasites and hosts. Less direct tests are possible for a wide range of other habitat factors. A postulated set of habitat changes should impact on other species who share that habitat, and these parallel changes should be reflected in congruence between trees. Conversely, it should not affect related species outside that habitat and should be reflected in a lack of congruence with those trees. Failure to find appropriate congruence suggests that the habitat factors have been misidentified.

The historical turn in the study of adaptation promises to lift adaptive explanation above the provision of just-so stories. But it has yet to be applied to adaptive studies of emotion. Some of the research that follows most closely in Darwin's footsteps succeeds in avoiding the worst pitfalls of adaptationism. Much of the rest is found wanting. Plutchik's ecological theory of emotion suffers particularly badly from the problems of adaptationism. Not only has it yet to undergo any of the tests outlined in the last section, it also suffers from another characteristic flaw of adaptationist reasoning. The theory does not establish the existence of the phenomena it purports to explain before it starts to explain them. Instead, it takes the success of the adaptive storytelling to bestow plausibility on the "facts" which it explains! To see how this happens it is necessary to understand how Plutchik generated the "emotion solid" (figure 3.3) which he sets out to explain. It was generated by semantic field analysis on a domain of English emotion words. This technique is the psychologist's equivalent of conceptual analysis. Competent speakers are asked to make comparisons between words, rating them on a scale of similarity or difference. The re-

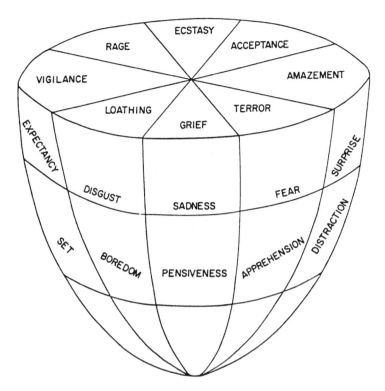

3.3. Plutchik's "emotion solid." The four pairs of "polar opposites" are supposed to correspond to four fundamental ecological variables. The vertical dimension represents intensity. From Plutchik (1970).

sults are factor-analyzed to discover the minimum number of axes of variation that can explain all the judgments. Because the number of factors obtained is notoriously artifactual, Plutchik uses a variant of factor analysis that places the words in a circle, all axes of which can be interpreted as corresponding to some dimension of difference. The way in which Plutchik constructed his model means that it is essentially a model of what English speakers *think* about emotions. Plutchik's method is based on the assumption that ordinary English speakers already have a correct theory of emotion! Once the emotion solid was derived, Plutchik interpreted it in terms of ecological categories that seemed to make some sort of evolutionary sense. The existing folk theory about the structure and function of the emotions is bolstered by backing it up with an evolutionary just-so story.

As usual, there is no great difficulty in telling a story in which a cognitive system with the structure and functions attributed to the emotion system by current English speakers would have been fitness enhancing.

One of the strengths of Robert Frank's ecological theory of emotion is that he has tried to establish that the traits for which he offers evolutionary explanations actually exist. He supports his account of the "sense of fairness" by citing experiments in which people punish those who have offered unfair bargains even when this is of no advantage to the person administering the punishment.

Darwin's own work holds up very well in the face of the problem of adaptationism. Darwin was continually aware of the historical and phylogenetic dimension of the evolutionary approach to emotion. His explananda were the well-defined facial expression syndromes he had uncovered by empirical investigation. He argued that these had an evolutionary basis by showing that the expressions were species-typical features of human behavior that did not seem to arise as a functional response to some universal environmental influence. He analyzed the syndromes into components, using anatomical techniques. Using this detailed set of characters he attempted to establish elements of a phylogeny for these characters, by looking for shared characters between human displays and those of other animals. Finally, he suggested an adaptive story in which expressions evolved by the successive modification to new adaptive needs of structures established to meet adaptive needs at an earlier stage in phylogeny. Despite his lack of rigorous modern phylogenetic techniques, Darwin's approach is adaptive-historical rather than adaptationist. In the next chapter I look at a modern theory of emotion that is built directly on the foundations established by Darwin. In the following chapter I look at theories like Frank's whose foundations are less secure.

4

Affect Programs
and Emotion Modules

4.1 Affect Programs

The experiments on facial expression reviewed in the last chapter have led to a revival of Darwin's approach to emotion. In the work of some authors, notably Paul Ekman, this approach has become linked to the idea of "affect programs." The central idea of affect program theory is that emotional responses are complex, coordinated, and automated. They are complex because they involve several elements. These are usually taken to include (a) expressive facial changes, (b) musculoskeletal responses such as flinching and orienting, (c) expressive vocal changes, (d) endocrine system changes and consequent changes in the level of hormones, and (e) autonomic nervous system changes. Emotion feelings and cognitive phenomena such as the directing of attention are obvious candidates to be added to this list. The affect program responses are coordinated because the various elements occur together in recognizable patterns or sequences. They are automated because they unfold in this coordinated fashion without the need for conscious direction. Ekman sometimes conceives affect programs as literal neural programs which coordinate the various elements in the emotional response. However, the phrase can be used in a more noncommittal fashion. The *affect program* is the coordinated set of changes that constitute the emotional response. I use the phrase in this sense.

The work of Ekman and his collaborators is of particular interest because they seem to treat emotion terms as the names of categories of psychological events in the manner I advocated in chapter 1. In that chapter I suggested that emotions should be identified with whichever theoretical entities psychology uses to explain the phenomena associated with those emotions. Science discovers that love is an evolved bonding mechanism or a social construction designed to subordinate women in the same way that it discovered that water is HOH and that barnacles are crustaceans. Ekman appears to argue for theoretical identities of this sort between the emotions and the affect programs. He claims to have uncovered six species-typical human affect programs. He has called these surprise, anger, fear, disgust, sadness, and joy.[1]

Ekman's claims have been controversial, and the reasons for this are as much philosophical as empirical. Many of Ekman's critics seem committed to the view that empirical discoveries cannot cause conceptual change. However, if an emotion like anger is identified with the relevant affect program, this will involve substantial revision of the concept of anger. Not everything ordinary speakers call "anger" will now be counted as anger, and many commonplace beliefs about anger will be rejected. The critics think it a problem that the proposed identity would induce these conceptual revisions. But this sort of revision is commonplace in the sciences. Modern systematics has led biologists to claim that Reptilia must either include birds or exclude crocodiles if it is to be retained as a real category. The discussion of Ekman's work by other authors shows just how far they are from appreciating these possibilities for conceptual change. A common criticism is that Ekman and authors who use similar techniques make subjects choose an emotion label from a limited list (Russell 1991c; Ratner 1989). If subjects were allowed to choose whatever term they wished, it is alleged, their agreement on what emotion is being expressed would disappear. Thus Ratner remarks, "One photo was variously described as amusement, gratitude, optimism, serenity and satisfaction (Izard 1980, 204). Yet the authors inexplicably state that the subjects expressed a common judgement that the photograph manifested joy!" (1989, 223).

Ratner's puzzlement would be resolved if he interpreted the claim that all the subjects have detected joy in the way I have suggested it should be interpreted. It does not mean that, of all the categories of positive emotion which are available in English, the subjects think *joy* is the best description of this face. If that was what Izard was claiming he would probably not written an experimental report which clearly contradicts this conclusion. Instead, the experiment is designed to show that all the observers are sensitive to a particular facial expression and that they assign it roughly the

---

1. Ekman and Friesen (1986) have argued for a seventh affect program, differentiated from the original disgust program and called contempt.

same significance. The authors code a wide range of positive emotion descriptors as joy because they have already chosen *joy* as a label for a facial expression that is known to be a pancultural human behavior produced in situations of positive emotion. The claim that the subjects all detected joy means that they all proved capable of identifying *this* face as an expression of positive emotion.

It may be that the conceptual change required to identify our emotion terms with the affect programs is too great. There are many examples of this in natural science. It has been known for centuries that any category wide enough to include all the true lilies will include garlic and onions, but ordinary folk have not started calling these vegetables lilies (Dupré 1981). But a failure to convert ordinary usage in this way would in no way discredit Ekman's work. If his empirical work is sound he would still have shown that in a certain limited range of instances what is going on when we describe people as angry is a particular affect program. He would have discovered a category of psychological state. If some wider psychological category can be found which includes a larger portion of the pretheoretic extension of the concept of anger, then anger can be identified with this category. The affect program might be one kind of anger. But if no such wider category exists it may be necessary to accept that anger is not a single object of study for psychology. If psychologists cannot induce suitable changes in the concept of anger they might give their own concept a new label like "affect program anger," just as botanists have given up the term *lilies* in favor of the family name *Liliaceae,* which includes onions, garlic, and much else.

4.2 The Evidence for Affect Programs

The experiments described in chapter 3 show that certain facial expressions of emotion are complex, coordinated, and automated. The affect program theory is on its home territory when discussing these elements. It is less clear that the other elements of emotional response possess the required characteristics. The affect program theory requires them to be coordinated with the facial expressions to form complex total-body responses. It also requires them to be found as widely across human cultures as the facial expressions. Opponents of the theory portray the other elements as either undifferentiated between different emotions or highly variable across persons and cultures.

The most heavily researched area after facial expression is the activity of the autonomic nervous system (ANS). Most of this research has investigated whether ANS response differentiates between emotions. Fortunately, this traditional question is almost identical to the question of whether emotional responses are coordinated in the way required by the affect program theory. To say that ANS activity differentiates among emotions is just to say that it is coordinated with other elements, notably facial expression, in recognizable patterns or sequences. There is also an important connection between the question of differentiation and the idea that emotional responses are the products of evolution. If ANS arousal is part of an adaptive response, it should reflect the forms of adaptive activity which the emotion is geared to. The ANS arousal associated with fear and anger might be similar, since fighting and flying require much the same physiological preparation, but it would be odd if sadness led to the same sort of preparations, since in sadness they could serve no useful function. A positive answer to the question of differentiation would therefore support the general psychoevolutionary approach, as well as the affect program theory.

Empirical research on the ANS was initiated by the desire to test the famous James-Lange theory of emotion (James 1884, 1893). According to this theory the consciousness of an emotion is the perception of autonomic nervous system changes which follow directly (by a reflex arc) upon the perception of some external stimuli. The causal sequence which brings about our consciousness of fear, for example, is as follows. First, we perceive a fearful object. This precipitates ANS changes as part of the flight response. The perception of these changes is what constitutes our consciousness of emotion. Walter D. Cannon (1927, 1931) argued that several experimental results tell against the James-Lange theory. Cutting the spinal cord and vagus nerves in dogs, for example, does not appear to inhibit their ordinary emotional reactions. They still exhibit anger, rage, and pleasure in handling, although ANS input must be much reduced. The response time of the visceral organs and their associated nerves also appears too slow to account for the rapid responses associated with such emotions as fear and startle. Cannon claimed that attempts to artificially induce the appropriate visceral changes by, for example, injecting adrenaline did not produce the emotional responses that the theory predicted. He also claimed that any stressful stimulus produces roughly the same set of ANS responses, so that differences in the feelings associated with various emotions could not be the result of different ANS feedback.

Later work went some way to rehabilitating the view that ANS arousal is differentiated among emotions. In a series of experiments, Ax (1953) and Joseph Schachter (1957) found that fear produces cardiovascular symptoms associated with elevated adrenaline (increased heart rate, increased stroke volume, and decreased peripheral resistance) whereas anger produces cardiovascular symptoms associated with noradrenaline and bears more resemblance to the physiological response to pain. These results are consistent with those of later authors such as Schwartz, Weinberger, and Singer (1981), who reported that anger differs from happiness, sadness, and fear in terms of diastolic pressure and heart-rate change. They also found that sadness inhibits the normal physiological changes brought on by exercise. At the present time the James-Lange theory is undergoing something of a revival. Antonio Damasio's recent best-selling account of research into the neural basis of emotion embraces James as the intellectual ancestor of his theory that emotion feeling is the perception in the neocortex of bodily responses to stimuli mediated through lower brain centers (Damasio 1994).

Philosophers have paid little attention to these experiments but have been inordinately interested in an experiment conducted by Stanley Schachter and Jerome E. Singer (1962).[2] Schachter and Singer suggest that physiological arousal is a necessary condition of emotion, but the sort of emotion which is experienced does not depend on the sort of physiological arousal. Instead, the very same arousal can be "labeled" as different emotions if different cognitive cues are available in the environment. Subjects interpret their arousal on the basis of the thoughts they are having at the time. There are obvious similarities between this theory and the hybrid propositional attitude–physiological arousal theories discussed in chapter 1. Schachter and Singer's results are frequently cited by adherents of those theories to relegate the physiology of emotion to a background role, so it is worth examining them in some detail.

Schachter and Singer put forward three specific hypotheses. First, a

---

2. It is necessary to keep a close eye on the initials. Stanley Schachter and Jerome E. Singer confront Joseph Schachter and Jefferson A. Singer from the last paragraph!

subject will label a state of autonomic nervous system arousal for which they have no other explanation in terms of the cognitions available to them at the time. Second, if the subjects are offered an immediate physiological explanation of their arousal, they will not feel the need to provide the arousal with cognitive labels. Third, an individual will consider their cognitions to be emotions only to the extent to which they are physiologically aroused. To test these claims, Schachter and Singer divided their subjects into four groups. One group was injected with a placebo. The remaining three groups were injected with adrenaline. Of these groups, one was told the genuine physiological effects that they would experience, another was told nothing, and the third group was misinformed about what they would experience. Each of the four groups was divided in two. One half of each group was subjected to conditions designed to produce happiness or euphoria and the other half to conditions designed to produce anger. These emotions were to be induced by the behavior of stooges placed with the subject and, in the latter case, by the use of impertinent questionnaires (Question 16: With how many men (other than your father) has your mother had extramarital relationships? 4 and under___; 5–9___; 10 and over___). Schachter and Singer gathered results by making secret observations of their subjects during the anger and euphoria conditions and by asking them to fill in questionnaires after the event.

The results gained by Schachter and Singer lent support to the three hypotheses. In accordance with hypothesis one, subjects in the euphoria condition reported euphoria and subjects in the anger condition reported anger. Hypothesis two was supported by the relative responses of the three adrenaline conditions. The group who were fully informed about the effects of the adrenaline injection showed and reported the least signs of emotional arousal. The group misinformed about the effects of the injection showed and reported the greatest degree of arousal and the group told nothing fell somewhere between the two. Hypothesis three was supported by the relative lack of response in the placebo condition.

Contemporaries of Schachter and Singer criticized various aspects of the experiment (Plutchik and Ax 1967) and there have been problems with its replication, but with hindsight there is a single, devastating objection. Since 1962 it has been well established that subjects who are unable to account for their own behavioral or physiological responses will invent an explanation from whatever cues are available in the environment and claim that the explanation results from their direct knowledge of their own mental processes. This phenomenon is known as *confabulation* (Gazzaniga and Smiley 1984; Nisbett and Wilson 1977). In the laboratory it has been observed in patients with lesions in the corpus callosum. They confabulate to explain the activity of the areas of the brain that can no longer communicate with the speech centers. In nature it is observed in patients suffering from Korsakoff's syndrome. These patients confabulate to explain their behavior when their damaged memory mechanisms have erased the memory of its real motives. It has even been suggested that a substantial amount of self-report in normal subjects may be confabulation. One would *expect* Schachter and Singer's subjects to confabulate in order to explain the abnormal arousal caused by adrenaline injections. The results obtained do not discriminate between this null hypothesis and the hypothesis that subjects were observing the normal arousal associated with the emotions they reported.

Schachter and Singer did not actually assert that ANS response is undifferentiated. At most, they asserted that differences were not the basis on which subjects label their emotions. Recent experiments have reinforced the findings of Ax and Schachter that there is substantial differentiation. Ekman, Levenson, and Friesen (1983) measured a number of different indicators of ANS arousal: heart rate, electrical resistance of the skin, skin temperature, and muscular tension. They plotted the patterns of relative change of these several different measures under different emotion-inducing conditions. The results appear to show characteristic patterns for several emotions. Not only was it possible to distinguish positive emotions such as joy from negative emotions such as fear, anger, and grief, it was possible to distinguish among those negative emotions. Similar results were obtained by Levenson, Ekman, and Friesen (1990). That paper describes forthcoming work extending these results to other cultures.

It seems that there is solid evidence of ANS differentiation, though obviously much more work is needed. The extent to which other elements, such as musculoskeletal responses and expressive vocal changes, are differentiated and coordinated is less clear. There is a great deal of anecdotal evidence supporting the view that musculoskeletal responses such as flinching or orienting to the stimulus are coordinated with other elements of certain emotional responses, but there has been no program of controlled experiment to compare with that on facial expression or ANS activity. It is often asserted that the voice differentiates between emotions. Zajonc claims that "we have no difficulty in identifying emotions expressed by members of unknown cultures speaking unknown languages" (1980, 153). However, in ordinary encounters, speech is supplemented by facial, behavioral, and contextual cues. Speech must be isolated from these cues before any real conclusion can be reached. The experiments Zajonc cites to support his claim show that we can recognize the emotional tone of passages of speech in our own language which have been deliberately degraded to remove semantic information (Dawes and Kramer 1966; Scherer et al. 1972). Scherer et al. (1991) showed that the classes of emotion which can be recognized in speech include those uncovered in the classic studies of facial expression. Unfortunately, Scherer's experiments were conducted with Western subjects, so it remains unknown whether recognition of emotion from the voice is possible across cultures. Component analyses would also be needed before it could be concluded that the vocal features which subjects recognize are the same as those used in their own culture and thus part of a pancultural affect program.

4.3 Affect Programs and Alternatives

Suppose that the many elements of emotional response are differentiated and coordinated in the way that affect program theorists maintain. The question then arises whether there are actual neural structures which can be regarded as programs controlling the emotional response. Ekman appears to believe that there are such programs. He offers the same argument for their existence in a number of places (Ekman 1972, 1973, 1980). The emotional responses in question are complex and coordinated. They also occur very rapidly after presentation of the stimulus. Their onset is typically involuntary, and they unfold without conscious direction (i.e., they are automated). In these respects they are rather like reflexes, but more complex and coordinated. The argument for the existence of literal neural programs is that these features of emotion can best be explained with the hypothesis that there is a single neural "program" that is triggered by the stimulus and controls the various elements of the unfolding response.

An important challenge to this argument is posed by Neil McNaughton (1989), who suggests that in a complex and apparently coordinated emotional response, a number of separate programs may be responding to different features of the stimulus situation. In standard environments, this creates the appearance of an integrated response: "The parallel organisation of the control systems of these different classes [*of bodily changes*], coupled with the orderly arrangement of the environment, would mean that a particular state of one effector system (say the autonomic) would normally be accompanied by a particular state of other effector systems" (McNaughton 1989, 38).

If McNaughton is right, then experimental manipulations which "factor" the normal stimulus situation should reveal that the response consists of parallel, independent components. McNaughton describes a simple example of this, due to Hofer (1972). Rat pups separated from their lactating mother exhibit a reduction in heart rate and characteristic behaviors, together forming a stereotyped separation reaction. Provision of a nonlactating foster mother returns the pups' behavior to normal but does not correct heart rate. Provision of frequent feedings with milk returns heart rate to normal but does not correct the behavior. The regular correlation of the two elements of separation distress is explained by the regular coincidence of the two eliciting features in the environment, not by any internal coordinating program. McNaughton suggests that similar environmental constancies may be responsible for the observed coordination of different bodily systems in more complex emotional responses.

McNaughton is able to provide an evolutionary rationale for the idea that emotional responses involve separate parallel systems. It is a commonplace that evolution does not produce optimal engineering solutions. Instead, it works by incremental changes from a historically determined starting point, each change offering some small advantage to the organism. In the case of an emotional response, the elements of the response are often independently adaptive. An animal's ANS and facial responses to danger are of value for quite separate evolutionary reasons. The first helps it to escape the danger, while the second is a means of intraspecific communication. They may, therefore, have evolved independently of one another and may well be controlled by separate mechanisms.

McNaughton's evolutionary rationale for separate "effector systems" seems compelling for responses to stereotypical situations. No natural environment will separate a rat pup from its mother without reducing the frequency of its feedings. So there is no adaptive reason why these responses should be linked together within the organism. But the story is less compelling for organisms which have to cope with novel stimulus situations. Emotions in humans, for example, are elicited by an enormously wide range of stimuli. A mere light on a control panel may precipitate fear or joy. The only thing which *all* eliciting situations for fear have in common is the extremely abstract property that, in the light of the organism's past learning history, they can be evaluated as dangerous. This makes it unlikely that each of these situations possesses a range of common features of a fairly immediate perceptual kind. But this is precisely what is required on the separate systems view, if the apparent coordination of elements in the emotional response is due to the coincidence of a number of separate stimuli in the normal eliciting conditions for the emotion.

This reply to McNaughton appeals to the fact that the occurrence of emotion in humans requires cognitive evaluation of the stimulus. It is not necessary to say much about the nature of these evaluation processes at this point. I turn to this topic in the next section. The mere fact that some sort of cognitive analysis is involved is enough to create difficulties for the separate systems view. However, McNaughton has another possible explanation for the apparent coordination of elements in the emotional response which avoids these difficulties. He suggests that the elements of the response may trigger one another in what he terms "dialectical interactions." This would allow the response to appear coordinated, without being directed by any central program. It is also quite compatible with cognitive evaluation of the stimulus. The evaluation of the stimulus could trigger one element in the response, and the rest could follow as the result of the interaction of peripheral systems. There is a certain amount of direct evidence for dialectical interactions. Ekman, Levenson, and Friesen (1983) found that ANS arousal could be produced more effectively by teaching subjects to form emotional facial expressions than by asking them to relive emotional experiences. The feedback from the somatic nervous system appeared to induce other elements of the emotional response. Ekman (1992) also found that subjects in a similar experimental situation made suitable self-reports of emotion. Many other theorists, including Darwin himself, have argued that voluntary facial expressions can induce or amplify emotion. Tomkins (1962, 1980) made this phenomena the center of an extensive program of research.

It is hard to see how to distinguish the affect program and dialectical interaction explanations of the coordination of emotional responses except by neuroscientific investigation. Both theories are compatible with the psychoevolutionary perspective on emotion. A suite of adaptive responses to a highly abstract class of stimuli can be triggered by a single central cognitive evaluation. Whether they are all triggered centrally or trigger one another as the result of peripheral interactions is of no evolutionary significance. It might be argued that the dialectical interaction model is more consistent with the incremental, historical nature of design by natural selection. There are two reasons why it would be a mistake to give too much weight to this argument. First, evolution has managed to design some fairly well integrated cognitive mechanisms. Humans integrate the data from their several senses into a single model of the world rather than processing the data from each modality in parallel, although the senses presumably evolved separately. Second, there is no a priori reason why a central neural program cannot be designed incrementally, its control of several independently adaptive responses being built up in an ad hoc fashion.

Actual localizations of neural circuits involved in emotional responses are available from a few animal studies. In a famous series of experiments J. P. Flynn studied aggressive behaviors produced in cats by direct neural stimulation (Flynn 1967, 1969). He identified clearly separate locations controlling two different stereotypic patterns of behavior. Stimulation of one site elicited the predatory aggression normally directed against prey species while the other elicited socially aggressive behavior normally directed against conspecifics. Similar research was conducted by Jaak Panksepp (1982). Panksepp suggests that four pathways which subserve emotional responses can be found in the hypothalamus. Panksepp calls these the "expectancy," "fear," "rage," and "panic" pathways. These experiments have some relevance to the debate over affect programs, but not enough to allow any very substantial conclusions to be drawn.

Perhaps the best way to think of the literal neural affect program advocated by Ekman is as a sort of ideal limiting case of a spectrum of possible relationships between affect programs in the sense of observed patterns of emotional response and underlying neural structures. In this ideal case, the observable pattern of behaviors is controlled by a literal neural program. At the other end of the spectrum, the organization of emotional responses that can be observed at the behavioral level may be quite invisible at the neural level. The fact that stimuli with a certain perceived ecological significance produce a clearly recognizable pattern of response may emerge from a disparate set of interactions among separate control systems. The program, in computational terms, is a virtual one, and the whole idea of an internal program may be rather misleading. Both alternatives, and various intermediate positions, are compatible with the affect program theory as I have described it.

4.4 Control Mechanisms for Affect Programs

I have tried to show that the output side of many emotional responses can be given evolutionary explanations. A natural further question is whether the input side can be explained in the same way. Are there evolutionary explanations of what triggers emotions, as well as of what happens when they are triggered? The first task is to outline what is known about the input side of emotional responses.

In a famous experiment on this subject J. B. Watson (1930) showed that newborn babies respond to loud sounds and loss of balance with fear, to prolonged restraint with rage, and to gentle forms of skin stimulation with pleasure. He argued that all other associations were learned. Recent research has added another extensive class of stimuli to Watson's list. Neonates are extremely responsive to the facial expressions of caregivers (Trevarthen 1984; Izard 1978; Meltzoff and Moore 1977). But the simple technique of testing for emotional response soon after birth makes no allowance for the emergence of new responses during development. It also fails to allow for "learning preparedness" (Seligman 1970). Experience may be needed to produce a response, but less experience may be needed to produce a response to one object than to another. These "prepared associations" and their converse "contra-prepared" associations can often be given evolutionary explanations.

There is experimental evidence for learning preparedness in the cases of fear and disgust. Seligman (1971) has argued that phobias are best understood as cases of highly prepared (often one-trial) learning of fear. He suggests that the stimuli for which humans are predisposed to acquire fear are those which would have been prevalent sources of danger during human evolution. Ohman et al. (1976) conducted conditioning experiments on human beings in an attempt to test a similar proposal. They found that associations between electric shock and classic phobic stimuli, such as snakes, were more resistant to extinction than associations established with a similar number of trials between shock and neutral stimuli, such as flowers, or arbitrary stimuli, such as shapes. They were also more resistant than associations between phobic stimuli and nonaversive stimuli, in this case sounds. They concluded that the association of certain classic phobic stimuli with danger is a prepared association in humans.

Disgust responses have been widely studied in animals under the heading of *taste aversion*. Many species exhibit a marked inability to associate anything but ingested substances with nausea and have remarkable capacities to identify and avoid noxious substances in their diet. Various authors have suggested the existence of specialized mechanisms for associating illness with tastes (Rozin and Kalat 1971; Garcia and Rusiniak 1980). Other authors (Logue et al. 1986) have attempted to show that a similar mechanism exists in humans. It appears that in humans, as in other animals, there is a tendency to acquire disgust for a taste which has been followed by illness, even where higher-level cognitive systems are aware that no causal connection exists between the food and the illness.

My aim in this section is to determine to what extent the input side of emotion could be given an evolutionary explanation. The data considered above suggest that most emotion-eliciting stimuli are learned. But they also suggest that the learning mechanism is biased. It is not a general-purpose mechanism, equally capable of learning any facts that the world may embody. Some kinds of fact are easier to learn, and some harder. Although the organism does not arrive in the world with a preconceived map of what is emotionally significant, it does bring with it some preconceptions about what is *likely* to be emotionally significant.

Most of these ideas about the input side of emotion are entirely consistent with an evolutionary account of the affect programs. An adaptive scenario can be sketched for the evolution of biased learning mechanisms as a way of determining which stimuli will elicit emotion. Affect programs are adaptive responses to events that have a particular ecological significance for the organism. The fear response is adapted to dangers, the disgust response to noxious stimuli, the anger response to challenges, the surprise response to novel stimuli. The local events which possess the properties of being dangerous, noxious, or novel may be very different from one environment to another. If affect programs are to be of significant adaptive advantage to an organism over an evolutionarily significant time period, it might well have been advantageous for them to be linked to some mechanism which can interpret the broad ecological categories of danger, novelty, and so forth, in the light of local conditions. So it is unsurprising that organisms have to learn which events in their particular environment should trigger the affect programs. There are, however, certain constancies in the environment which a learning system can be preprogrammed to take account of. The disgust response is designed to prevent the ingestion of noxious substances. It would be extremely inefficient if the disgust response were to be elicited by nongustatory stimuli, however well those stimuli might correlate with illness. Such responses would be useless and probably counterproductive. It might therefore be advantageous to have a constraint on the learning mechanism which restricts disgust to gustatory stimuli in organisms that select food by smell, as observed in rats, or color stimuli in organisms that select food by sight, as observed in quail. The other sort of constraint on learning discussed above, a preparedness to interpret certain stimuli as having a particular ecological significance or a reluctance to interpret other stimuli in this way, also has possible adaptive advantages. A prepared learning mechanism of this sort could combine flexibility in the face of environmental variation with the advantages of inheriting the experience of past generations.

It is also possible to sketch adaptive scenarios for the evolution of the neonate's sensitivity to the facial expressions of caregivers. Learning the significance of the facial expressions of conspecifics would be a complex and probably lengthy task, but it would be advantageous to have this ability available as early as possible. First, responding appropriately to the emotional state of caregivers may be directly advantageous to the infant. There is a less obvious advantage, however, which may in fact be more important. The significance of events in the current environment can be very rapidly assessed by noting the assessment of those who have already lived in that environment. Very few children have been hurt by snakes, or spiders, or the dark, but it seems that only a slight demonstration of revulsion or anxiety by adults is needed to produce powerful aversions to these things in the young (Klinnert et al. 1983). An early capacity to interpret the emotional responses of adults would facilitate learning of this kind.

Finally, it may be possible to give an evolutionary explanation of the irrational persistence of judgments about the emotional significance of the environment. A single aversive experience or a single display of fear by a caregiver may result in a fear of, say, the dark that will be retained despite any amount of information about the harmlessness of darkness. Emotional responses do not seem to adjust themselves as readily as beliefs when new information is acquired about the environment. Sustained counterconditioning seems to be needed to delete an assessment once it has become linked to an affect program response. This may be due to the evolutionary advantages of false-positive responses. The costs of failing to respond to dangers, challenges, noxious stimuli, and so on may well outweigh the costs of responding unnecessarily. Failing to respond to danger may lead to death, while responding unnecessarily merely wastes a little energy. In evolutionary terms, phobias and irrational distastes may have much to recommend them.

These putative evolutionary explanations have the "how possibly" form typical of adaptationist reasoning. They sketch plausible scenarios for the evolution of the various features discovered by psychologists. But as the discussion in the last chapter showed, it is a mistake to put too much weight on such storytelling. The most basic trap to avoid is that of taking the empirical findings about the emotion system to be confirmed by their evolutionary plausibility. Past experience suggests that *whatever* was discovered would have been made to look evolutionarily plausible. Only actual empirical psychology can provide good grounds for theories about the structure of the emotion system. The second trap to avoid is taking the mere plausibility of an evolutionary explanation as adequate confirmation of that explanation. The literature on evolutionary optimality models shows that intuitions about the plausibility of models presented in nonquantitative, narrative forms are of no use in assessing those models. It is just too easy to generate plausible models. Some authors have suggested that we should be impressed by certain sorts of precise quantitative fit between an optimality model and the actual state of the organisms in a population (Orzack and Sober 1994) but no suitable quantitative elaborations of models of the emotion system exist to allow this sort of testing. The obvious way to test some of the stories I have told in this section would be to develop them to the point where they have implications about where in the sequence of mammalian evolution the traits concerned should appear and to test these implications using the comparative method.

4.5. Emotions and Modularity

In this section I want to consider the relationship between the affect program system and higher cognitive processes. Unfortunately, I cannot do much more than gesture at what I mean by *higher cognitive processes*. The history of cognitive science has been marked by success in understanding the operation of specialized mechanisms such as the visual system, while only the sketchiest accounts exist of the mechanisms underlying activities such as reasoning, theorizing, and planning. My own understanding of higher cognitive processes centers on the idea that they are the processes in which people use the information of the sort they verbally assent to (traditional beliefs) and the goals they can be brought to recognize (traditional desires) to guide relatively long-term action and to solve theoretical problems.

It seems clear that emotions are sometimes triggered as a result of higher cognitive processes. A complex chain of reasoning may reveal that an entirely novel stimulus is dangerous, and fear ensues. It seems equally clear, however, that on other occasions, emotions are triggered despite, or in opposition to, higher cognitive processes. In some cases a conscious evaluation calls for an emotional response, but none occurs. In other cases, a conscious evaluation of a stimulus reveals that it does not merit an emotional response, and it receives one nonetheless. Emotional responses can also occur in response to stimuli that have not been detected by higher cognitive processes. Zajonc (1980, 1984b) lists a range of experiments tending to show that emotional responses can be triggered when the information that triggered the response is unavailable for any higher cognitive purposes. In chapter 2 I referred to these last two cases as "reflex emotion."

Ekman has argued that the independence of emotional responses from rational evaluations, and the speed of onset of many responses, suggests that they can be triggered by an evaluation system independent of higher cognitive processes. Ekman calls this the "automatic appraisal mechanism." The AAM would have some form of memory, storing information about classes of stimuli previously assessed as meriting emotional response. The AAM would receive perceptual information, presumably at quite a basic level of analysis, and compare this to "memories" which would take the form of generalizations about the significance of certain perceptible features. I do not mean to imply a physiological separation between the memory and the decision-making system, only to distinguish two functional aspects of the AAM. The two might be physiologically identical, in the manner of some connectionist systems. The effect of the AAM would be to allow a more rapid response to important events than would be possible if it were necessary to evaluate their significance using all available information. It would also cause the organism to be conservative, producing an emotional response more often than was actually necessary. Zajonc is less specific, but argues that "affect and cognition are under the control of separate and partially independent systems, that can influence one another in a number of ways, and that both constitute independent sources of effects in information processing" (1980, 151).

Zajonc grounds this view on a collection of results in which there is an apparent emotional response but no evidence of higher cognitive activity, or in which higher cognitive activity of an appropriate sort can actually be ruled out. I described some of these results in section 2.2. In two of these experiments melodies and figures were presented to subjects for very short periods. Although recall memory for these items remained at chance levels, the classic "exposure effect" on preferences was produced. Subjects significantly preferred items to which they had been repeatedly exposed to other similar items. This seems to show that information had reached affective mechanisms without reaching the mechanisms governing recall.

Ekman's AAM and Zajonc's emotion system possess many of the features which Jerry Fodor (1983) lists as characteristic of modular cognitive systems. The systems operation is *mandatory* (Zajonc's term is "inescapable"). People often respond with fear or anger to a given stimulus whether they choose to or not. The system is largely *opaque* to our central cognitive processes. People are aware of its outputs, which are the emotional responses themselves, but not aware of the processes that lead to them. Finally, and most important, the system is *informationally encapsulated*. It cannot access all the information stored in other cognitive systems, and it can store information that contradicts that other information. Conscious beliefs concerning, for example, the harmlessness of earthworms do not get taken into account when the system is deciding upon a response. Informational encapsulation is one of the most important features of modular systems, since it captures what is meant by their "separation" from other processes, such as those leading to longer-term, planned action.

The data on the triggering of emotional response reviewed in the last section lend themselves very naturally to a modular interpretation. The data suggest that the rules governing the acquisition of information about what is emotionally significant are importantly different from those used to acquire information on other topics. This in turn suggests that a distinct psychological system is involved.

The modularity of the systems which trigger affect programs differs in one important respect from that of the perceptual input systems which constitute Fodor's paradigm. The output of perceptual systems is a mental event, a perception, whereas that of the emotion system is behavioral. But this does not conflict with the Fodorean approach to modularity. Fodor establishes the notion of a modular system by analogy with reflexes, which, of course, have a behavioral output. Fodor draws the analogy in the following, typically Fodorean, words:

> Reflexes are informationally encapsulated with bells on . . . you have come to know perfectly well that under no conceivable circumstances would I stick my finger in your eye . . . Still, if I jab my finger near enough to your eye, you'll blink. To say, as we did above, that the blink reflex is mandatory is to say, inter alia, that it has no access to what you know about my character or, for that matter, to any other of your beliefs, utilities and expectations. For this reason the blink reflex is often produced when sober reflection would show it to be uncalled for . . . it is prepared to trade false positives for speed.
>
> That is what it is like for a system to be informationally encapsulated. If you now imagine a system that is encapsulated in the way that reflexes are, but also computational in the way that reflexes are not, you will have some idea of what I'm proposing that input systems are like. (1983, 71–72)

The proprietary appraisal mechanism for the psychoevolved emotional responses would be a module of this sort—a system akin to a reflex in its encapsulation and mandatory operation, but with relatively sophisticated information processing arrangements for the interpretation of the stimulus.

Various authors have given an evolutionary slant to the notion of modularity. Fodor draws on Rozin (1976) and others to give an evolutionary explanation of the continued existence of modules in organisms such as ourselves which are capable of more general intelligence. Modules have their origin in phylogenetic predecessors who did not have general intelligence. They provide relatively unintelligent but effective ways of performing certain low-level cognitive processes such as perception (and, I would add, immediate emotive response). The question is therefore not why we have them but why we have retained them. Fodor argues that the very unintelligence of modular systems gives them a number of advantages over general intelligence. Among these are the very short response times that can be obtained by having a mandatory system and a limited database. If a system is mandatory, there is no decision time incorporated in the response time. If the system operates on a limited database, which is chosen for its relevance to the question at hand, the procedures through which it must go in order to make its decision may be more rapid. Finally, Fodor suggests that there are penalties to allowing our higher cognition to interfere with certain other processes. In the case of perception he points out that it is vital for an organism to be able to accept data which contradict even its most centrally held beliefs. If perception is an entirely top-down process then the perception of novelty is impossible. The modularity of our perceptual processes means that we are compelled to consider data hostile to our present beliefs even if, eventually, we decide not to change them on the basis of those data.

Similarly, the modularity of our emotional responses can be seen as a mechanism for saving us from our own intelligence by rapidly and involuntarily initiating essential behaviors. If central cognitive processes conform more or less closely to rational decision theory and implement plans designed to maximize expected outcomes, there may be evolutionary advantages in retaining more cautious and conservative mechanisms to handle certain vital responses. Zajonc (1980) comments on this fail-safe aspect of emotional response:

> If the rabbit is to escape, the action must be undertaken long before the completion of even a simple cognitive process—before, in fact, the rabbit has fully established and verified that a nearby movement might reveal a snake in all its coiled glory. The decision to run must be made on the basis of minimal cognitive engagement. (1980, 156)

The affect program responses seem to fit this model quite well. In the case of the fear response, no matter what our higher cognitive processes tell us about the current situation, if we have experienced an object as harmful in some past segment of our learning history, the AAM will trigger our fear affect program and this will initiate expressive facial changes and the necessary autonomic nervous system changes for a flight or fight response.

Once again, these evolutionary interpretations take the form of nonquantitative, narrative presentations of optimality arguments. All the reservations outlined above apply to them. They cannot take the place of actual empirical findings in assuring us that the emotion system really is modular. They themselves must be treated as "how possibly" explanations until they are properly confirmed. One way to begin confirming them might be to construct quantified versions of them. Some of the considerations adduced by Fodor and Zajonc should be mathematically interpretable using signal detection theory, a branch of optimality modeling which looks at the optimal relationship between incoming information and behavioral output. However, an optimality approach to these particular features is made less appealing by the fact that they are secondary adaptations based on retained features from earlier phases of evolution. If they are optimal, it is in the sense that they represent the best place you can get to from a particular starting point, not the best place you can get to overall. Considerations of history like this are hard to build into mathematical optimality models. They pose no problem, however, for the historical and comparative approach to testing adaptative stories which I recommended in the last chapter. Even in their current sketchy form Fodor's and Zajonc's theories imply that the existing affect program system is phylogenetically more ancient than higher cognitive processes. This claim is eminently testable.

One reason to take Fodor's and Zajonc's ideas seriously is that they fit with what is currently known about the neural basis of emotional responses. This suggests that they are subserved by neural circuits in the limbic system, the phylogenetically old portion of the cortex which surrounds the brain stem, or in associated brain-stem structures. The hypothalamus and amygdala seem to play a crucial role in much of the brain activity underlying the affect program responses (the central role of the hypothalamus has been recognized since the pioneering work of Walter D. Cannon [1927, 1931; see also Papez 1937]). This limbic localization of our phylogenetically ancient, pancultural elements of emotional response seems fairly secure (see chapter 7 of Damasio [1994] for an accessible recent survey).

Zajonc has argued that the localization of emotion in the limbic brain implies that emotional responses must have evolved earlier than the intelligent, flexible cognitive systems characteristic of humans and other large mammals. As noted above, this would support his ideas about the evolution of emotion:

The limbic system that controls emotional reactions was there before we evolved language and our present form of thinking . . . When nature has a direct and autonomous mechanism that functions efficiently—and there is no reason to suppose that the affective system was anything else—it does not make it indirect and dependent on a newly evolved function [*cognition*]. It is rather more likely that the affective system retained its autonomy, relinquishing its exclusive control over behavior slowly and grudgingly . . . These conjectures make a two-system view more plausible than one which relegates affect to a secondary role mediated and dominated by cognition. (1980, 169–70)

4.6 A Tentative Model

The theories considered in this chapter suggest a tentative picture of the psychology of the affect program emotions: surprise, fear, anger, disgust (contempt?), sadness, and joy. These emotions consist of complex, coordinated, and automated responses. These may either be coordinated by some central program or result from characteristic patterns of interaction between the various bodily systems involved in the response. There is a flow of perceptual information to the mechanisms controlling these responses which is separate from the flow of information from perception to the higher cognitive processes responsible for intentional action. This element of modularity is required to account for the lack of fit between emotional responses and conscious evaluations of the significance of stimuli. In some cases higher cognitive processes may be able to trigger emotional responses directly,[3] but in other cases the associations which lead to the response must be separate from the evaluations made by higher cognition.

The modular system which triggers emotion has an interestingly biased mechanism for learning. The biased nature of the learning mechanism provides a further reason for thinking of the emotion-triggering system as independent of higher cognitive processes, since the biases seem to be specific to the learning of emotional responses. The isolation of the triggering system from higher cognition need not be complete. It may be that rational

---

3. Creating emotion by imagining emotionally significant stimuli may be an example of the direct effect of central cognitive processes. On the other hand, this may work via the generation of visual and other sensory imagery. It would then be an internal analogue of the triggering of emotion by the visual arts.

evaluations of stimuli as emotionally significant can cause the triggering system to be sensitive to those stimuli in future instances. I know of no experimental literature that would allow this to be determined at present. There are also results which seem to show that higher cognitive processes can affect the initiation of emotions in much the same way that they affect the perception of pain (Melzack 1973). Lazarus, Coyne, and Folkman (1984) cite a number of experiments in which the effect of a stimulus situation on emotion, as measured by ANS arousal and self-report, was influenced by manipulating the interpretation of the stimulus by higher cognitive processes.

Finally, Ekman's work on cultural display rules suggests that other cognitive processes can block the display of automatic emotional responses by recruiting the bodily systems involved for other purposes. The fact that the response cannot be blocked before it influences the facial musculature provides further evidence for the informational encapsulation of the emotion triggering system.

The model just described makes it possible to dissolve the various puzzles raised by the propositional attitude theory of emotion. The idea that emotional evaluations are informationally encapsulated gives us what Michael Stocker was looking for in chapter 2 when he talked of "emotionally held" thoughts. The content attribution "S is afraid of spiders" implies that S evaluates spiders as dangerous. But this evaluation can be made by two separate psychological systems. If it is made by higher cognitive processes, then S may not exhibit the emotional response. If it is made by the modular "automatic appraisal mechanism," then S may not admit to believing that spiders are dangerous. Folk-psychological content attribution will be unproblematic when both systems evaluate the stimulus in the same way. When they disagree, however, we get some of the problematic cases described in chapter 2. Reflex emotions occur when the automatic appraisal mechanism evaluates the situation in a way which conflicts with its evaluation by higher cognitive processes. Unemotional evaluations occur when a situation is evaluated by higher cognition as having some ecological significance, but the automatic appraisal mechanism does not recognize this significance. Objectless emotions occur when affect program responses are inappropriately triggered as they sometimes are in epileptics (MacLean 1980). The model does not immediately explain how emotions are triggered by imaginary objects but it makes this a practical question for psychology, rather than a philosophical paradox.

Examples of emotions which do not fit the model spring immediately to mind. Love, in its romantic sense, is hardly going to be analyzed as a rapid response which had survival value for our phylogenetic predecessors (though lust, of course, plausibly might be). It is therefore important to understand that the model is not intended to cover all the mental events which it is good English to call *emotions* or *emotional*. The model hopes to deal with a class of short-term emotional responses many of which are homologues of responses in other species. These emotions exhibit to the greatest extent those properties which mark off emotions from such mental states as judgments and beliefs, features like "passivity." I argue in part 2 that these states, the phenomenologically compelling, occurrent instances of anger, fear, joy, sadness, disgust, and surprise, act as a paradigm for the folk-psychological conception of emotion.

One reward of the narrow focus of the current model is its greater explanatory power. I argued in chapter 1 that the cognitive theory, even if successful in its own terms, would explain very little about emotion. The affect program theory, however, explains a great deal about the responses with which it deals. It explains why they consist of both physical responses and assessments of the significance of the environment. The physical response is adaptive in the perceived ecological situation. It provides testable hypotheses about the origins of many details of each response. It also provides testable hypotheses about the origin of the mandatory and opaque quality traditionally referred to as the "passivity" of emotion (Peters 1962). These features may well be explained by the evolutionary advantages of modularity. The question I turn to in the next chapter is whether these powerful explanatory tools can be applied to a wider range of emotions.

5

The Higher Cognitive Emotions: Some Research Programs

5.1 The Need for a Theory of Higher Cognitive Emotions

When a theory of emotion has some success in explaining aspects of some emotions, its adherents typically try to apply the theory to all emotions. Some theorists do this by stipulating that mental states which do not fit the model are not emotions. Other theorists claim that all emotions will eventually be explained by the favored model when it has been adjusted or extended. Propositional attitude theorists and social constructionists have used both strategies to oppose "naturalistic" views of emotion, but they are not the only sinners. In this section I want to suggest that the success of the affect program model does not warrant either of these strategies. The model is a good one, but there are many emotions that it does not explain and there is no reason to suppose that any eventual successful treatment of these emotions will be an outgrowth of the affect program approach.

The affect program system creates brief, highly stereotyped emotional reactions. It has only limited involvement with the cognitive processes which control longer-term action. The stimulus appraisal which initiates an affect program reaction is to a large extent informationally encapsulated. The subsequent complex set of actions unfolds automatically, and it is difficult to interfere with these actions voluntarily. There are a large number of emotions which do not conform to this model. In many instances of guilt, envy, or jealousy the subject does not display a stereotypical pattern of physiological effects. In addition, these emotions seem more integrated with cognitive activity leading to planned, long-term actions than the affect program responses. There are even instances of categories like anger and disgust, the very categories which affect program research has done so much to illuminate, that do not involve the relevant affect programs. Competent members of the speech community call people "angry" or "disgusted" when they have not displayed the appropriate facial expressions or ANS activity. It would be possible to stipulate that instances of anger, disgust, etc., in which the affect program symptoms are not present are not really instances of those emotions or are not emotions at all, but this would serve no useful purpose at this stage of our inquiry. I suggest in part 2 that emotion concepts may evolve to fit the affect program model as knowledge of that model is disseminated, but for now it is clear that people classify as anger, disgust, etc., states that do not involve the affect program responses. These responses are no less worthy of investigation than those which fit the affect program model.

There are other reasons to look beyond the affect programs for an understanding of emotion. The affect program system appears to be effectively the same in all human populations (pancultural) and effectively the same in the many individuals that possess it within each population (polymorphisms do not take the form of alternative repertoires of affect programs). Other emotional phenomena show much more variation both across and within populations. Some emotions are common in one population and absent in another. The Japanese experience an emotion known as *amae,* which involves a highly rewarding sense of being dependent on another person or organization. Something about human development in Japan induces this feature of the psychological phenotype in a way that human development in Europe does not. Other emotions are present in one individual but not in another. The thrilling humiliation so familiar to Leopold von Sacher Masoch was not familiar to the majority of nineteenth-century Austrians.

The second tempting response to the success of the affect program model is to suggest that all emotions are based on or include the known affect programs. Emotions which do not fit the affect program model are blends of more than one affect program, or affect programs occurring at the same time as some other mental activity. The strategy of treating emotions that do not fit the affect program model as blends of the six or seven "basic" emotions can be used to address the issue of individual and cultural variation. The same basic emotions can then be ascribed to all individuals and cultures and the differences attributed to different characteristic blends called forth by local conditions. I have severe doubts about this strategy. This is not because there are no blends of basic affects. It seems clear from the work of Ekman and others that there can be blends of the various affect programs. Blends are caused by the cooccurrence of elicitors for different programs. A program of research into these blends is well worth pursuing. What I am skeptical of is the idea that the whole domain of emotional phenomena can be addressed by a judicious admixture of the six or seven basic affects. The affect program states seem an inadequate basis for understanding the whole domain of emotion in at least four ways. First, the functional situations that elicit the six or seven affect programs do not cover the whole range of functional situations which seem to elicit emotions. Situations that elicit jealousy or moral indignation do not differ from each other merely in the proportions of danger, conspecific challenge, noxiousness, and loss that they involve. They have their own specific significance for the organism. We might call this problem the "inadequate functional breadth" of the basic affects. Second, many of the states currently included under the label "emotion" are sustained responses, not brief responses like the affect programs. Third, many emotions do not have any stereotypical immediate behavioral and physiological consequences. A blend of two or more affect programs ought to have a distinctive set of consequences like those seen when affect program emotions in Ekman's Japanese subjects interacted with the conditioned smile. Finally, and most important, blending the basic affects does not address the concerns about cognitive involvement described above. Some emotions seem to be highly integrated with complex, often conscious cognitive processes in a way that is quite alien to the affect program model. These emotions play a role in motivating considered plans of action rather than in triggering rapid, reflexlike responses. Blending several reflexlike responses does not produce something more cognitively involved.

A more promising way to expand the affect program approach is the hypothesis that other emotions are affect programs accompanied by distinctive higher cognitive activity. This allows the introduction of new elements into each emotional response while preserving the central role of the affect programs. Antonio Damasio attempts something very like this.[1] He distinguishes "primary" and "secondary" emotions. Primary emotions

1. The main elements of the theory can be found in chapter 7 of Damasio (1994). A similar extension of affect program theory was put forward by Leventhal (1984), in which the level of cognitive involvement of different emotions reflected various Piagetian developmental stages.

are very much like the affect programs. They are stereotyped responses involving several bodily systems and triggered very directly by sensory input without the mediation of higher brain centers. They are localized in the limbic system. Damasio's description of the primary emotions is based on some of the same research that I have cited in support of the affect program model. Secondary emotions occur when these primary emotions are triggered by activity in the prefrontal cortex (this localization claim concerning higher cognitive emotional activity is the central concern of Damasio's research). Damasio believes that primary emotions are innate while secondary emotions are acquired. He seems to mean this dichotomy to apply to both the input and output sides of emotion. On the input side, primary emotions are triggered by stimuli to which the organism is intrinsically sensitive from early childhood. Secondary emotions are triggered by stimuli to which the organism has become sensitized through experience. On the output side, primary emotions have stereotypical physiological consequences. In secondary emotions these effects are modulated in ways that reflect individual development. Damasio's theory is rather like the "subsumption" theory favored by some social constructionists (e.g., Ratner 1989). There are universal emotional reactions that are the result of evolution, but in adult humans these are subsumed in more complex reactions that reflect culture and individual development. The difference between Damasio and the social constructionists is that he thinks the underlying "biological" reactions help to illuminate what is going on in the complex adult emotions, whereas the constructionists think them a distraction from the real business of emotion theory.

My worries about Damasio's proposal do not concern his fascinating neurological research, but the broad theoretical framework that he uses his findings to support. As always, this framework is greatly underdetermined by the data. I suspect that the decision to treat the cognitively involved secondary emotions as necessarily involving the activation of primary emotions reflects certain background beliefs about emotion rather than anything in the evidence. There is a widespread view in European culture that emotions are involuntary biological responses which must be contrasted to cold, rational, intelligent responses. I showed in chapter 2 how this belief caused some propositional attitude theorists to find in their analyses of the concept of emotion the requirement that an emotion cause involuntary physiological arousal. I suggest that this belief has also influenced Damasio in his claim that all emotions involve primary emotions as elements. But although the belief that emotions are involuntary and biological is widespread, it does not completely dominate everyday thought about emotion. People count as emotions responses which involve complex, often conscious thought and little involuntary physiological arousal. Because of this, other philosophers have been able to use the analysis of emotion concepts to *denounce* the view that emotions are irrational and involuntary (e.g., Solomon 1977; Greenspan 1988). They have used emotion concepts to draw convincing folk-psychological sketches of people who are envious, disgusted, or jealous in virtue of patterns of belief and desire, without the activation of involuntary physiological responses. Some of the research I describe in this chapter concerns the possible evolutionary origins of characteristic patterns of cognition which resemble these purely cognitive emotions. This research should not be hampered by the insistence that it respect one strand rather than another of people's none too coherent intuitions about emotion. It should not be assumed that everything which counts as an emotion must involve the activation of ancient, pancultural, involuntary responses. In particular, higher cognitive activity need not trigger affect program responses in order to be counted as emotional.

Damasio's use of biological and evolutionary ideas in his distinction between primary and secondary emotions runs into the problems discussed in section 3.3. I reviewed there well-known problems with the traditional innateness concept (Bateson 1991; Gray 1992). Calling a trait innate suggests at least four different things: (1) that it is found in an individual because of their ancestry rather than their current environment; (2) that its growth does not depend on that environment for anything but basic sustenance; (3) that it is present at birth or early in development; and (4) that it is part of the "nature" of the species (which itself has multiple meanings). But all of these properties can vary independently of one another. The result of this mismatch between concept and reality is that when theorists discover that one element of the innateness concept applies to a trait, they are liable to assume that the other elements must also apply. This assumption is often mistaken. The internal logic of the innateness concept seems to drive several of Damasio's conclusions about emotion. Because the primary emotions are innate emotions which humans are "wired to respond with" (Damasio 1994, 131), they must be present in early infancy and not depend on complex environmental and social inputs for their emergence. They will also be the same in all people, for they are part of biological human nature. Secondary emotions, on the other hand, are acquired emotions. They are therefore not part of a universal human nature and can display variation both within and across cultures. This leads to the further conclusion that secondary emotions must be given less direct evolutionary explanations than primary emotions. Innate primary emotions can evolve but acquired secondary emotions must be the product of the local environment acting on some very general resources which are products of evolution. Most of these conclusions are highly questionable.

The powerful stereotype of an innate reaction is probably responsible for the strangest omission in Damasio's theory. He does not consider the possibility that the input and output sides of his primary emotions might fall on different sides of the innate/acquired dichotomy. I described in chapter 4 the evidence that highly stereotyped, pancultural emotional responses are nonetheless triggered by stimuli that reflect an organism's individual learning history. Damasio cites the authors who produced this research, but nevertheless assumes that stereotyped reactions mediated in the limbic system (primary emotions) will be triggered by stimuli which do not require a learning history. Conversely, he assumes that emotional reactions which are produced by "acquired" stimuli must have more variable physiological consequences than "innate" emotions. Nothing in Damasio's research forces him to adopt these views. Much of Ekman's research suggests that they are false. Damasio's assumption that "innate" stimuli trigger stereotypic responses and "acquired" stimuli trigger varied responses reflects nothing but the powerful grip of the innate/acquired dichotomy.

The idea that higher cognitive emotions have less direct evolutionary explanations than primary emotions is also highly problematic. Damasio's model of the secondary emotions makes them classic Lorenzian learned responses. They are the response to a particular environment of an evolved mechanism which is capable of indefinitely many different responses: "Prefrontal response . . . comes from *acquired* rather than *innate* dispositional representations, although, as discussed previously, the acquired dispositions are obtained under the influence of dispositions that are innate" (136; italics in original). The actual details of secondary emotions are thus screened from evolutionary explanation. Only the general capacity of the organism to acquire some secondary emotions or other can be explained by evolution. This restriction on the scope of evolutionary explanation is another presupposition forced on Damasio by the innate/acquired distinction. Evolution is presumed to operate by creating traits that emerge in almost any environment, depending only on internal factors like genes and quite general "environmental support" like adequate nutrition. Since higher cognitive emotions would presumably not develop normally in individuals brought up in an impoverished developmental environment without social contact, they cannot be products of evolution. I described in chapter 3 what is wrong with this picture. The developmental mechanisms that create evolved traits exploit all sorts of reliable features of the developmental environment. I described there how the sexual behavior of rhesus monkeys, a paradigm example of an evolved trait, depends for its development on suitable social interactions during infancy. These facts about development block any simple inference from the fact that a trait has a complex dependence on environmental inputs to the conclusion that it does not have a direct evolutionary explanation.[2] Complex social interactions were present in the evolutionary past and the developmental system of *Homo sapiens* evolved to make use of them. The "evolutionary psychologists" who are discussed later in this chapter attempt to give direct evolutionary explanations of higher cognitive emotions.

There is at present no framework for thinking about emotional phenomena which involve higher cognition that is anything like as well established as the affect program model of relatively automatic, short-term responses. I have argued that there are no solid grounds for supposing that all higher cognitive emotional phenomena will turn out to involve the affect program phenomena as components. Research into higher cognitive emotions should be pursued directly, not only as an extension of research into pancultural, automated, involuntary emotional responses. In the rest of the chapter I outline some current programs of research into the higher cognitive emotions, argue against certain presuppositions built into these research programs, and sketch what I believe would be the most productive research agenda.

5.2. The Evolutionary Psychology Program

The evolutionary psychology program is the successor to the sociobiology of the 1970s. Sociobiology tried to explain human behavior using tools

---

2. My argument here parallels Barkow, Cosmides, and Tooby's (1992) attack on the "standard social science model." Note that the entire tendentious inference that I am criticizing can be hidden in the simple phrase "it is not innate."

from population genetics and evolutionary game theory. In many cases it interpreted observed behaviors as "evolutionarily stable strategies" (ESSs)—traits which cannot be outcompeted by any mutant form. Evolutionary psychology adds to the tools of sociobiology an approach to the explanation of behavior derived from the computationalist school in cognitive science and the Chomskyan tradition in psycholinguistics. The manifesto of evolutionary psychology is Jerome H. Barkow, Leda Cosmides, and John Tooby's *The Adapted Mind*—a collection of articles defending the program and applying the program to various aspects of psychology.

Evolutionary psychology makes a great deal of the distinction between the *adaptiveness* of a biological trait and the fact that the trait is an *adaptation*. Adaptiveness is a measure of a trait's current effect on an organism's reproductive fitness. An adaptation is a trait which can be explained as the result of natural selection. Adaptiveness is neither necessary nor sufficient for a trait to be an adaptation. A vestigial trait like the appendix is an adaptation although it is no longer adaptive. The ability to read has been adaptive for much of human history but reading is generally thought to be a side effect of other, more ancient cognitive abilities. Evolutionary psychology claims that the human mind is a bundle of cognitive adaptations. It does not claim that these adaptations are currently adaptive. The environments in which most humans live are very different from those which they occupied during most of their evolutionary history. The behaviors we observe in modern humans may not be ESSs in their modern settings.

Evolutionary psychology takes from cognitive science and psycholinguistics a particular sort of concern with mental mechanisms. It accepts the characterization of the levels of explanation in psychology proposed by David Marr in his influential book *Vision* (1982). Marr proposed that an adequate approach to psychology must make use of three levels of description. The highest level describes the task which the psychological system accomplishes. In the case of vision, Marr claims that the system takes patterns of stimulation on the retina and produces an interpretation of the world in terms of moving, three-dimensional objects with color. The intermediate level describes how the system computes information in order to accomplish this task. In the case of vision, it details the algorithms by which retinal patterns are transformed into representations of the world. The lowest level describes how these computational processes are implemented in the brain. The computationalist school of cognitive science assigns to psychology the job of describing the intermediate level—the information-processing methods used by the mind to perform its tasks. Describing the physical machinery that implements those methods is the job of the neurosciences, with the results of psychology acting as an important and perhaps essential heuristic. What evolutionary psychology adds to this conventional picture is the idea that evolutionary theory provides a way of describing the mind at the highest level, the level of task description. This has a number of payoffs (Tooby and Cosmides 1992). First, since computationalists have always recognized that a task description is an important, and perhaps essential, heuristic for finding algorithmic-level descriptions, evolutionary analysis becomes an important heuristic in the search for psychological theories. In some cases the task description derived from evolutionary theory coincides with that of common sense. Cognitive scientists already knew the task description of the visual system. In other cases it is novel. Cosmides and Tooby (1992) provide a novel task description for human reasoning which is based on game-theoretic models of the evolution of cooperation. The second way in which the evolutionary perspective assists psychology is that knowing the problems that certain mental mechanisms must solve provides a general "solvability criterion." This is a first filter on proposed theories about those psychological mechanisms. Cosmides and Tooby argue that a mechanism for negotiating social exchange that is vulnerable to people not honoring their bargains could not have evolved and so can be ruled out a priori. Finally, the evolutionary perspective has an explanatory and organizing role. It makes sense of all sorts of otherwise senseless detail uncovered by psychology. The idiosyncratic rules followed by the rat in rejecting food items after illness fall into place when understood as a poison-avoidance mechanism.

Evolutionary psychologists believe that the clear distinction they draw between adaptation and current adaptiveness and the stress they place on mental mechanisms rather than behavior will allow them to escape the strictures leveled at first-wave sociobiology (e.g., Kitcher 1985). There is some truth to this, but three very important reservations about the evolutionary psychology program remain unaddressed. First, its adherents make a strong commitment to the view that human cognitive adaptations are monomorphic. Many human traits like eye color and height are polymorphic, with different individuals inheriting different developmental potentials. But according to evolutionary psychology any mental differences between individuals, with the exception of mental illnesses, are responses to the local environment. Every human individual begins life with the potential to develop the same evolved cognitive structures. I argue below that there is no reason whatever to suppose that the mind is monomorphic. My second reservation concerns evolutionary psychology's favored model of development. Evolutionary psychologists are aware of the vital role of nongenetic developmental resources in the development of psychological traits. They recognize that human culture is a key developmental resource and that it has played a key role in the evolutionary process. Nevertheless, I argue below that evolutionary psychology does not go far enough in this regard. The program would be improved if it used a developmental systems framework to think about the role of cultural and other "environmental" factors in psychological development. My third reservation about the program concerns its commitment to an adaptationist model of evolutionary theory.

The shortcomings of the adaptationist program were discussed in section 3.6. The adaptationist supposes that selective problems are very strongly associated with particular solutions to those problems. This belief licenses two sorts of inference. First, adaptationists think they can infer the solution from the problem. If they know what adaptive problems an organism has faced, they can infer what adaptations it will possess. Second, adaptationists think they can infer the problem from the solution. They think that by looking at the complex forms evolution has produced, they can infer the ecological interactions between ancestral organisms and their environment that produced those forms. I suggested in chapter 3 and have argued elsewhere (P. E. Griffiths 1994, 1995, n.d.) that both these inferences are unreliable. Problems and solutions do not correspond in such an obvious fashion. Evolutionary psychologists are aware of the most egregious error of adaptationist reasoning. They accept that the solution cannot simply be inferred from the problem. A hypothesis about mental structure cannot be proved merely by producing an adaptive scenario in which that mental structure would be advantageous. An empirical demonstration that the mind is actually structured in that way is also required—"Although selectional thinking is an important source of inspiration for the evolutionary psychologist, nature always gets the last word" (Symons 1992, 143–44). But although nature gets the last word, the evolutionary psychologist thinks that the fact that a particular feature "makes evolutionary sense" is a reason for taking seriously even quite marginal data suggesting that it actually exists. If nature disagrees with the adaptationist about what should have evolved, then she has to shout. If she agrees, then she has only to whisper. This is what is meant by saying that adaptive thinking has heuristic value. A hypothesis backed by a plausible adaptive scenario is more likely than the alternatives. This suggests that evolutionary psychologists do not accept one of the central claims of recent antiadaptationist writing, which is that adaptive scenarios are so easy to come by that they provide little or no support for the existence of the features they predict.

The passage in Symons (1992) from which I just quoted is a good example of how little support narrative presentations of adaptive scenarios provide. Symons is discussing the claim that men are universally attracted to nubile young women. He notes that there is substantial empirical support for this claim. But he also says that the claim receives additional support from the fact that it "make[s] excellent adaptive sense" (1992, 143). Men who preferentially mated with women who had just begun menstruating and had not yet borne a child would be at an evolutionary advantage. It is at this point that I am skeptical. Suppose the empirical data resolves itself so as to indicate that more mature young women are maximally attractive. Will it not then "make excellent adaptive sense" that these older women were better bets in the ancestral environment? They had more skills in foraging, or more resource holding power within the band, or had already proven their fertility by bearing a child. The adaptive story cannot enhance the credibility of the data because an equally good story would be available for many of the alternative findings.

The other form of adaptationist reasoning favored by the Darwinian psychologists is inferring the problem from the solution. Tooby and Cosmides (1992) describe this explanatory strategy as "reverse engineering." Looking at the performance profile of a cognitive adaptation allows the evolutionary psychologist to deduce the evolutionary forces that have produced it, just as taking apart a piece of machinery allows a rival company to work out how it was produced. The problem with this strategy is that an adaptive explanation can be very plausible but false. This is obvious when there are several well-developed adaptive explanations, as there are for the explosion in brain size in hominid evolution. The runaway selective process initiated by the invention of transmitted cultural skills, the "machiavellian" needs of a social primate or the importance of thermoregulation on the savanna might all have been the motor of evolutionary change in this case. The adaptationist normally recommends further development of each hypothesis so that its predictions become more detailed. The hope is that there will eventually be only one candidate that correctly predicts the observed traits. But an adaptive hypothesis can be falsified even when it adequately predicts the observed trait and has no rivals. If McKitrick (1993) is correct, low birth weight in bears is not related to hibernation. That hypothesis explains the trait and has no rivals but is contradicted by the comparative data. Low birth weight evolved before hibernation and is preserved on branches of the phylogenetic tree where hibernation never originated. The adaptationist presumably thinks that a really detailed adaptive scenario that predicts the observed traits is so likely to be true that it is not worth running the battery of available comparative tests. This is a quite extraordinary view. There are many other examples of comparative tests falsifying very plausible adaptive hypotheses.[3] The adaptationist neglect of comparative tests is profoundly unscientific. It systematically ignores chances to bring current presuppositions up against empirical data. That is a recipe for reinforcing existing assumptions and slowing down theoretical advance.

The adaptationist program not only lacks positive heuristic value in psychology, it may have a substantial negative heuristic effect. It can induce complacency in the face of unreliable or ambiguous data, because that data or interpretation of the data "makes adaptive sense." Parent-offspring conflict is a good example. Many sociobiologists were impressed by Robert L. Trivers's demonstration that the long-term interests of parents need not be identical with those of their offspring (Trivers 1974). There is an appealing story according to which the parent wants to conserve its resources for future offspring, whereas the offspring wants as much as it can get. This model was taken to confirm observations of squabbling between parents and offspring around the time of weaning in primates, including humans. It also created the expectation that offspring would deceive their parents about their needs in an attempt to get more resources. These ideas still

3. Taylor 1987; Basolo 1990; Gray and Craig 1991. See also examples in Brooks and McLennan 1991; Coddington 1988; Felsenstein 1985; Harvey and Pagel 1991; Lauder 1981, 1982, 1990; Lauder, Armand, and Rose 1993; Miles and Dunham 1993.

have currency in the evolutionary psychology literature. Parent-offspring conflict is "inherent to the human condition" (Pinker and Bloom 1992, 483) and its "inevitability" is cited in support of the existence of psychodynamic mechanisms of deceit and self-deceit (Nesse and Lloyd 1992). Yet the empirical evidence for parent-offspring squabbling over weaning is very weak. Patrick Bateson (1994) summarizes various studies which failed to find aggressive interactions at weaning in a wide range of species, studies which found offspring weaning themselves, and studies which found both parties engaging in reliable signaling in order to coordinate weaning. These behaviors offer rich opportunities for adaptive explanation, but their discovery has been hindered by devotion to a simple a priori model of the evolutionary problem that behaviors surrounding weaning were supposed to solve.

One reason for the popularity of the adaptationist program is the mistaken impression that the alternative is to eschew evolutionary thought as a source of insight into organic form. Nothing could be further from the truth. The alternative to the adaptationist program is a richer approach to evolutionary explanation. This "adaptive-historical" approach recognizes the essential historicity of evolutionary explanation.[4] This historicity has more than one aspect. First, there is the role of historical contingency in evolution. The outcomes of evolutionary processes do reflect the ecological relationship between organism and environment, but they also reflect stochastic factors in the selection process and the availability and order of occurrence of alternative forms. The role of these factors in determining outcomes makes it impossible to read back and forth from problem to solution and solution to problem in the manner of the adaptationist. Instead, empirical methods for the reconstruction of history, especially modern cladistic versions of the comparative method, are central to the study of adaptation. Optimization theory and game theory do not explain form; they suggest adaptive hypotheses for comparative testing. A second aspect of historicity is the importance of phylogeny to thinking about evolution. Living organisms are at the end of lines of descent which pass through many different ecologies. The form which results from any one phase of

---

4. Various aspects of a historical approach to the study of the adaptive origins of form can be found in Felsenstein 1985; Taylor 1987; Coddington 1988; O'Hara 1988; Brooks and McLennan 1991; Harvey and Pagel 1991; Miles and Dunham 1993; Griffiths 1994, n.d.).

adaptation reflects the previous form of the organism as well as the ecology it encountered. Generalizations about the effects of particular ecological factors are likely to be richer and more reliable when confined within taxonomic groups that approach the "problem" with a common inheritance (I suspect that the idea that niches or adaptive problems cannot be identified apart from the organisms which fill or solve them is simply an alternative formulation of the same idea).

Kim Sterelny (personal communication) has suggested that claims about human cognitive adaptations will be more difficult to subject to rigorous comparative testing than many other aspects of evolution. Human cognitive adaptations are supposed to have evolved after the separation of hominids from other primates. *Homo sapiens* is the only living representative of the lineage involved. It is therefore not possible test hypotheses about these adaptations by looking at the distribution of homologous traits in related taxa. This is a legitimate worry, but it should not be overstated. Natural history can creep up on the period in which our lineage became distinctively human from both sides (evolutionary psychologists tend to refer to this period as "the pleistocene"). I have already described attempts by emotion theorists to creep up on the pleistocene from behind in chapters 3 and 4. Darwin and his modern successors found extensive homologies between human emotions and those of other primates. New findings about the psychological and neurological bases of emotion can only enrich this collection of homologies. Similar results should be possible in many other areas of psychology. The discovery of primate homologies does not simply illuminate the history of the homologous structures themselves. Those structures and their history provide a framework with which evolutionary scenarios for uniquely hominid cognitive structures must be consistent. This consistency requirement creates extensive opportunities for testing those scenarios.

The possibility of creeping up on the pleistocene from in front has been created by developments in molecular biology and historical linguistics. There is a discernible phylogenetic structure within the species *Homo sapiens,* as there is in most widespread species. Modern molecular biology makes possible extensive investigations of the history and biogeography of human populations (Cavalli-Sforza et al. 1994). Further access to this structure comes from historical linguistics. Phylogenetic trees for human populations can be constructed on the basis of their languages. The congruence between the structures discovered by these two means is very consider-able (Penny et al. 1993). These discoveries make it possible to discern ho-mologies within *Homo sapiens* and to infer the "ancestral" condition of many traits (the condition which existed before the separation of current human populations). The access to history provided by these methods is limited by the fact that human populations only began to separate one hundred fifty to two hundred thousand years ago. Nevertheless, determin-ing whether a trait was ancestral in humanity as a whole should be an essential precursor to any attempt to explain that trait by conditions in "the pleistocene." Hypotheses about the evolution of aesthetic preferences for landscape (Orians and Heerwagen 1992) or of sexual attraction might well be eliminated by such a test. This test should also be applied to many of the emotional dispositions postulated by Robert Frank (1988) and dis-cussed below.

An adaptive-historical approach to evolution can play a heuristic role for psychology, although not quite in the way outlined by current evolu-tionary psychologists. The evolutionary psychologists' heuristic is sup-posed to take three forms. First, adaptive thinking is to provide the task descriptions for cognitive mechanisms. An adaptive-historical approach to psychology would be more skeptical of the possibility of using a priori reflection on what would be likely to evolve as a heuristic for finding cogni-tive adaptations. The new approach would suggest a phylogenetic heuristic for psychology, which would look for cognitive systems in humans which are elaborations of mechanisms seen in other species and which seem likely to have existed in a common ancestor. In this way the adaptive-historical approach revives neglected elements of the evolutionary approach to be-havior of classical ethologists like Lorenz and Tinbergen. The evolutionary psychologists' second proposal is that evolutionary theory can provide gen-eral "solvability constraints" that narrow down the class of possible psy-chological mechanisms. Once again, the adaptive-historical approach would suggest a more phylogenetic perspective. Rather than ruling out certain classes of mechanism on general grounds we would take note of patterns in the comparative data. For example, the North American coy-ote's poison avoidance mechanism uses taste to potentiate food odors, while on the same prairie the red-tailed hawk uses taste to potentiate visual food cues. The two species solve the adaptive problem in a way that reveals their kinship to the laboratory rat and laboratory pigeon respectively (Garcia and Rusiniak 1980). It would have been very surprising if the mechanisms had been reversed. Finally, the evolutionary psychologists look to evolution to make sense of the eclectic collection of mechanisms that make up the mind. Adaptive thinking is supposed to reveal the true purpose of these mechanisms. An adaptive-historical approach would welcome the construction of adaptive scenarios for known behavioral regularities and/ or cognitive mechanisms. But these scenarios are hypotheses awaiting test by the comparative method. Furthermore, well-constructed adaptive hypotheses will themselves have historical content. They will suggest that at a certain point in a lineage an ancestral form already equipped with such and such features acquired some new feature. The order imposed on the findings of psychology by this sort of adaptive reasoning will have a phylogenetic dimension. Tooby and Cosmides (1992) expect cognitive traits to make sense as a suite of adaptations fitting humans to their pleistocene "environment of evolutionary adaptedness." I expect them to make sense as a series of traits acquired, retained, and modified as the lineage leading to *Homo sapiens sapiens* passed through many speciation nodes and many different selective environments. The origin of these traits will be reflected in their distribution in the nested hierarchy of primate taxa, hominid taxa, and human populations.

I argued in chapter 3 that Darwin's perspective on emotion was adaptive historical rather than adaptationist. This accounts for the great productivity of the research traditions derived from Darwin as compared to those inspired by more adaptationist conceptions of evolution. It is this phylogenetic perspective on behavior which Lorenz identifies as Darwin's great legacy to ethology (Lorenz 1965). If Darwinian psychology can retain its evolutionary and phylogenetic perspective on the mind while shedding its adaptationism, then it will truly deserve its name.

5.3. The Evolutionary Psychology of Emotion

Tooby and Cosmides (1990b) predict what a future evolutionary psychology of the emotions will be like. Adaptive thinking reveals that an emotion must be a set of behavior-regulating algorithms which are deployed in response to frequently recurring ecological situations: "Each emotion state—fear of predators, guilt, sexual jealousy, rage, grief, and so on—will correspond to an integrated mode of operation that functions as a solution designed to take advantage of the particular structure of the recurrent situation these emotions respond to" (Tooby and Cosmides 1990b, 410). They go on to list the eight properties of environment and mechanisms that will characterize each emotion and the seventeen classes of biological process that should be partly governed by emotional state. It is clear from their citations of Ekman that they regard the affect program theory as a contribution to this research program. However, the affect program states do not fit Tooby and Cosmides' prescription very accurately. Tooby and Cosmides expect emotions to be under the control of a mechanism that integrates a number of perceptual cues to determine if a situation is appropriate for an emotion. This is fine in itself, but they go on to suggest cues such as "looming approach of a large, fanged animal" for fear and "seeing your mate have sex with another" for a postulated emotion of sexual jealousy. The modular appraisal mechanisms of affect program states simply do not embody knowledge of the evolutionary past in this form. I described in section 4.4 how the systems controlling affect programs are sensitive at birth to only a few stimuli especially relevant to the neonate. For example, they respond to the facial expressions of caregivers. As the individual develops, these systems become sensitive to a vast range of other cues. These cues are acquired through the individual's own experience and, more important, through observation of the emotional responses of adults with experience of the current environment. Insofar as the mechanism reflects details of the evolutionary past, it does so in the form of learning preparedness. It is easier for the mechanism to acquire certain cues than others. These facts mean that an examination of the cues to which an adult responds is likely to reveal more about the current environment than the hunter-gatherer lifestyle of the pleistocene. I had a phobic response to exposed electric wires for some years after receiving a severe shock. In this case, evolution has favored keeping up to date.

Tooby and Cosmides' description of the seventeen adaptively plausible effects of emotion is more promising as a framework for the output side of the affect program theory. They list all the known classes of output, including communicative expressions, physiological changes, stereotyped behavior, and the direction of behavior. The rest of their extensive list covers more subtle cognitive phenomena such as recalibration of the parameters of memory, learning, and decision mechanisms. The cognitive effects of the affect programs have not been extensively investigated and anecdote and introspection suggest that this will be a fascinating subject.

Tooby and Cosmides, however, tend to assume that emotions will be strongly integrated into the cognitive processes leading to long-term planned action. The affect programs, as far as is known, are reflexlike. Their effects are mainly short-term and seem to compete with higher cognitive processes for control of motor systems, rather than being integrated with them to determine how motor systems will be affected. The prospect of finding "recalibration" effects of the affect programs on other cognitive processes goes some way to ameliorate this impression, but these effects still require a specific affect program response to initiate them. They will not occur in some weaker form if the stimuli are insufficient to elicit the affect program. If Othello's sexual jealousy had been an affect program or a downstream cognitive effect of such a program, then he would have had to catch Desdemona in bed with Cassio, or at least have seen the handkerchief, before his jealousy was initiated. Tooby and Cosmides seem to have provided a framework for the study of the higher cognitive emotions rather than the affect programs.

Some fascinating work that goes some way to fill in this framework is Robert H. Frank's book *Passions within Reason: The Strategic Role of the Emotions* (1988). Frank provides a worked-out version of the hints at a theory of emotion found in the work of many sociobiologists (Weinrich 1980). The best known of these is the discussion of the moralistic emotions in Robert L. Trivers's classic article "The Evolution of Reciprocal Altruism" (1971). Frank develops these hints into the "commitment model" of emotion. Emotions often lead people to behave in ways which conflict with calculative rationality. Loyalty leads someone to keep an agreement, even when this brings them no advantage and there is no possibility of retribution. Resentful or vengeful people often cause further harm to their own interests in order to revenge themselves on someone who has injured them. Decision-theoretic models which assume that agents maximize their individual welfare do not predict these decisions. A strong emotional response to perceived exploitation (the "sense of fairness") may also lead people to refuse to participate in an arrangement because they believe that the other party is exploiting their bargaining position to ensure an uneven distribution of the spoils. This is a further departure from rational decision theory, because however uneven the distribution of the economic product there is still an absolute gain to be had by participating in the transaction. All these "irrational" behaviors have something in common. If an individual were known to be committed to them in advance, they would be treated differently by other agents. This different treatment can have advantages. If a person is known to be loyal, one can make mutually advantageous but unenforceable agreements with them. If a person is known to be vengeful, then it is unwise to wrong them. A person with a sense of fairness may be offered a fair deal because they will turn down anything less. Frank proposes that "social" emotions including anger, contempt, disgust, envy, shame, and guilt may be irruptive motivations designed to enforce commitment to strategies that would otherwise be disrupted by the calculations of self-interest.

Frank suggests an important role for emotions in forging alliances. There are many cooperative arrangements which it would not be rational to agree to without some assurance that the other party will voluntarily keep their side of the bargain. In the classic one-shot prisoners dilemma it is advantageous for both prisoners to cooperate by keeping silent and thus foil the justice system. But it is impossible for them to do so by simple agreement, since the authorities can offer incentives to each prisoner which make it rational for them to "defect" whether or not the other prisoner keeps the agreement. If both prisoners are rational, they both break the agreement and end up with an inferior outcome to that which the agreement would have produced. Only if the prisoners are irrationally loyal can they keep their agreement and foil the authorities. Frank argues that many cooperative outcomes can be achieved with the aid of "irrational" behavioral dispositions associated with emotions such as guilt and shame. These emotional states act as internal guarantors of alliances.

One of the strengths of Frank's work is that he tries to establish that the traits for which he offers evolutionary explanations actually exist. For example, he is able to cite several experiments supporting the existence of a sense of fairness. In one experiment pairs of players were asked to divide ten dollars between themselves. Player 1 was given the chance to propose a division of the money, player 2 the chance to accept or reject the proposed division. If player 2 rejected the division, the money was lost to both. Since the players never met again, there was no question of player 2's establishing a precedent, and to reject any deal at all was to throw money away. Nevertheless, player 2 frequently rejected unfair offers. The average division in cases where agreement was reached was only 61 to 39 percent in player 1's favor (Guth, Schmittberger, and Schwarze 1982). A later experiment showed that the average person in a similar game was happy to lose up to $2.59 rather than accept an unfair bargain (Kahnemann, Knetsch, and Thaler 1986). A follow-up to this experiment cast light on the motivation of the "fair-minded" players. Players were offered the choice of dividing twelve dollars on a fifty-fifty basis with a player known to have proposed an unfair bargain to a third party or ten dollars on a fifty-fifty basis with a player known to have proposed a fair bargain. Seventy-four percent of players chose to sacrifice the extra dollar to punish the unfair player. This suggests that the financial sacrifice in the original experiments was made in order to punish player 1. The next step in the evolutionary investigation of these behaviors, following the adaptive-historical principles I have recommended, would be a comparison of human behavioral tendencies with the emerging literature on punishment in social primates (Clutton-Brock and Harvey 1995) in the hope of establishing homologies.

Unfortunately, not all of Frank's explanations of emotions are backed up by experimental results. He suggests that love is designed to ensure commitment to the pair bond after a partner has lost the qualities for which they were initially valued. Despite some admirable efforts to find objective evidence of selflessness in relationships, Frank is open to the charge that he has constructed a "just-so story" for something that is a normative ideal rather than a description of actual human behavior. Melvin Konner (1982) argues that societies have only rarely established pair bonds on the basis of romantic love and suggests that if this emotion had a biological function it would be to facilitate adultery and abandonment rather than continuation of the pair bond.

Frank's theory depends on the ability of individuals to communicate their emotions, and hence their behavioral dispositions, to one another. Verbal threats and promises are insufficient, as they are not strong guarantors of future behavior. Direct testing of the disposition by looking at past instances is often impractical. The connection between facial behavior and emotion might help to solve this problem. Frank and his associates conducted a series of experiments in which subjects demonstrated a significant ability to predict who they could rely on in situations akin to the prisoner's dilemma on the basis of unrelated social interactions. They presumably succeeded in communicating aspects of their personality to one another, and it is at least plausible that the facial behaviours associated with affect programs played a role here. However, there is no reason to restrict the range of behaviors used to those uncovered by Ekman and his colleagues. Nonverbal communication of all sorts, both pancultural and culture specific, may play a role in communicating Frank's emotional dispositions.

Signals of this type (intention signals) are inherently evolutionarily unstable. Any individual that can mimic the signal without having the behavioral disposition will be able to reap the rewards of the cooperative agreement or to deter exploitation without incurring the costs. The mimic strategy will spread until the signal is no longer associated with the behavior. As this happens it will be less and less advantageous to respond to the signal. Eventually, the whole signaling system will break down. Maynard Smith (1982) discusses this problem at length and concludes that one possible result is a cycle in which new signals repeatedly evolve while old ones are discredited. Trivers (1971) suggests that an elaborate and unstable system of signaling, cheating, and detecting cheating will result. Frank himself constructs a model in which cheaters coexist stably with genuine cooperators. If it is possible to detect cheats, then cheats will not drive out honest signalers. But if there is a cost involved in detecting cheats, then cheats will not themselves be eliminated. The proportion of cheats will merely be driven down to the point where the chance of meeting a cheat is too small to make it worth paying the cost of checking. Those who rely on signals will tolerate a reduction in their reliability rather than pay the cost of detecting cheaters or the cost of ignoring honest signals. So there is no a priori reason to rule out the sort of signal system Frank proposes.

5.4 Higher Cognitive Emotions and the Affect Program Theory

The general conception of an emotion in Frank's theory is an irruptive pattern of motivation. People have general goals and use means-end reasoning to derive immediate goals from these. They may, for example, want a job because it increases their purchasing power and gives them a social position. But according to Frank they can be deflected from this goal-seeking process by emotion. Loyalty to a sacked friend can prevent them from taking the job. On some occasions this can be fitted into the overall pattern. Good relations with this friend are a subgoal derived from a general goal of social integration. This subgoal has now come into conflict with subgoals derived from another source. But many emotional behaviors resist this sort of explanation. They are not plausibly derived from preexisting goals. The schoolboy who secretly breaks a piece of expensive school equipment after being caned does not seek anything but revenge.

There are two fundamentally different ways to introduce these irruptive patterns of motivation into psychology. The first is to explain them as the further effects of the existence of affect program states. Frank seems to take this view. He suggests that the conscious affect (feeling) associated with emotion acts as an internal source of reinforcement for behavior. Behaviors which would be reinforced by external rewards are punished by these internal reinforcers, and vice versa. This view of the effects of emotion is entirely consistent with the affect program theory. The affect program theory can (and should) incorporate emotion feelings either as an additional element of the program or as the perception of the physiological elements of the program. Feedback from the facial musculature is a popular candidate for the source of emotion feelings (Tomkins 1962; Izard 1971; Ekman, Levenson, and Friesen 1983). Damasio (1994) has an ambitious theory in which a continuous flow of information from the body in the form of feelings is central to most mental functions. But the effects of affect programs on cognition need not be restricted to the reinforcement of certain behaviors by feelings. The affect program theory could incorporate the direct effects on other cognitive processes envisaged by Cosmides and Tooby. The occurrence of an affect program could, for example, call up memories associated with that emotion. It could cause more or less cautious learning rules to be deployed, as appropriate. It could call into play special decision rules, such as making risk-averse choices in the context of fear.

The second way to introduce irruptive motivations into psychology would be to postulate them as additional pieces of mechanism. These need not be related to the known affect programs. Under certain ecological conditions people experience characteristic irruptions of motivation not derived by means-end reasoning from preexisting goals. There is a positive argument for keeping this theoretical option open. This is the problem of the inadequate emotional breadth of the affect programs referred to at the beginning of this chapter. There are six or seven affect programs, each with its particular ecological category of elicitor. None of these ecological categories corresponds closely to the classes of social situations appropriate to guilt or shame. There are obvious links between anger, a known affect program, and vengefulness, one of Frank's postulated higher cognitive emotions, but it is not clear that the anger affect program plays a role in all vengeful behavior. Anger is a common part of bargaining interactions as well, but once again there seems no reason to believe that the operation of Frank's sense of fairness always involves the occurrence of the anger program. In general, insisting that higher cognitive emotions must involve the occurrence of one of the known affect program states seems an unmotivated and restrictive assumption on future research. Researchers developing Frank's ideas should be free to look for characteristic patterns of irruptive motivation that stand alone as pieces of psychological mechanism.

The idea that the higher cognitive emotions are the immediate effects of the occurrence of affect programs should be clearly distinguished from the idea that the affect programs have a role in the ontogeny of these emotions. Frank's references to emotions as internal reinforcers are unhappily ambiguous in this respect. An "immediate effect" conception of an emotion like guilt would claim that this characteristic pattern of motivation is a response to the unpleasant sensations produced by the fear and sadness affect programs. An ontogenetic conception of the role of the affect programs in producing guilt would be very different. It might postulate that the occurrence of the fear and sadness in social exchange situations during infancy leads to the existence of the motivational complex of guilt in the adult. The occurrence of guilt in the adult, however, need not involve the occurrence of the affect programs. Hypotheses of this sort are plausible because the affect program responses are present from earliest infancy. They are likely to play a role in the development of many other affective phenomena. But this hypothesis is quite distinct from the hypothesis that other affective phenomena actually involve the affect programs as components or immediate causes.

5.5 Evolutionary Psychology and the Monomorphic Mind

I described above the commitment of the evolutionary psychology program to certain forms of adaptationist reasoning and my reservations about this aspect of the program. My second major reservation about the current evolutionary psychology program was its commitment to the doctrine of the monomorphic mind or "psychic unity of humankind" (Tooby and Cosmides 1992, 79). Tooby and Cosmides argue that as far as their evolved minds are concerned all human beings have the same developmental potential. Any differences that exist in the cognitive adaptations of individuals or groups are not due to genetic differences. This is an extraordinarily strong claim. It asserts not merely that all cognitive adaptations are pancultural (found in all human populations) but that these adaptations are universal (found in all human individuals). This would make cognitive adaptations highly atypical human traits. Most human traits display considerable heritable individual variation. All human beings have eyes, but these eyes exhibit heritable differences in color, size, shape, acuity, and susceptibility to various forms of degeneration over time. Much of this heritable variation may be presumed to reflect genetic differences. It has been known for half a century that wild populations of most species contain substantial genetic variation, and humans are no exception. According to the latest estimates the average heterozygosity of human populations (the proportions of loci for which more than one alternative allele exists in the population) falls between 21 percent and 37 percent (Cavalli-Sforza, Menozzi, and Piazza 1994).

Tooby and Cosmides (1990a, 1992) offer a single, simple argument for the conclusion that the genes involved in producing cognitive adaptations will be the same in all human individuals:

> Complex adaptations necessarily require many genes to regulate their development, and sexual recombination makes it combinatorially improbable that all the necessary genes for a complex adaptation would be together at once in the same individual, if genes coding for complex adaptations varied substantially between individuals. Selection, interacting with sexual recombination, enforces a powerful tendency towards unity in the genetic architecture underlying complex functional design at the population level and usually the species level as well. (Tooby and Cosmides 1990b, 393)

The authors apply this argument only to psychological adaptations, but its logic extends to all traits with many genes involved in their etiology. In fact, their argument seems to imply that every member of a breeding population has all the complex adaptive traits observed in that population! Since this is obviously false, Cosmides and Tooby suggest that a universal genetic program must contain environmentally triggered alternative pathways which account for all the variants seen in the population. The observed individual, seasonal and geographic variation in populations is real, but it does not reflect any genetic variation within populations. If correct, Tooby and Cosmides' conclusion would be surprising in the extreme. There is considerable variation in the complex adaptive traits displayed in populations and there is considerable variation at the genetic level, but these two phenomena are entirely unconnected!

The shortcoming of Cosmides and Tooby's argument are all too obvious. It assumes that development is a mechanical consequence of the exact sequence of the genome. A particular phenotypic outcome requires the same alleles to be in the same sequence on the same chromosome. If the genetics of complex adaptations worked like this then it would be a miracle that anything complex was ever inherited. Even if both parents *were* homozygous at all relevant loci, the genetics of complex traits would be horrendously disrupted when crossing over occurred during meiosis. What Cosmides and Tooby seem to have overlooked is the phenomena described by the geneticist C. H. Waddington as "developmental canalisation" (Waddington 1959). Development is buffered against genetic variation as well as against environmental variation. Waddington captured this idea by picturing the developmental system of an organism as a landscape of hills and valleys. Waddington compared the developing organism to a ball rolling down a path dictated by the contours of this landscape. A suitable landscape will take the ball to the same destination from a wide range of starting points. This is not to deny the importance of genetic variation in evolution. Waddington conceived of the developmental landscape as "held down" underneath by individual genes, changes in which would affect the shape of the landscape. The developmental system is simultaneously the product of the genes and the determinant of their significance. In recent years this idea has come to be expressed in the language of complexity theory. Stuart Kauffman (1993) and others have attempted to understand development as a complex system for which certain developmental outcomes are attractors (Goodwin, Kauffman, and Murray 1993). The parameters for any particular "run" of this system are the particular sequence of genes. Changes in these parameters will affect many aspects of the run, but will only rarely enable the system to escape from the strong attractors represented by the typical form of the species. The idea of developmental canalization explains how the observed genetic variation in natural populations is compatible with the observed stability of phenotypic outcomes. It does so in a way that also allows the existence of the observed geographic, seasonal, and individual variation in the phenotypes of a single breeding population. There is no reason to suppose, as Cosmides and Tooby do, that this variation represents the response of a single genetic program to different environmental triggers.

One reason for the popularity of the doctrine of the monomorphic mind is that it seems like a bulwark against racism. If all human beings have substantially the same genes, then racial differences are superficial and modifiable. This inference is questionable in itself, but even if it were correct it would not be necessary to embrace the monomorphic mind in order to avoid racism. It is important to distinguish pancultural traits from universal traits. The fact that racial differences in various cognitive traits are insignificant does not show that individual differences in those traits are insignificant. The affect program research showed that the ability to produce and recognize certain emotions is widespread in all human populations. This does not show that there are no differences between individuals in their ability to produce or recognize those emotions. If human phenotypic variation follows the pattern observed for genetic variation then within-group differences should dwarf between-group differences (Lewontin 1972; Cavalli-Sforza, Menozzi, and Piazza 1994, 19). This suggests that individual differences in the emotion system may be substantial and important despite the lack of between-group differences. Furthermore, between-group differences need not be of a kind that would support anything like a race concept. The evidence is now largely in to show that neither racism nor universalism is correct. Ten years ago David Hull wrote, "As a biological species we are seamless but not homogeneous. Various groups of people at a variety of levels of generality exhibit statistical differences. *Homo sapiens* is polytypic." (1986, 8). Looking at modern gene map of *Homo sapiens,* one is hard put to sustain any other conclusion.

5.6 Evolutionary Psychology and Developmental Psychology

My third major reservation about the current evolutionary psychology program concerns its picture of developmental biology. Although the theoreticians of evolutionary psychology have a remarkably sophisticated approach to development, they are ultimately unable to escape the pernicious dichotomies between nature and nurture, genes and environment, and biology and culture. But evolutionary psychology has gone a remarkably long way towards escaping these dichotomies. Its adherents go well beyond the truism that evolved traits develop through the interaction of genetic and environmental factors. They realize that nongenetic factors cannot be reduced to a standard background against which the genetic program unfolds. Many evolved traits require highly structured nongenetic inputs, and differences in these inputs may give rise to different evolved traits. There are polymorphisms due to the environment, as well as polymorphisms due to genetic differences. This sophisticated theoretical position was forced on evolutionary psychology by the doctrine of the monomorphic mind. The combination of this doctrine with some standard views about behavioral evolution implies that there must be environmental polymorphisms.

It is typical of behavioral and cognitive traits that their fitness is frequency dependent. The value of a strategy depends on the strategies adopted by other players. Because of frequency dependence the only evolutionarily stable state in many model systems is one in which players adopt a range of different strategies. An equilibrium exists when these strategies coexist in proportions that make the average payoff to each strategy equal. There are two different ways in which an evolutionarily stable state of this kind can be maintained in the population. First, the population could be polymorphic with respect to this behavior. A proportion p of individuals are honest signalers and $1 - p$ are cheats. Second, the population could be monomorphic with every individual adopting the same "mixed strategy." Every individual would be honest in interactions p of the time and cheat in interactions $1 - p$ of the time.

Human behavioral evolution seems overwhelmingly likely to have involved frequency-dependent selection. In a whole host of human interactions from mating to trading the best strategy depends on what mix of strategies the rest of the population adopts. While there are behaviors that lend themselves to interpretation as mixed strategies, there also appear to be behavioral polymorphisms, with each individual committed to one strategy. But a genetically maintained polymorphism is ruled out for Tooby and Cosmides by their acceptance of the doctrine of the monomorphic mind. The solution to this paradox is that polymorphisms can be maintained by environmental factors. The situation with cognitive adaptations may be the same as that which obtains with life-history adaptations in many other species. A single type of genome supports a range of developmental outcomes. Genetically identical beetles may develop into large, heavily armed males or into small inconspicuous males as a result of encountering different population densities as juveniles. The two "morphs" maintain a balanced polymorphism, where the fitnesses of the two types are roughly equal. Tooby and Cosmides represent cases like this using the idea of a disjunctive developmental program. The instructions guiding development have the form "If environmental condition A obtains; develop on pathway 1, if environmental conditions B obtain, develop on pathway 2; . . . etc." The idea of a disjunctive developmental program allows the environment to play an informative as well as a supporting role. The environment is not just a standard background to development. Differences in the environment account for some of the variance in evolved traits seen in populations (figure 5.1).

Tooby and Cosmides' view of development has a lot to offer besides making polymorphisms consistent with the doctrine of the monomorphic mind. Tooby and Cosmides claim that their conception of developmental programs will allow them to overcome the sharp divide between biological and cultural traits that has hindered attempts to think clearly about human evolution. Culture has traditionally been supposed to refer to the information inherited outside the genome. It is also supposed to explain the characteristic pattern of within-group similarity and between-group difference seen across human populations. Tooby and Cosmides (1992) argue that these patterns need not be explained by "transmitted culture" in which individuals pass on mental representations by imitation and inculcation. The alternative to transmitted culture is what Tooby and Cosmides christen "evoked culture." Evoked cultural traits are those which reflect the response of a disjunctive developmental program to local environmental conditions. Evoked traits exhibit the pattern traditionally associated with "cultural" traits but are not explained by cultural transmission. Tooby and Cosmides argue that particular cultures are constructed by a complex interaction of evocation and transmission. The realm of the cultural is not distinct from that of the biological.

There is much that is promising in this approach to development but the evolutionary psychologists do not go far enough in integrating intrinsic and environmental factors into a single "developmental system" and hence are unable to entirely escape the biology/culture divide. The idea of a developmental system was introduced in section 3.3. The developmental system of an organism is the entire set of factors which are reliably present in each

Chapter Five

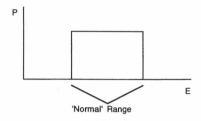

(a) 'Closed program'

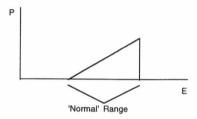

(b) Disjunctive program, continuous
variation

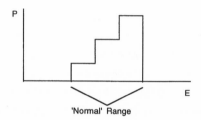

(c) Disjunctive program, discontinuous variation

5.1. Developmental Programs as envisaged by Tooby and Cosmides (1992). P = Phenotypic outcome, E = environmental variable. "Normal" range is interpreted as the range of environments experienced by ancestors.

generation of that lineage of organisms and whose interaction reconstructs the typical life cycle of the lineage (Oyama 1985; Griffiths and Gray 1994). Tooby and Cosmides take one major step towards a developmental systems conception of evolution. They recognize that the genes must be embedded in a complex cellular environment in order to have any significance at all. Much of this environment of methylation patterns, membranes, and cell organelles cannot be constructed without its own involvement and must therefore be inherited in parallel with the nuclear genetic material to initiate a new life cycle (Jablonka and Lamb 1995; Jablonka and Szathmáry 1995). Tooby and Cosmides recognize these facts by defining the developmental programs as the entire zygotic machinery passed from one generation to the next (1992, 78). But they are unwilling to extend the program any further. The program unfolds against the background of an environment whose contents it anticipates. This is very different from a developmental systems conception, in which the elements of the environment necessary for the construction of the life cycle are part of what the organism inherits. The social interactions that induce normal psychosocial development in the rhesus monkey (section 3.3) are as much part of its developmental system as the endoplasmic reticulum of its maternal gamete. The nuclear genetic material, the zygotic machinery, and the social environment are all "inherited." They are all passed on from the last generation to the next and interact to reconstruct the life cycle.

The idea of a disjunctive developmental program sounds as if it is a substantial hypothesis about the mechanism by which the phenotype is constructed. This in turn makes it sound as if the developmental systems alternative is substituting a vague hypothesis for a precise one. But a "disjunctive developmental program" is actually only a description of the pattern of variation in developmental outcomes and says no more about actual mechanisms than the developmental systems reformulation. Calling a trait the outcome of a disjunctive genetic program means nothing more than that the environment accounts for some of the variance in that trait in the population.

What makes the notion of a disjunctive developmental program appear more substantial is a version of the innateness fallacy (described in section 3.3 and revisited earlier in this chapter). The notion of innateness conflates the two independent claims that a trait has an evolutionary explanation and that it is insensitive to environmental variation. In the same way, the claim that a trait is the result of a disjunctive developmental program conflates the claim that it has one of the norms of variation sketched above with the claim that the elements of the program were selected for producing this norm of variation. It is only this implicit claim about selection that makes it incorrect to say that a socially deprived macaque is following the disjunctive program "if not allowed to play as an infant, do not finish copulations as an adult" or that a victim of the drug thalidomide is following the disjunctive program "in a thalidomide-rich environment develop rudimentary limbs." The "program" produces this response but this is not one of the outcomes that it was selected to produce. The ability to make these distinctions creates the impression that a disjunctive developmental program is something more than a description of the observed pattern of developmental outcomes. It *is* something more than this, but not because it says anything specific about developmental mechanisms. Instead, it ascribes the pattern to a specific historical cause. This gives it many of the same pitfalls as the innateness concept. It tempts theorists to slide back and forth between a thesis about development and a thesis about evolution without realizing that they are doing so.

Tooby and Cosmides' failure to incorporate the environmental inputs in development into their "developmental programs" causes them to miss some of the roles of environmental factors in evolution. They think developmental programs evolved in an environment which contained varying circumstances, but which on a larger scale of space and time constituted a single "environment of evolutionary adaptedness." If a developmental program produces an adaptive result today it is because it finds the same environmental factors that existed in that original environment. The "evoked" cultural traits are part of a universal human heritage which reflects a single pleistocene environment of evolutionary adaptedness. The only alternative to this universal human nature is traditional "transmitted culture." Every adaptive cognitive trait is either part of the universal human nature or is learned from the other members of the culture in accordance with the traditional conception of culture. The biology/culture divide is alive and well despite all their efforts to subdue it.

A full-fledged developmental systems conception creates a wider range of options. Each organism inherits a range of developmental resources which interact to reconstruct the phenotype. Variation in any of these can be a source of adaptive innovation. In Tooby and Cosmides' approach variation in environmental resources must be either anticipated in the program or a source of abnormality. The developmental systems formulation shows that it can be a source of evolutionary innovation. The behavior of Malaysian barn owls is a good example. This population was introduced from the United Kingdom a few decades ago. In the UK the species is solitary and hunts by searching an individual territory. In Malaysia it is gregarious and hunts the abundant rat populations of the rubber plantations using a sit-and-wait strategy (Lenton 1983). There is no reason to suppose that this is the expression of a disjunctive program selected in ancestral birds who lived in conditions of abundance. An even more striking example occurs in the fire ant *Solenopsis invicta*. This species has two types of colonies. There are monogynous colonies with single, large queens and polygynous colonies with multiple, smaller queens. The differences between queens are induced by the type of colony in which they have been raised, as shown by cross-fostering experiments. Exposure of eggs from either type of colony to the pheremonal "culture" of a polygynous colony produces small queens who found polygynous colonies. Exposure of either type of egg to a monogynous pheremonal "culture" produces large, monogynous queens (Keller and Ross 1993). Without the experimental intervention most workers would have assumed that the two subspecies were genetically distinct. In fact, the few genetic differences between the two types seem to be responses to the different selection pressures in the two nest types. The norm of variation of these ants is not the result of a disjunctive developmental program in Tooby and Cosmides' sense because the two types breed true in nature. Under natural conditions offspring of monogynous queens do not get raised in the pheremonal environment of polygynous nests, so they have not been selected for the ability to respond to this treatment. Rather than a disjunctive developmental program, this is another example of a disruption of the nongenetic elements of the developmental system inducing a new, adaptive, and self-replicating variant.

Although the idea of innovation due to variation in the environmental elements of the developmental system is easiest to grasp from dramatic cases like these, it is an equally useful formulation for mundane cases of habitat or host imprinting. Wherever the developmental system incorporates a stable feature, disruption of that feature is a potential source of innovation. This has enormous implications for the relationship between evolved psychological traits and culture. It is no longer necessary to assimilate all cultural differences in the psychological phenotype either to a disjunctive human nature designed for hunter-gatherer societies or to culture as traditionally conceived—a set of ideas and practices transmitted by inculcation and imitation. Instead we can construct a quite general model of psychological development and distinguish within it many sources of difference. The developmental system which constructs the psychological phenotype includes traditional biological factors such as genes and traditional cultural elements such as stories and norms of behavior. It contains many other resources, from child-care practices to landscapes. All of these may differ across cultures and induce variants of human psychology. Within this general formulation we can sketch many different forms of development and transmission. In some cases cultural variation may be sustained by traditional mechanisms like learning and imitation. In others it may be sustained by the effects of child-care practices or the physical environment. Only some of this variation is of interest to evolutionary theory, but the difference between that which is of interest and that which is not does not turn on whether it involves traditional biological resources like genes or cytoplasmic traces. Variation is of interest to evolution whenever it is reliably self-replicating. This is demonstrated by cases like the owls and the fire ants described above. If a child-care practice is stably transmitted in a lineage and affects the psychological phenotype, then its invention constitutes microevolution as surely as a change in an allele at a locus.

5.7 The Heterogeneous Construction of Emotions

The phrase "heterogeneous construction"[5] is meant to convey the idea that the psychological phenotype is constructed through the interaction of traditional "biological" factors, traditional "cultural" factors, and factors that are hard to classify in terms of that dichotomy. The developmental systems tradition also conceives the interaction of these factors in a richer way than either the evolutionary psychologists or the social constructionists. Reasonable members of both schools subscribe to the truism that human psychology requires both genetic and environmental inputs to its development. They use opposite but symmetrical assumptions to minimize the impact of this concession. On the one hand, evolutionary psychologists have tended to follow the earlier sociobiologists in supposing that the evolved features of human psychology will emerge in all humans who have the relevant genes and cellular machinery and an environment in the normal range. No environment which produces a functional human psychology can avoid producing the evolved features. On the other hand, social constructionists embrace the "social determinist" view that biology provides only a broad constraint on the range of outcomes that can be pro-

5. I owe this phrase to Peter J. Taylor, who uses it to express the impact on scientific theories of all sorts of factors, the "internal," the "external," and the hard to classify!

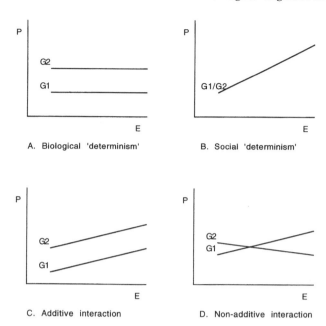

5.2. Assumptions about norms of reaction. P = phenotypic outcome, E = environmental variable, G = genetic variable (or other conception of "biological" variable). All variables are shown confined within their "normal" (historic) ranges.

duced by environmental factors. Our biology prevents us from becoming Superman at one end and becoming chimpanzees at the other. Within those constraints, only social factors affect what is produced. Carl Ratner tells us that "the vestigial elements of animal emotionality which we have inherited are empty shells which become subsumed under social-psychological processes" (1989, 218–19).

Both these views make strong and unwarranted assumptions about the forms of "norms of reaction." Each proposes that changes in one of the variables of a norm of reaction has no effect on the outcome (except at the extremes, where it has catastrophic effects). These two assumptions and some simple alternatives are shown in figure 5.2. In figure 5.2 B it is assumed that all the variance between individuals is accounted for by environmental factors. This is the social constructionist view of human psychology. In figure 5.2 A it is assumed that in any normal range of environments the differences between individuals will depend only on differences in their genes. This traditional biological determinist view is modified in two ways by the evolutionary psychologists. First, they extend the biological variable G to include the entire machinery of the fertilized egg. They call this a developmental program. This makes little difference to the picture. Second, they expect this developmental program to be disjunctive. Genetically identical individuals need not develop the same psychology irrespective of the environment. They are programmed to develop differently depending on the environmental cues they encounter. In effect, the evolutionary psychologist allows that development may resemble figure 5.2 C or 5.2 D, but insists that every such departure from 5.2 A must have an adaptive explanation.

The idea of an additive interaction pictured in figure 5.2 C is a slightly less restrictive conception of the relationship between biological and cultural variables. It allows that both types of variables may have some effect on the outcome. But it assumes that a particular change in one variable has the same effect on the outcome no matter what value the other variable is set at. The addition of a certain developmental factor will always produce a certain sort of difference in the phenotypic outcome. This allows Stephen Goldberg (1973) to argue that although the effect of the hormone testosterone depends on other factors, the fact that men have higher levels of this hormone than women means that they will always be more aggressive. A general assumption that interaction is additive also underlies a piece of reasoning used by many social theorists to dismiss the idea that genes affect human behavior. The argument starts from the premiss that there are many radically different forms of human society and that genetic differences across these societies are minimal. It concludes that the genes have no interesting role in the production of the features that differ across those societies. A change in the human genome might create some overall change affecting every human culture, but it would not affect the differences across cultures. But this argument assumes that the norm of reaction for every other possible human genome is parallel to that for the current human genome. In other words, it assumes that interaction is additive. Despite the wide appeal of the additivity assumption, there is little reason to suppose that it is correct. The geneticist Richard Lewontin has famously argued that norms of reaction will often be nonadditive (Lewontin 1974).

Developmental systems theory (DST) drops all these assumptions. It takes figure 5.2 D as the central picture of development and subsumes all the other figures as special cases. DST also adds a temporal dimension to the norm-of-reaction concept. The effect of a developmental resource may depend on when it is present as well as on whether it is present. DST goes beyond even the most sophisticated evolutionary psychologists' picture of development by not demanding an adaptive explanation for every departure from figure 5.2 A. This means that the environment can be a source of novelty. This account of the construction of the (psychological) phenotype provides the best framework for thinking about cultural variation in emotion. It provides a new perspective on variant psychologies, conceiving them as evolved from a single psychological phenotype in a common ancestor by the incorporation into the developmental system of variants of some of the developmental resources. This makes it possible to discern the common origins of two emotional responses without having to factor the responses into identical (evolved) and different (cultural) elements. A developmental systems conception can hypothesize common origins on the basis of all sorts of abstract resemblances, just as we might hypothesize a common origin for two homologous features on the basis of something as abstract as the common relative position of those parts in early ontogeny. Two emotional responses in different cultures might be homologous in the same distant way that the hammer and anvil bones in the mammalian ear are homologues of bones in the reptilian jaw.

The developmental systems perspective has a further advantage in that it separates questions about the historical source of a trait from questions about its development. Humans have had a culture since before they were human. Culture is a key resource for the construction of the psychological phenotype. The fact that the development of a trait has a complex dependence on culture does not show that an evolutionary perspective cannot throw light on its origins. The developmental systems theorists are free to concentrate on the question of how the emotional phenotype is constructed. They do not have to concern themselves with whether the emotion in question is biological, in which case they must assimilate its construction process to that of a highly entrenched morphological feature, or cultural, in which case they must treat biological factors as a uninteresting background. They are free to look at the heterogeneous construction of emotion. The social constructionist literature which I review in the next chapter need not be read in the first instance as showing that emotions have no evolutionary origins. It can also be read as a fascinating contribution to developmental psychobiology. If emotions depend critically on factors such as cultural models of appropriate behavior, then the evolutionary questions remain to be addressed. How ancient are those models? How long ago did the human psychological phenotype come to depend on this particular source of developmental information, and how much has that resource diverged between different human groups since that originating event?

6

The Social Construction of Emotion

6.1 What Is Constructionism?

The constructionist approach is inspired by the apparent variation in emotional phenomena across cultures. This variation is of many kinds. Most radically, some cultures seem to have their own, proprietary emotions. The Japanese experience an emotion called *amae,* sometimes described as a deeply gratifying sense of childlike dependency on a person or institution (Morsbach and Tyler 1986). This is not easy to identify with any emotion experienced in Anglo-Saxon societies. Even where it seems possible to identify the same psychological condition across cultures, the wider phenomena associated with the emotion may differ greatly. If an emotion sharing cognitive and physiological elements with *amae* were found to occur in Anglo-Saxon society, it would be appear very different because it would not find the other social factors with which it usually interacts. Finally, an emotion may be more prominent in one culture than in another, in the sense that the emotion is experienced more often and that people use the emotion concept to articulate ideas about what constitutes a successful or unsuccessful life. Love seems to be particularly prominent emotion in our own culture. Observations of these sorts of variations give rise to the idea that emotional phenomena are part of the local culture in the same way as the local religion or system of gender relations. Although I have distinguished various ways in which emotional phenomena differ among cultures, social constructionists have treated them all in much the same fashion. They have tried to deny that there is any essence to an emotion which can be reidentified across different social contexts (Armon-Jones 1986a). Rather than saying that the same emotion has different effects or is interpreted differently, they have claimed in every case that different cultures have different emotions.

The social constructionist program has two things to offer to a general treatment of emotional phenomena. First, it suggests that elements of the local culture such as social roles and conceptions of appropriate behavior may feed by several different routes into the construction of the emotional phenotype. These contributions can be assimilated to the program of heterogeneous constructionism which I sketched in the last chapter. I hope to show that these insights of social constructionism are perfectly compatible with what is known about the evolutionary basis of emotion. Second, the social constructionists suggest that much of what people say about their emotions is not a transparent description of their psychological processes. Certain emotional responses may be the acting out of myths about the mind in the same way that ghost possession is the acting out of metaphysical beliefs. If correct, this strongly supports my general conclusion that we will need conceptual revision in order to construct a scientific psychology of emotion.

In order to gain the benefit of the insight that certain emotions are "social constructions" it is necessary to reject attempts to water down the notion of social construction so that it applies to everything and offers no particular insights about anything. There are two very different models of the social construction of emotion in the literature. I call these the *social concept* model and the *social role* model. The social concept model is most clearly expressed by Solomon (1984), although it can found in most of the authors whose primary discipline is philosophy. Solomon begins by asserting something like the propositional attitude theory of emotion defended in his earlier work (Solomon 1977). To have an emotion is to make a certain judgment about the world. In fear, the current situation is dangerous; in love, it is romantic; in *amae*, it is perhaps maternal. Unlike the traditional propositional attitude theory, however, the social concept model suggests that the categories into which the world must be classified in order to produce an emotion are "cultural" rather than "natural" categories. This distinction is explained by Claire Armon-Jones: "Emotions are constituted by non-natural attitudes, these being acquired in, and explicable by reference to, specifically socio-cultural contexts . . . such attitudes and their external referents are either irreducibly, or significantly socio-cultural in nature" (1986a, 36–37).

So natural and nonnatural propositional attitudes are those whose *objects* are "natural" or "cultural" respectively. I take it that the belief that

I am about to be accused of treason is an example of an attitude with a
"cultural" object. The belief that I am about to be eaten might be an example of a belief with a "natural" object. Since emotions involve beliefs and
desires with cultural objects, they will vary from society to society. As Solomon puts it, "Emotions are conceptual constructions, and as go the concepts, so go the emotions as well" (1984, 252); and Ratner: "The fact
that adult human jealousy is constructed from social concepts means that
cultures lacking these concepts should experience no jealousy. This situation characterises the Eskimo who accept extra-marital sexual relations
without jealousy" (1989, 213).

The social concept model concerns itself primarily with the construction of categories of eliciting situations for emotion. It is a model of the
emotions themselves only because an emotion is identified with the thought
that the eliciting situation is present. The second model of social construction concerns itself more with the construction of the output side of emotion, the sequence of events that manifests an emotion. I call this the social
role model of construction. A clear presentation of this model can be found
in the work of the psychologist J. R. Averill. Averill defines social constructionism as the view that

> an emotion is a transitory social role (a socially constituted syndrome)
> that includes an individual's appraisal of the situation, and is inter-
> preted as a passion rather than as an action. (Averill 1980a, 312)

A social role is a characteristic pattern of behavior found in a particular society. The existence of such roles often appears to have a function,
either for the individuals who play the role, or for the society as a whole,
or for both. The role of father, for example, is both a way for a man to
define his authority and responsibilities in our society and a way that a
particular kind of social order is maintained. A *transitory* role is a role
like "understanding friend" or "stern teacher"—a set of behaviors that a
person deploys on an occasional basis, usually in a specific type of social
situation. Averill suggests that "being angry" or "being in love" are also
roles that people adopt in certain situations and that reflect society's conception of what is appropriate in that situation.

Another part of Averill's definition, the idea that emotions are interpreted as passions, helps make the social role idea more plausible. Emotions are normally thought to just happen, rather than being put on or

acted out. They are passions rather than actions. But according to Averill, the belief that emotions are difficult or impossible to control is a myth which helps the emotion to fulfill its various functions. Our helplessly "suffering" an emotion is part of the role we take on.

> Take anger as a case in point. There is a general cultural prohibition against intentionally harming another; however, under certain circumstances . . . retaliation may be expected, and even demanded; it must, however, be carried out in such a manner that the individual does not willingly violate the general cultural norm against injuring another. Being "overcome" by anger is one way of meeting this dual standard. (Averill 1980b, 66)

Many people find the idea that emotions are "disclaimed actions" intuitively implausible. Constructionists try to shake this intuition by describing disclaimed actions in distant cultures whose myths have no grip on us. Averill provides a particularly striking example in his discussion of a New Guinean socially constructed illness. The Gururumba people experience the state of "being a wild pig" (Newman 1964). In this state they run wild, looting articles of small value and attacking bystanders. The Gururumba think the wild-pig syndrome is caused by being bitten by the ghost of a recently dead member of the tribe. They believe that this releases impulses suppressed by society and civilization. The syndrome is treated as a disease by the tribe. The antisocial behavior is tolerated to a quite remarkable extent. The disease either runs its course or is ritually cured. Wild-pig behavior is largely restricted to males between the ages of twenty-five and thirty-five. At this age men are likely to be under considerable economic pressure following the acquisition of a wife. Wild-pig behavior seems to occur when a man cannot meet his financial obligations. After a display of wild-pig behavior the individual receives special consideration with respect to these obligations. Newman convincingly explains wild-pig behavior as a device by which a man can obtain this consideration without denying the fact that the demands made on him are legitimate. The behavior is an action, but is not acknowledged as such either by the individual or by society. It is part of the wild-pig role that wild-pig behavior is involuntary.

In a recent book on multiple personality syndrome (MPS) Ian Hacking describes a form of social construction very similar to that seen in the Gururumba (Hacking 1995). According to Hacking the modern symptomatology of MPS evolved hand in hand with theories of the disorder. By channeling their distress into forms recognized by current theory, individuals were able to gain social acceptance as "sick" and to receive positive feedback from therapists, support groups, and so forth. In the early days of the modern MPS epidemic individuals rarely presented with the full range of symptoms. Distressed individuals were "trained" in the production of MPS symptoms, first by expert therapists and later by a voluntary movement of laypersons. Today, with the help of literature and television talk shows, patients are able to produce the symptoms without individual tuition. MPS has become part of the local culture in countries suffering the MPS epidemic.

A similar explanation might be given of the syndrome found in a number of southeast Asian societies and referred to as *amok*. This syndrome consists of indiscriminate attacks on others and usually culminates in the killing of the person who runs *amok*. *Amok* is traditionally triggered by perceived dishonor. Cases are cited of Westerners living in Asia running *amok*, presumably by example. Once again, this can be interpreted as a disclaimed action. The man running *amok* is not pretending to be in a frenzy, but he would not be in the frenzy unless he had learned that this is an appropriate response to certain unbearable social pressures. He is acting out a social role, part of which is that he is not in control of his actions. It might be argued that a similar syndrome now exists in Western culture. Men who believe that none of their options allows them self-respect exhibit a rather stereotypical pattern of behavior, probably derived from contemporary action films. They shoot at a large group of people, not necessarily people associated with their misfortunes, before being shot or shooting themselves. They purport to be "out of control" and are treated as such by society, yet their behavior is under the fairly precise control of a recently developed model of how one might behave in such a situation.

Averill suggests that emotions can be disclaimed actions of this sort. People display the behavior that they have learned is socially appropriate in that situation. Neither the individual nor society, however, acknowledges that this is what is happening. Instead, they represent the behavior as a natural and inevitable response to the circumstances and outside the control of the individual. Averill argues that we construct emotions because as supposedly passive, unavoidable states they obtain special privileges for those who suffer them. The Gururumba's constructed spiritual disorder helps individuals cast off social ties and allows society to reduce the implicit challenge to its moral order by blaming the event on ghosts. Similarly, social ties can be cast off with the assertion that one is carried away by love without questioning the legitimacy of those ties.

Although the idea of disclaimed action is central to Averill's presentation of constructionism, the social role model need not depend on it. Averill insists at several points that a socially constructed response must be "improvised," that is, planned by the agent using their knowledge of cultural norms. But this is far too narrow a conception of how cultural norms can influence behavior. A driver's response to an intersection is presumably socially constructed, since it is an acquired behavior in which the subject attempts to conform to cultural norms for the situation. Nevertheless, it can and should be so inculcated as to be produced without conscious direction (sometimes even without its production being consciously registered by the subject). Socially constructed emotional responses may be automatic in the same way. The emotion need not be the product of a cultural model in the synchronic sense that the individual produces it in order to conform to the model. The emotion may depend on the model in the diachronic sense that the existence of the model in the culture helped shape what is now a relatively automatic reaction to certain situations. We might call this the *reinforcement* version of the social role model, as opposed to the *disclaimed action* version.

At some points, Averill seems to recognize this possibility. In response to the accusation that his account of improvisation is implausible as an account of actual mental processes preceding each emotional response, he remarks that

> it is true that most people do not become emotional in order to fulfil some social obligation. But a role analysis is no more objectionable in this respect than is an analysis in terms of biologically based adaptive patterns . . . any specific episode of anger, love, . . . etc., may meet no social need. But if on the average, or over the long run, such emotional syndromes conform to social norms, then their net result will be functional within the social system (Averill 1980a, 336)

The idea in this passage seems to be that people do not deliberately produce emotions in order to obey cultural norms. Instead, the existence of those norms creates something akin to a pattern of reinforcement which shapes people's behavior so that it conforms to the norms. So although emotions achieve various individual and societal goals, the individual need not have a plan to achieve their goals when they produce the emotion. The wider society need not have a plan to achieve *its* goals when it accepts the emotion. The goals explain the behavior only because they explain why behavior of that sort has been reinforced.

I have discussed two models of the social construction of emotion, the latter of which has two important variants. The social concept model suggests that to have an emotion is to think of the current situation as one which is culturally appropriate to a particular emotion. The social role model suggests that having an emotion is manifesting the behavior that constitutes a culture's model of a particular emotion. The social role model has two variants, the disclaimed action version, in which the behavior is driven by a deliberate attempt to conform to a social role, and the reinforcement version. In the reinforcement version the social role is not internalized as a direct cause of behavior, but behavior is brought into conformity with it by patterns of reinforcement in the cultural environment.

6.2 Getting Constructionism Right

The social role model of the social construction of emotion is superior to the social concept model. It can incorporate all the insights of the social concept model, and that model itself turns out to be either grossly inadequate or a perverse and inconvenient way to state the social role model. Furthermore, the social concept model inevitably leads to a conflation of the various senses in which things can be socially constructed.

The insight behind the social concept model was that a key part of emotional "competence" in a culture is knowing when to emote, as well as how to emote. This idea is already present in the work of social role theorists such as Averill, who defined an emotion as "a transitory social role (a socially constituted syndrome) *that includes an individual's appraisal of the situation,* and is interpreted as a passion rather than as an action" (Averill 1980a, 312; italics added).

A social role is not just a pattern of behavior. A proper grasp of the social role of "mother" includes a conception of when maternal behavior is appropriate and an interpretation of mothering, perhaps as a natural and inevitable response to children, or perhaps as a moral duty. Emotions resemble other social roles in these respects. So the insights of the social concept model can be incorporated into the social role model simply by including in the social role the act of believing that a suitable elicitor is present.

The inadequacy of the social concept model can be brought out with an obvious objection. The model seems to rule out the possibility that two cultures could demand different emotional responses to the same situation. Surely a culture could prescribe a complex social role, whose elements are unique to that culture, as a response to dangers or to infants? The fact that another culture has the concept "danger" or "infant" would not prove that it has the same emotion. The social concept model makes the identity of a socially constructed emotion depend solely on the situation that elicits the emotion. This seems to gratuitously neglect many other elements. When confronted with this objection adherents of the social concept model typically deny that two cultures can share a concept unless the concept has exactly the same connotations for both cultures. If two cultures have different emotional responses to infants, then they must have different concepts of infant. They are therefore not really responding to the same situation. Thus, for example, Rom Harré asserts that two cultures cannot share the emotion of fear if one regards fear as shameful and the other praises it (1986, 10). There are many reasons to reject this view of concepts. It seems to imply a holism about meaning so extreme that it would exclude the possibility of successful communication except between doppelgängers. But there is no need to appeal to such general considerations here. In this context the holistic view of conceptual identity is merely a perverse attempt to explain the output side of emotions. The concept of the eliciting situation is supposed to determine in and of itself exactly what should be done in any situation where someone has the emotion! Whereas a social role theorist would say that fear is a social role that people produce in response to what they interpret as danger, the social concept theorist claims that fear is just the interpretation of the situation as dangerous. To account for the other aspects of emotion, the social concept theorist adds that the concept of danger is the concept of a situation where certain sorts of objects recognized as threats in our culture are present and which calls for the production of a certain range of behaviors (perhaps different ones for different objects) and for having certain sorts of thoughts about the kind of psychological state one is in. We can reject this as nothing more than poor conceptual analysis. The concept of danger does not include a full specification of everything our culture believes about fear. That is why we can make sense of the possibility of other people having different attitudes to danger.

A related reason to reject the social concept model is that it inevitably leads to a conflation of various senses in which a mental state can be socially constructed. Notice that the social concept model argues that an emotion is the thought that a situation is of a certain type. It is because these types are social constructions that emotions are social constructions. So the primary things that are socially constructed are the categories into which the world is classified. But there are at least three important senses in which categories can be socially constructed. First, there is the trivial sense in which all concepts are socially constructed. In this sense, the concepts of electron, magnesium, and clade are social constructions, as well as the concepts of citizen, member of parliament, and licensed dog owner. None of these *concepts* can exist independently of a community of speakers and thinkers, and each was created by a sociolinguistic process.

In the second, stronger sense, citizens, members of parliament, and licensed dog owners are social constructions while electrons, magnesium, and clades are not. The *categories* referred to in the first list are social constructions, whereas those referred to by the second list are not. The categories electron, magnesium, and clade would exist (their members would have certain properties in common) whether or not the concepts of those categories had been formulated. The elements described by the periodic table do not need the activities of a community of speakers and thinkers to make them differ in atomic weight and number. Modern systematics was not needed for evolving lineages to speciate.[1] The category of MPs, however, depends for its existence on the formulation of the concept of a member of parliament. Were it not for the sociolinguistic activities centered on this concept, the members of parliament would have nothing in common to differentiate them from nonmembers. According to Hacking the same is true of multiple personality syndrome. The potential to develop MPS could be developed very differently. Another society might make

---

1. There are, of course, many social constructionists who would deny that there are any categories of this kind, but most social constructionists about emotion seem to accept that there are.

something very different of the individuals who are now made into sufferers of MPS. That society might also make some cases of MPS into one alternative way of being and others into another alternative way of being. This way of grouping would find as much justification in the occurring phenomena as the current groupings. Hacking describes his view as *dynamic nominalism*. Dynamic nominalism differs from simple nominalism in that the members of a category do share something over and above the fact that they are members of that category. However, the fact that the members have these shared properties reflects the existence of the category and the social practices in which it is embedded (Hacking 1995).

The third sense of *socially constructed* is the sense expressed when someone remarks that a thing is "just socially constructed" and infers from this that no such thing exists. It would be natural to say this about Newman's condition of ghost possession. Ghost possession is not a category like electron which exists independently of our social practice, but neither is it like member of parliament or licensed dog owner. Most people would happily admit that the only difference between MPs and non-MPs is that we as a community treat these people in a particular way. This realization has no effect on the social practice in which the concept of MP is embedded. But it would make all the difference in the world to the Gururumba if they believed that the only difference between wild-pig men and other men is the decision of the men to be wild pigs and the decision of the community to treat them as such. The Gururumba practice of ghost possession rests on a collective pretense that this is not the case. Socially constructed categories in this third sense are social *pretenses* that cannot survive the realization that they are merely our inventions. The general acceptance of Hacking's analysis of multiple personality syndrome would have a corrosive effect on the social practices of the modern MPS community. Another Western example of this third sort of social construction may be the social construction of gender. Our social practices have been transformed by the growing acceptance that traditional gender characteristics are not the inevitable effects of biological sex.

So the claim that categories are socially constructed turns out to be doubly ambiguous. In a trivial sense all concepts are socially constructed. In a more substantial sense a socially constructed category is one partly dependent on the sociolinguistic process that creates the concept of that category. Within this more substantial sense of "socially constructed" there

1. Trivial Constructionism	
A concept exists because of sociolinguistic activity involving the concept.	
2/3. Substantial Constructionism	**2. Overt Construction**
The category corresponding to a concept exists (its members have something in common) because of sociolinguistic activity involving the concept.	The nature of the category is, or can be, known to those who use the concept without disrupting the process by which the category is constructed.
	3. Covert Construction
	Knowledge of the nature of the category by those who use the concept would disrupt the process by which the category is constructed.

6.1. Three kinds of social construction. See text for explanation.

are two very different kinds of socially constructed entities (figure 6.1). First, there are overt social constructions like members of parliament. It can be openly acknowledged that this category groups together individuals whose common nature is a product of the sociolinguistic process that produces the concept of a member of parliament. Second, however, there are covert social constructions like wild-pig men. These are categories that are ontologically on a par with overt social constructions but are treated by the community as if they corresponded to independent distinctions in nature. They are treated in the same way as categories like chlorine or motor-neuron disease.

Averill and other advocates of the social role model think that emotions are social constructions in the third sense—covert social constructions. Emotions are a society's collective pretense that people are subject to certain natural and involuntary "passions." Solomon and other adherents of the social concept model, however, seem to think that emotions could be social constructions in the second sense—overt social constructions. Solomon argues that emotions are social constructions because "getting angry is making an indictment (whether overtly or not). It involves concepts and evaluations that are clearly learned and, in their specifics, learned only in the context of a particular society with certain kinds of ethical views and theories" (1984, 250).

His argument seems to be that emotions are social constructions because an emotion is the thought that the current situation falls into some category and that category is a social construction (second sense). An exactly parallel argument would suggest that believing someone to be an MP is a socially constructed mental state, because the category of MPs is a social construction (second sense). If this is Solomon's argument for constructionism, then he must think emotions could be *overt* social constructions.

Other passages suggest that Solomon is using a slightly different argument for constructionism. The passage just cited continues, "This is not to deny that one might find anger (or some similar emotion) in every society," and elsewhere Solomon does not "foreclose the probability [*sic*] that some emotions are specific to *all* cultures" (1984, 249; emphasis in original). The argument here seems to be that emotions are social constructions because an emotion is the thought that the current situation falls into some category and all categories are social constructions (first sense). If this is the argument, then Solomon's social constructionism is just another way of asserting that emotions are thoughts. This is a plausible interpretation, since Solomon's earlier work on emotion centered on the claim that emotions are evaluative beliefs (Solomon 1977).

I suggest that most of what is interesting about social constructionist theory rests on the idea that emotions are covert social constructions. Both the constructionist positions I have attributed to Solomon are too weak to be interesting. If emotions are social constructions merely because they are thoughts and all concepts are social constructions, then every thought is a social construction in the same sense. An emotion has the same status as the thought that chlorine has more than one isotope. Surely the work of Averill and others points to a more interesting hypothesis than this. Even the less trivial of the two positions is pretty weak. It claims that anger is a social construction in the same sense as the thought that something is illegal or foreign. The objects of these concepts depend for their existence on the sociolinguistic practice that involves these concepts. But there is no sense here of the radical nature of Averill's proposal. People live quite happily with the idea that laws and nations are social constructions. The suggestion that love and anger are not natural and inevitable parts of human being provokes anger and denial in a large part of the population. It runs counter to the view of these emotions that many people live by. Solomon's constructionism is missing something that makes emotions vastly different from laws or nations. It is missing the fact that emotions are interpreted as passions rather than actions.

There is a fundamental tension in the work of Solomon and other authors who have come to constructionism from the old propositional attitude theory. These authors have spent their careers denouncing the "cultural myth" that emotions are irrational, involuntary, and natural. They have claimed that when properly understood, emotion terms refer to judgments about the world, which are voluntary and subject to rational and moral standards. These same theorists now want to embrace the view that emotions are created and constituted by cultural myth making! The obvious way to combine these views would be to say that in emotion we act out the cultural myth that there are irrational, involuntary, natural states called emotions. But to say this, the adherents of the propositional attitude school would have to admit that their old conceptual analyses of what ordinary speakers mean by emotion terms were mistaken. Because they are unwilling to do this they are unable to come to terms with many social constructionist ideas. For example, one of Averill's key ideas is that emotions fulfill their social functions precisely because they are accepted as natural and involuntary.

The problems I have documented in this section can be avoided without difficulty simply by adopting the social role model. Constructionism is the view that emotions are transitory social roles that are interpreted as passions rather than as actions.

6.3 The Problem of Sincerity

The social role model of social construction claims that cultural models of emotion help to produce the emotional behaviors that conform to those models. I have argued that in some cases the role of cultural models may be diachronic. They act during the agents' development by structuring the patterns of reinforcement in the cultural environment so as to produce automatic behaviors that conform to cultural norms. Many constructionists, however, have focused on cases where the cultural model has a synchronic role in guiding behavior. According to this version, the emotional response is produced "strategically" with the intention of extracting a suitable response from others. But the emotional response is interpreted by the agent and their community as natural and involuntary. The action is "disclaimed." Such a theory owes a more precise account of "disclaimed action." It must avoid the trivializing conclusion that these cases are merely ones where someone pretends to have an emotion. I approach this problem by asking when, on a constructionist account, a disclaimed action emotion is sincere.

The obvious way to make a disclaimed action seem sincere is to say that the agent is not aware of what they are doing. The plan behind the emotional response is unconscious. There are obvious parallels with the medical category of "abnormal illness behaviors" in which the strategic purpose of the "symptoms" is not consciously available to the patient. But constructionist theorists have been hostile to the idea of unconscious states. They have followed the example of Jean-Paul Sartre in suggesting that people know why they produce emotions, but deceive themselves about this. The difference between self-deceit and deceit of others serves to distinguish socially constructed emotions from mere pretenses of emotion. Self-deceit is then explained in a way that does not involve unconscious processes. In this section I will show that this rejection of unconscious processes is a mistake. No adequate account of either disclaimed action or self-deceit is possible without the use of unconscious processes. In any case, the constructionist hostility to unconscious processes is unwarranted. The notion of unconscious information processing is ubiquitous in modern cognitive science and the traditional philosophical arguments against this notion are fatuous.

Sartre's (1962) theory of emotions has had a major influence on many social constructionists. In Sartre's asocial form of constructionism emotions are disclaimed actions, but they are explained in terms of individual psychodynamics rather than the surrounding social order. Sartre claims that emotions are actions that we perform in order to obtain psychological rewards, primarily the avoidance of stress. He describes emotion as "magical consciousness." In becoming emotional we return to a way of confronting the world which we adopted as helpless children. Instead of confronting the world as it is and taking appropriate action we distort or annihilate our perception of it. So when a person faints in terror, their aim is to remove the object of terror from their consciousness. The whole essence of emotion is self-deceit. People are emotional about what they cannot face up to and being emotional consists precisely in not facing up to things.

Most people deny that whenever they have an emotion they go through the psychodynamic processes described by Sartre. This denial is often pretty convincing. So Sartre owes us an account of why people do not seem to recall the thoughts he attributes to them. The obvious response would be that the thoughts are unconscious, but Sartre sees positing an unconscious as just one more way to escape from the conclusion that we live our lives in a state of self-deceit and "bad faith." Instead, he offers an account which is supposed to avoid the need for unconscious processes. This appears to be seminal for later constructionist rejections of the unconscious (Warner 1986; Harré 1988). Sartre begins with a version of the well-known distinction between having a thought and thinking that you have that thought. A moment ago I was conscious of being on an airplane. Now, having chosen this as an example, I have an additional state—I am conscious that I am conscious of being on an airplane. As well as thinking that I am on an airplane, I am thinking that I am thinking "I am on an airplane." The first thought is a representation of a state of affairs and may function to guide my behavior. The second is a representation of the state of affairs of my having the first representation. These sorts of representations are sometimes called first- and second-order mental states. A second-order state has a first-order state as its object. Sartre suggests that in self-deceit a first-order state of pretending guides the agent's behavior. So the agent is consciously pretending. However, there is no second-order state which is a representation of this fact. The agent is not conscious that they are consciously pretending. This account is supposed to establish that self-deceit is not an unconscious process. Instead, it is a conscious process that we are not reflective about.

Sartre's account simply misunderstands what unconscious mental processes are. Consider David Armstrong's famous example of "coming to" at the wheel on a long drive (Armstrong 1980). Behavioral evidence persuades us that the driver's behavior before they "came to" was guided by a representation of the road. The driver adjusted the wheel to stay on course. In this sense the driver was "conscious of " or "aware of " the road. But they were not aware of this awareness, nor can they recall it. So in another sense, the driver was unconscious of their environment and of their decision making. The point of this example is that there is a sense in which a person is "conscious" or "aware" of any fact that is represented in a state that helps to guide their behavior. They have first-order consciousness of all such facts. But to have an unconscious thought is not to lack first-order consciousness. If a thought lacks first-order consciousness it just doesn't exist! To say that a thought is unconscious actually means that the person has no second-order consciousness of that thought. They are not conscious of being conscious. It is this second-order consciousness which the long-distance driver briefly loses. This is what makes their thoughts about the road unconscious thoughts. So the states of conscious pretense without consciousness of pretending which Sartre makes so much of are paradigmatic unconscious thoughts. Sartre's claim that they are conscious states fails to distinguish the first-order sense of conscious from the second-order sense.

Sartre's account of self-deception has been endorsed and elaborated by contemporary social constructionists. C. Terry Warner uses such an account in his analysis of anger (Warner 1986). He argues that it is of the essence of anger for it to be disproportionate and exaggerated. The prime drive of an angry person is to deceive themselves about how unreasonable they are being. Like Sartre, Warner is extremely hostile to unconscious processes. He tells us that they are self-contradictory and involve conceptual confusions, although these contradictions and confusions are not spelled out in detail. Having rejected the unconscious, Warner tells us that "on the agentive view, her self-deception is not a matter of concealing a belief, but a matter, we might say, of believing perversely" (1986, 164). The self-deceiver does not have unconscious processes in which they decide that it would be to their advantage to believe the opposite of what the evidence suggests. Instead, they simply form a "perverse belief" given the evidence at their disposal. A similar account is endorsed by Rom Harré (1988). But none of these accounts even begins to explain self-deception. They make a complete mystery of the fact that self-deceiving beliefs serve the interests of the agent, or reduce their psychological stress, or in some other way are not random with respect to the agent's circumstances. If no information is processed in order to form the belief, or to decide which "perverse" rules of evidence are to be used, then the fact that the self-deceptive belief fits the agent's circumstances is magical. The need to explain this fact cannot be sidestepped merely by announcing that the agent "believes perversely" or in Harré's phrase that they "choose an alternative scheme of rhetoric." Some sort of process must control these activities and agents are not conscious of any such processes. So there are unconscious processes involved.

It is a mystery to me why the belief that unconscious mental states are somehow problematic persists. We know that it is impossible to account for the operation of the visual system or the balance system without the idea that these systems contain representations of states of affairs and information transformations that are not accessible to introspection and verbal report. If this idea is unproblematic here, why should it be problematic for a case like self-deception? One reply, albeit a feeble one, is that there is some different between these mechanical or biological processes and cognition proper. But the "confabulation" studies of Nisbett and Wilson (1977) and others have provided documented empirical evidence of very complex reasoning which is unavailable for report. A split-brain subject is presented with a cue that determines their choice of one of a range of actions. The cue is presented to sensory apparatus connected to the hemisphere that lacks connections to the speech areas. The cue might be a word flashed on a screen. The subject will respond to the cue, perhaps by choosing the object named by the word from a selection in front of them. But when asked why they chose that particular object, they tell an implausible story unconnected with the cue. The subject's response to the cue was mediated by a process of reasoning that they cannot introspect or report.

This sort of result has given rise to a philosophical discussion of the "computational unconscious" (e.g., Dennett 1982). The computational unconscious consists of mental states and processes that the agent cannot introspect or verbally report because information about them is not available to the mechanisms underlying introspection and verbal report. The concept of the computational unconscious has obvious relevance to the debates over emotion and self-deception. Georges Rey (1988) has discussed how the distinction between reportable and unreportable mental representations can be built into a computational account of the undamaged human mind and how this can be used to explain phenomena like self-deception and weakness of the will. Unfortunately, the social constructionist literature seems to have taken no account either of philosophical discussion of the computational unconscious or of the empirical findings on which it is based.

The computational unconscious can be used to give a relatively unproblematic account of the sincerity of disclaimed action emotions. An emotion of this kind is sincere simply when the subject is unaware that it is a disclaimed action. The motivation and planning underlying the response is not accessible to introspection or verbal report. The agent's belief that the state is natural and inevitable is sincere, because they have no access to the evidence against this view. This definition has the nice property of automatically making all the relatively automatic responses that conform to the "reinforcement" variant of social role theory sincere as well.

One of the advantages of this computational conception of the unconscious is that it does not make the distinction between conscious and unconscious processes too rigid. A process which is perfectly capable of being consciously monitored may proceed unconsciously because of an unconscious, or even a conscious, decision not to monitor it. A failure to monitor of this sort can happen whenever we direct our attention to a task or have it compelled by some striking feature of the environment. Other mental activity, such as reception of sensory information irrelevant to the object of attention, goes unnoticed, although it may still be playing a vital role in such important activities as navigating our way around the room. Disclaimed action emotions can therefore be more or less sincere, depending on the extent to which the subject realizes that his responses are voluntarily initiated or exaggerated. It is possible to distinguish a whole range of possibilities, such as straightforward pretending, mere inattention to one's motivation, self-deceit, and real deep-seated inability to get at one's motivation. At least this many ways for emotion construction to be hidden are recognizable, and it is a considerable virtue of an account to be able to fit them all in.

In cases of straight pretending, all or most of the processes leading to the constructed emotion are monitored by consciousness. In cases of mere inattention, the subject is unaware of the process of emotion construction simply because their attention is directed elsewhere. Minor interventions, such as another person's pointing their motive out to them, or a moment's reflection, may be enough to make them give up the emotion or change to pretense or self-deceit. The term *self-deceit* itself probably covers a number of very different processes. There will be cases in which the subject would have been conscious of the processes leading to the emotion if they had not been consciously motivated to direct their awareness elsewhere. Critics of the use of unconscious processes to analyze self-deceit (such as Sartre and Harré) have focused on the apparent regress involved in talking of decisions to engage in self-deceit. They argue that a further decision is needed to deceive oneself about this decision, and so on ad infinitum. But there are a whole range of options which this objection ignores. In some cases, the subjects' unawareness of their intention to deceive themselves may be merely due to inattention, as described above. In other cases, the initial decision to engage in self-deceit may itself be unconscious. The final category of unconsciousness listed above is deep-seated unconsciousness. Here I have in mind cases in which the emotional response is akin to multiple personality disorder as described by Hacking (1995). There is no need for the agent to engage in any decision to hide the construction of the emotion from consciousness, as it never had any tendency to manifest itself consciously. Mental effort is needed to bring the underlying processes to consciousness, not to suppress them. It may not even be possible to become conscious of some processes. The cognitive mechanisms that produce the response may be firmly informationally isolated from those serving introspection and verbal report.

This account of the unconscious production of emotions fits disclaimed action into the framework of conventional cognitive psychology. The disclaimed action version of the social role model of social construction can take its place alongside the reinforcement version.

6.4 Social Construction and Heterogeneous Construction

Two important options for explaining emotion emerge from the social constructionist literature. They are the two versions of the social role model of social construction. In the reinforcement version the social role is embodied in social practices in such a way that it produces a pattern of reinforcement. This leads the adult to produce behavior that fits the social role. It is not necessary for the adult to have any mental representation of that social role or to have any motive for conforming to it. In the disclaimed action version the social role that constitutes the emotion is produced as "strategic behavior." The agent has a representation of the social role and conforms their behavior to the role in order to achieve certain rewards. In some cases these are rewards in a straightforward sense, such as being excused for an act of violence. In other cases the reward may be the minimal one of having some sort of guidelines for action in an otherwise baffling situation. The importance of this sort of reward should not be underestimated. It may be the prime reason for the production of something like the "Rambo" behavior syndrome in Western males which I described above.

I suggested in the last chapter that many of the insights of social constructionism could be incorporated into a general model of the "heterogeneous construction" of the emotional phenotype. I also suggested at the beginning of this chapter that social constructionism reveals that some emotions are mythical. The two versions of the social role model lend themselves to these two very different fates. The idea that some emotions are disclaimed action leads to the conclusion that these emotions are mythical. The idea that some emotional responses develop because of reinforcement by the surrounding culture fits in with the idea of heterogeneous construction.

The idea of reinforcement by the local culture fits the heterogeneous construction model because this sort of developmental influence can interact with traditional "biological" processes to determine the adult emotional phenotype. Interactions of this sort can even affect the expression of the affect programs. Paul Ekman (1971, 1972) has discussed this phenomenon under the heading of "display rules." These are rules dictating when the effects of affect programs should be suppressed or accompanied by other displays. They are inculcated during a person's upbringing and, like many other motor skills, they become automatic and involuntary in the adult. In studies of facial expression in Japanese and American students Ekman and his collaborators found that the Japanese suppressed their facial expressions in the presence of authority figures. They superimposed voluntary muscle movements so as to produce a polite smile. These voluntary movements were initiated so quickly that the initial emotional expressions could be detected only by using frame-by-frame analysis of videotapes. The output side of the affect program responses appears to be deeply developmentally entrenched. Their emergence in the infant conforms to the classic biological determinist model, in which almost any environment that supports survival to adulthood supports development of the trait. This means that the effects of different developmental environments take the form of supplementary elements, designed to either suppress or enhance the effects of the program. The Japanese students give us an example of a supplementary element designed to suppress the response. Darwin's (1872) claim that Europeans supplement the pancultural elements of anger with involuntary fist clenching provides an example of enhancement.

I argued in chapter 5 that there are likely to be more developmentally plastic emotions. I described research suggesting that these might take the

form of irruptive patterns of motivation affecting the higher cognitive processes which control long-term, planned actions. The effects of reinforcement by the local culture on these emotions may be more profound than
its effect on the affect programs. Rather than the local culture producing
additional, supplementary elements that accompany universal responses,
it may produce variants of a common ancestral response. Frank (1988)
suggests that humans have evolved a sense of fairness which causes them
to bear costs rather than accept grossly unfair divisions of the economic
product of a transaction. The idea of heterogeneous construction suggests
that this disposition need be neither universal nor uniform for Frank to be
correct. Some cultures may have developed in a direction that modifies
or even eliminates this disposition during development. So heterogeneous
constructionism alerts researchers to look for variation across cultures in
the emotions suggested by evolutionary theorists. Conversely, the idea of
heterogeneous construction suggests the search for cross-cultural resemblances in the emotions described by social constructionists. European culture makes a strong connection between guilt and responsibility. Other
cultures have emotions that resemble guilt (Harré 1986) but lack the strong
connection to responsibility. People experience these guiltlike emotions
simply because they have been a part of some event that is regarded as a
bad thing. The social constructionist claims that these emotions are not
the same emotion as guilt. From the viewpoint of heterogeneous construction the resemblance is as interesting as the difference. It suggests that both
emotions may be variants of a response to situations in which a social
norm has been violated and that they may share important developmental
resources. Obvious topics for research would include both the age at which
the emotional phenotypes of these cultures diverge from one another and
the inputs that produce this divergence. If experiences of punishment play
a key role in the ontogeny of guilt, then the occasions on which punishment
is meted out might be critical.

Emotional responses that owe their form to patterns of reinforcement
produced by the local culture can be smoothly integrated into the heterogeneous construction program for studying emotion. But emotional responses that are disclaimed actions cannot. This is not because their development does not fit the heterogeneous constructionist model. Disclaimed
actions will fit the heterogeneous construction model in the general sense
that their development depends on the co-occurrence of factors tradition-

ally regarded as biological and those traditionally regarded as cultural. Darwinian psychologists have written at length about the possible adaptive advantages of self-deception (Nesse and Lloyd 1992). Producing strategic behaviors that are interpreted as natural and involuntary may be an ancient human trait. The nature of the strategic behaviors people produce and of the interpretations put upon them are likely to vary with the local culture. Disclaimed action emotions will reflect the local conception of emotion in the same way that multiple personality syndrome reflects local conceptions of that illness. This pattern would also resemble the pattern of variation in schizophrenic delusions, which typically reflect the local religious culture. So in this general sense, disclaimed action emotions are the products of a process of heterogeneous construction, just like "reinforced" emotions. The problem with disclaimed actions is not how they are constructed, but how they are implemented. Emotional responses which are disclaimed actions are essentially pretenses. They can be sincere only in the way that abnormal illness behavior or ghost possession can be sincere. The subject does not have conscious access to the causes of their behavior and provides an erroneous explanation of their behavior that masquerades as an introspective report. The reason that disclaimed action emotions cannot be smoothly integrated into the heterogeneous construction program for studying emotion is that they are attempts to mimic other emotional responses. There is a whole layer of mechanism in their production that is absent in other instances of emotion. This makes it inappropriate to try to explain them in the same way as other emotional responses. It would be like trying to explain ghost possession using conventional models of parasitic disease.

Both culturally reinforced and disclaimed action responses are represented in the local cultural milieu as universal and natural responses that are not actions to be explained by the agent's goals and intentions. In the case of culturally reinforced responses, only the first half of this interpretation is false. The responses are not universal and natural. Contrary to local belief, they reflect the local culture. But the local culture is right to insist that they are not actions. Culturally reinforced responses are not pretenses. The psychological processes that produce them do not have the "hidden layer" seen in disclaimed action. A well-enculturated agent does not have an intention to experience guilt or to manifest its symptoms. In the case of disclaimed actions both elements of the local interpretation are false.

These emotions are reflections of the local culture *and* they are actions which can be illuminated by looking at the agent's goals and intentions.

6.5 The Limits of Social Constructionism

Social constructionism about emotion has been taken up enthusiastically by a number of philosophers, notably Rom Harré. These authors have argued that all or most emotions are socially constructed. While I am sympathetic to the idea that social constructionism can illuminate an important class of emotional phenomena, Harré and others have greatly exaggerated the range of phenomena that it can explain. They have argued that "naturalistic" accounts, such as those canvassed in the earlier chapters of this book, have no important role in explaining emotion. Harré (1986) claims that the extent of cultural variation in emotions suggests that most emotional phenomena are to be understood in the light of the local culture: "There can be little doubt that, even if there are some universal emotions, the bulk of mankind live within systems of thought and feeling that bear little but superficial resemblances to one another" (1986, 12). He supports this contention with examples of "cultural variation among emotion systems." Harré's strategy is to show that emotion has the pattern of between-group difference and within-group similarity that has traditionally been thought to require a cultural explanation, as opposed to biological explanation. However, the idea that this pattern precludes biological explanations is problematic. I discussed in chapter 5 the attempt of evolutionary psychologists to explain some instances of this pattern as "evoked culture" (Tooby and Cosmides 1992). These psychologists suggest that a flexible genetic program may produce characteristically different outcomes in different cultural circumstances. I also outlined my preferred "developmental systems" approach. I suggested that psychological phenotypes are heterogeneously constructed through the interaction of stereotypically biological resources like genes, stereotypically cultural resources like moral norms, and resources that are hard to classify in terms of that dichotomy, like experiences of play. Any of these resources may "mutate" in a way that causes the change to be replicated in the next generation and thus leads to heritable change in the resultant phenotype. The developmental systems approach suggests that emotional phenotypes will diverge across human populations due to the incorporation of different extragenetic resources into the developmental system. This leads to a rejection of the idea that the emotional phenotype should be divided into universals to be explained by biological evolution and variable features to be explained by cultural evolution. Instead, emotional phenomena should be grouped together at various levels of generality in a way that reflects patterns of descent. This system of classification will extend from very broad homologies ranging across species to very narrow homologies ranging across human populations. These narrow homologies will reflect recent events of human microevolution, such as changes in "cultural" elements of the developmental system. A nested, genealogical classification of this sort will allow the formulation of whatever evolutionary explanations are available. An *evolutionary* explanation is one that explains the possession of a trait by certain individuals as a result of its inheritance from a common ancestor and suggests that the form of that trait can be illuminated by considering the historical process that produced it (see section 3.3).

Harré's strategy is based on the mistaken idea that variation in a psychological trait across cultures shows that this trait is "cultural" and hence precludes evolutionary explanation. In furtherance of this strategy he adopts a sort of holistic essentialism about emotions. Two psychological traits cannot be identified on the basis of any degree of resemblance short of being completely identical. He claims, for example, that if the moral connotations of emotion words differ across cultures, the emotions referred to must be different. Catherine Lutz (1986) shows that a state called *metagu* (usually translated as "fear") is praised in the Ifaluk atoll culture, while fear is usually condemned in our culture. Harré argues that these two psychological states cannot be the same emotion because they have different moral connotations for those who possess them. It would be "gross mistranslation" to equate them. His second example of cultural variation is that a "strong" form of an emotion can exist in one culture while only a "weak" form exists in another. He alleges that Spaniards more readily and acutely feel embarrassment at the social ineptitude of others. They have a special, albeit phrasal, name for this feeling. This point relates to Heelas's extremely useful notion of *hypercognition*. Heelas (1986) argues that emotions may be hyper- or hypocognized by cultures. Roughly, this means that people talk about them more, or talk about them less. As a result, it is claimed, they classify more or less of their emotional life in those terms, and attribute and self-attribute those emotions more or less often. Love, for example, may be hypercognized in our culture when compared to some others. Harré's third example of cultural variation is more substantial. He claims that emotions go in and out of existence within a single culture. His example is *accidie,* a form of depression and boredom found among early Christian hermits and medieval monks. Harré, with Finlay-Jones, has written a paper on this emotion (1986). This paper, however, suggests that accidie is a state found in many modern subjects but nowadays not distinguished from other varieties of depression. This doesn't fit very well with the claim that emotions come and go with the flow of history. It suggests that what's going on is hyper- and hypocognition.

I find Harré's summary of the evidence for cultural variation in emotions unimpressive. It's supposed to support the thesis that the elements in emotion that are common to all cultures are trivially small. If anything, it does the opposite. Even when a culture ultrahypocognizes an emotion, as it were, observers who retain the appropriate concept seem to be able to find the phenomenon. The phenomena do not disappear, as they should do if wholly dependent on the culture's ideas about them. The immediate cause of these very different interpretations of the evidence is simple. I am assuming that an emotion can be "the same" in some important sense despite differences in some of its properties. Emotions, like other biological traits, can be classified at various levels of generality. Philosophers of social construction like Harré, Claire Armon-Jones (1986a, 1986b), and Carl Ratner (1989) attempt to deny that there is any "essence" to an emotion that can be reidentified across time and culture. Change in any aspect of an emotion changes its identity. They have devoted a great deal of effort to showing that there are no legitimate ways of classifying emotions that would allow them to be identified across cultural contexts. They have looked at proposed essences for emotions and argued that they do not have the potential to explain most of what interests us about emotion. If this were true, then it would be possible only to produce explanations of the emotions found in a particular culture. But the philosophers of social construction have simply not looked at the strong candidates for emotional essences. They have consistently chosen to attack straw persons. The brunt of their attack has been borne by a straw person called "naturalism."

The naturalist theory of emotions which Harré, Armon-Jones, and other philosophers of social construction combat is supposed to represent a central tendency in the work of theorists who stress the evolutionary roots of emotional responses. Paul Ekman, Carroll Izard, Robert Plutchik, and R. B. Zajonc are obvious candidate naturalists. According to Armon-Jones, the naturalist argues that emotions are "universal and natural dispositions" (1986b, 64) to respond in a certain way to certain stimuli. Fear of the dark might be such a natural disposition. Constructionism supposedly has the advantage over naturalism of being able explain fear in situations that "do not naturally warrant fear" (65). Armon-Jones's example at this point is a tribe whose children fear their elders and the neighboring tribes. It is a problem for her "naturalist" that

> while actions such as "fleeing" take the same form whether culturally or naturally determined, they are not identical in respect of the attitudes which give rise to them . . . members of these societies, in prescribing "fear", are endorsing a response which, in so far as it is related to cultural beliefs and moral values, is distinct from, and not strictly derivable from, natural "fear". While this distinction is compatible with the existence of natural "fear", it does call into question the naturalists' account of socialised "fear" as explainable in terms of natural "fear" in virtue of their sharing the same qualitative features and causal conditions. (1986b, 66)

While not exactly transparent, this passage gives important clues to what is going on in Harré's and Armon-Jones's work. They want to classify emotions in terms of what causes them. If an emotion output is caused by spiders and exposed electric wires in one culture, but by scorpions and witch doctors in another, then it's a manifestation of different emotions. The "naturalist," who maintains that emotions are the same across cultures, is then forced to argue that emotions have the same causes in all cultures, which is implausible. Unfortunately, other theorists don't classify emotions by what causes them, so this argument never gets off the ground. The candidate "naturalists" listed above all believe that people are afraid of different things in different cultures. These differences reflect differences in beliefs and learning history. Most "naturalists" give broad, functional definitions of appropriate elicitors. Fear should be elicited by dangers. These broad definitions get filled in in the light of local conditions. Contact with exposed electrical wires will be recognized as a danger in New Zealand; it may not be recognized on Ifaluk atoll.

To get their argument against naturalism off the ground, Harré and

Armon-Jones need a further argument to establish that there can be no taxonomy of emotions which abstracts away from the particular causes of an emotion. I have been able to find only one argument for the view that there is nothing to an emotion over and above the things which cause it and the behavior it causes. In this argument Armon-Jones proceeds by assuming that "inner essences" identifiable across cultures would have to be feelings and then attacking the feeling theory of emotion with neo-Wittgensteinian ideas:

> Emotion feeling is constituted by those attitudes appropriate to the emotion . . . "fear feeling" would not remain unchanged [*across cultures*], but rather would be qualitatively different to the extent that the attitudes constitutive of the emotion feeling are specifically cultural. (1986b, 66; see also 1986a, 40–41)

But the feeling theory is another straw person. The main candidates for the "essences" of emotions which remain constant across cultures are behavioral syndromes, neural structures, and sets of beliefs and desires. The first of these taxonomizes emotions on the basis of their effects alone. The second and third postulate some sort of "inner essence." All three will do the job of giving identity across cultures to emotions while allowing them to have different particular causes.

The view that the essence of an emotion is a set of beliefs and desires is, of course, the traditional propositional attitude theory. Armon-Jones does discuss the propositional attitude theory but never seems to notice the threat it poses to her own view. Like Solomon, she sees it as the first step towards the "social concept" model of emotion described earlier in this chapter:

> The attitudes regarded by contemporary theorists as constituting emotions share the feature [*of constructionism*] that they can in principle be acquired by training. While we regard some attitudes as natural (e.g.: the desire to eat; the evaluation of wild beasts as dangerous), we regard other attitudes as dependent on training and the introduction to custom (e.g.: the desire to be polite; the evaluation of a Matisse as delicate; the belief that theft is a crime). (1986a, 43–44)

What Armon-Jones does not seem to appreciate is the use of abstraction to create cross-cultural definitions of emotion. The propositional attitude theorist says that fear is the belief that something is dangerous and the desire to avoid harm. As I showed in section 2.7, this is an abstract scheme intended to capture all the different sets of beliefs and desires that might, in different cultural contexts, constitute fear. This is precisely the sort of cross-cultural essence that Armon-Jones wants to deny is possible. Fear in all cultures is some set of attitudes that amounts to the belief that one is in danger and the desire to avoid the danger. Envy in all cultures is some set of attitudes that amounts to "wishing to have what someone else has and which is important for the subject's self-definition" (Ben-Zeev 1990, 489). The propositional attitude theorist can predict that an emotion will look very different in another culture, either because of differences in the specific local attitudes that fit the general schema or because of the other propositional attitudes common in that culture. The causal relations of propositional attitude systems are, after all, holistic. Which experiences cause and what action results from certain propositional attitudes vary as a function of the other attitudes the agent holds. So even if an emotion schema was filled in by similar propositional attitudes in two cultures, the similarity might be unrecognizable without a comprehensive grasp of local conditions and the culture of the inhabitants.

The other candidate cross-cultural "essences" are behavioral syndromes and neural programs. Armon-Jones does not discuss these, but it can be assumed that she would take the usual constructionist line. Authors like Ratner (1989) admit that a few innate, universal elements of emotional responses can be found but argue that these either disappear with socialization or become an insignificant part of more complex, learned responses: "The vestigial elements of animal emotionality which we have inherited are empty shells which become subsumed under social-psychological processes" (1989, 218–19). In a similar vein Averill remarks that "biologically determined reactions form a relatively small class of emotional reactions. Their primary importance is that they may be incorporated as elements into other kinds of emotion" (Averill 1980b, 39). There are two main problems with this way of dismissing "biological" perspectives on emotion. First, there is the cluster of confusions caused by subscribing to the traditional concept of innateness. Ratner seems to think that an evolved emotional response must be present at birth and cannot need social inputs to construct it or sustain it. Averill's talk of "biologically determined" responses suggests a similarly narrow conception of evolved responses. I discussed in section 3.3 and in chapter 5 the way in which the notion of innateness allows people to slide back and forth between a trait's having an evolutionary explanation and its being insensitive to environmental variation. Ratner uses this slide to move from the fact that a trait depends on the environment to the conclusion that it has no evolutionary explanation. But in fact, evolved traits are heterogeneously constructed. Normal psychological development in humans includes nurturing, a speech community, and many other elements of culture. An impoverished view of psychological development, obsessed with untenably rigid distinctions between biology and culture and between innateness and learning, makes it very hard for Ratner to appreciate the explanatory potential of "naturalistic" theories.

The second problem with the constructionists' dismissal of this sort of naturalism is their apparent lack of interest in putting emotions into general categories of any sort whatever. It is all very well to insist on the diversity of emotions across times and cultures, but if there is to be any explanation at all emotions will have to be categorized in a way that abstracts away from detail. If most of the interesting features of a particular emotion depend on some cultural model that plays a role in its construction, then emotions of that sort may have to be classified in terms of their descent from a common cultural origin. Thus, although love in Western teenagers is a unique phenomenon, it can be understood as derived from cultural models that go back to the Middle Ages. There may even be more general explanations of the tendency of societies to generate emotions of a particular sort to fulfill social functions. These explanations will require suitably general categories of emotions drawn from some future sociology. Abstracting away from detail is an essential step in giving explanations. "Naturalism" is just another way of doing this. It suggests that emotions in different times and cultures might usefully be grouped together on the basis of patterns of resemblance among them. Such groupings make it possible to offer explanations. For example, they make it possible to explain why fear and *metagu* in Harré's own example have so much in common despite the radically different social roles they play. This explanation cannot be rejected on the grounds that the two differ from one another in respects outside the scope of the explanation.

The extreme holism about emotion favored by Harré and Armon-Jones cannot be sustained for long even in their own writings. Armon-

Jones quickly finds herself recognizing the same emotion in quite different cultural settings. This happens when she considers "inappropriate emotions." Cases in which an emotion occurs in a socially inappropriate situation are of two basic kinds (Armon-Jones 1986b, 71). In the first kind, an inappropriate emotion occurs because the subject has false beliefs. This is no problem for the constructionist. The emotion is not culturally appropriate to the situation the agent actually faces, but it is appropriate to the situation the agent *thinks* they are facing. The second kind of inappropriate emotion occurs when the agent perceives the situation correctly, but still behaves strangely. Armon-Jones argues that in these cases the inappropriate response is either a response which was culturally prescribed in childhood and has been inappropriately retained or the result of a deviant upbringing which may have inculcated emotions that were not culturally prescribed at any stage. She remarks that "the second case in which an emotion involves culturally inappropriate attitudes can be explained by the constructionist as non-paradigmatic, and as liable to deprive the agent of his status as someone in possession of normal sensibilities" (1986b, 71).

Armon-Jones is treading on very thin ice here. She has been trying to show that the identity of an emotion depends on the class of situations which elicits it. But if this were the case, then people who had the sort of abnormal social training she suggests would not have recognizable emotions with abnormal elicitors; they would have emotions which their compatriots would be at a loss to identify. Yet Armon-Jones seems to accept that recognizable emotions can exist in deviant contexts. From a theoretically uncommitted viewpoint this is the right thing to say. Pedophiles find sexual relations between adults and children delightful and pleasant to contemplate. What is strange about them is that they feel *these* emotions rather then those an average person would feel. We do not contemplate them like Mr. Spock observing the earthlings, unable to comprehend these strange "emotions." But although this seems to be the right account of the inappropriate emotions, by giving it Armon-Jones is saying something radically at odds with the rest of her theory. She is admitting that an emotion can retain its identity even if it occurs apart from the culturally appropriate situations which she says give the emotion its identity.

Harré and Armon-Jones do not provide any effective argument against a propositional attitude account of the identity of emotions across cultures and have not even deigned to produce arguments against the various biologically and physiologically based accounts described in chapters 2 and 3. Ratner and Averill do argue against such views but these arguments rest on crude conceptualizations of development which I have already rejected in earlier chapters. The extreme holism which rejects all cross-cultural identities is unsustainable even in the work of those who subscribe to it. There is no compelling reason to think that social constructionism is the sole or main illuminating perspective on emotion. The heterogeneous construction program, which gives due weight to biological factors, gives a far more promising account of most developmentally variable emotions.

II

The Nature of
Psychological Categories

7

Natural Kinds
and Theoretical Concepts

7.1 Emotions as Natural Kinds

This second part of the book looks at emotion and emotions as "natural kinds"—categories that supposedly correspond to some real distinctions in nature and around which theories are structured. My starting point is that emotions are the referents of the kind terms of theories that deal with emotional phenomena. Anger is the thing referred to in theories that successfully explain the phenomena associated with the vernacular use of the term "anger." The theories considered in part one each focused on a different portion of the pretheoretic domain of emotion. Each has its successes in its chosen area and faces obvious problems in others. In order to successfully explain emotion it may be necessary to reconceptualize both emotion and individual emotions like love and anger. The aim of this reconceptualization will be to put like with like. Phenomena with the same explanation should be placed together and phenomena with different explanations drawn apart. In some cases there is no good reason to put the things that fall under a traditional concept together in one category. Aristotelian physics placed all objects outside the orbit of the moon in a single category of superlunary things. We now know that this is as arbitrary a way of grouping objects together as one could hope to devise. Nothing follows from the fact that an object is superlunary other than the fact that it is superlunary and trivial transformations of this (e.g., it is not sublunary). There is no epistemic payoff to be had by using this category.

The need for reconceptualization as new information comes to light should come as no surprise. Conceptual change of this kind has been a major concern of both philosophy of science and philosophy of language for the last twenty years. The initial impetus for this discussion was the eclipse of "description theories" of the meaning of theoretical terms. Reconceptualization in the light of empirical findings is ruled out by description theories. The current conceptualization of a referent cannot be mistaken, because it defines what can count as a referent for that term. Some form of description theory underlies most philosophical work on emotion, as I showed in chapters 1 and 2. Authors like Wayne C. Davis (1988) believe that they can find out the nature of fear itself by analyzing ordinary speakers' understanding of the word "fear." This is because they take the meaning of "fear" to be exhausted by the descriptive content which the term has for ordinary speakers. Only something which fits this description could count as fear. The philosophy of emotion is an odd backwater. The rest of the philosophical community was shaken out of its complacency on this issue by the "causal" theories of reference proposed by Saul Kripke (1980) and Hilary Putnam (1975). Causal theories of meaning and their causal-descriptive successors (Devitt and Sterelny 1987) were designed to explain the phenomena of reference. Kind terms in language and concepts in people's minds have some referential relationship with cats and dogs, electrons and quasars. The causal theory aimed to replace the view that this relationship is one of description with the view that it is one of causation. My concept of cat is about cats because its existence depends on cats by the particular kind of causal pathway appropriate to "being about."

The causal theorists' account of reference allowed them to tackle two vital issues in the philosophy of science. These are the transtheoretic identity of theoretical terms and conceptual revision. The idea of transtheoretic identity arises because of the intuition that people with radically different theories can talk about the same things. We can disagree with an ancient who thinks that the *stars* are fixed points on the crystal spheres of heaven. So it seems that the same theoretical term can occur in two very different theories. This intuition runs counter to the idea that the claims of different scientific paradigms are incommensurable (Kuhn 1970). Causal theories back up this intuition by arguing that an important component of meaning remains constant across radical shifts in theory. This component is the actual reality with which language users interact. The second issue which causal theories tackle is the way in which theoretical concepts in science are revised as theory changes. Changes in scientific theory can cause people to revise their judgments about both the intension and extension of a theoretical term. The discovery that biological taxa are groups of organisms descended from a common ancestor caused systematists to decide that birds are reptiles, a revision that is now spreading to the wider speech community via books and films. The intension of the term "reptile" changed as well as its extension. Gary Larson's cartoon of an alligator telling the prosecutor "Of course I did it in cold blood you fool—I'm a reptile" will be merely puzzling to the next generation. The causal theory explains change in intension and extension in the following manner. The "stereotype" of a term is a set of beliefs about its referent. These beliefs pick out a particular set of instances as the term's extension. Changes in the intension of the term are changes in the stereotype which occur when new discoveries are made about the referent of the term. When the stereotype changes in this way it may also pick out a different extension.

The rejection of description theories of meaning implies that understanding fear involves learning about the psychological state to which the term "fear" refers, not just analyzing current beliefs about fear. The real nature of emotion will be revealed by the theories which best explain emotional phenomena, even if these theories depart substantially from preexisting beliefs. Emotions "really are" whatever those theories describe, just as pretheoretic kinds like heat, fire, and iron "really are" what is described by the physical sciences, and species "really are" Darwinian entities. Things have moved on considerably since the early causal theories of reference, but this central insight has not been lost. My aim in this chapter is to show that the very latest work on theoretical terms, and the categories that they represent, is as incompatible with the a priori, conceptual approach to emotion as were the crudest causal theories. In fact, what Richard Boyd (1991) has called the "enthusiasm for natural kinds" in the human sciences has carried the debate right into the emotion theorists' backyard.

7.2 Natural Kinds and Realist Metaphysics

The idea of a natural kind is the subject of long philosophical tradition. The central theme of this tradition is that there are underlying explanations of the correlations of properties that allow us to sort things into distinct kinds. Theory construction "cuts nature at its joints" when it puts together things whose resemblance to one another has such an underlying explanation. When organisms are divided into species or substances divided into chemical elements, they are divided in ways that are *projectable*. The correlations of properties that these categories represent can be relied upon to hold up in new instances. A new organism that passes the test for membership of a species will have the other features characteristic of the species but not specified in the test. What is more, when new knowledge is acquired about some members of the category, it can be reliably projected to the others. The existence of natural kinds thus provides the ontological element of a solution to the problem of induction. The epistemic element of a solution requires a way of identifying the natural kinds.

Causal theorists like Putnam gave the natural kind concept a strongly realist interpretation. The adherents of a scientific theory are committed to some account of the ultimate nature of reality. They identify the natural kinds in their theory with constituents of this reality. This interpretation reduced the appeal of the causal theory of reference to more empiricist philosophers of science. In recent years Putnam himself has eschewed realism (Putnam 1994). He now proposes that the world cannot be clearly separated from the mind that understands it. Categories are dependent in some way on the theoretical concepts that represent them. Moving away from realism in this way robs the causal theory of its simple explanations of how concepts retain their identity when theories change and how changes in theory cause changes in the extension and intension of concepts. In the first case, the theory-independent kinds with which thinkers are in touch are no longer available to anchor their concepts. In the second case, some new account more internal to the scientific project itself is needed of what justifies a decision to change the extension or intension of a term. If categories are in part dependent on our theories, then they cannot one-sidedly dictate how our theories should develop.

Richard Boyd has argued that the theory of natural kinds can be made independent of general metaphysical realism (Boyd 1991). The postulation of natural kinds is necessary to understand certain elements of scientific practice. Theorists aim to use concepts which are projectable, since only projectable concepts are of any use in induction or explanation. An examination of scientific practice shows that projectability is judged on the basis of background theories. Concepts are designed to pick out categories which have a role in the current best theory of the domain. The fact that the current best theory is committed to the existence of these categories is what makes it reasonable to think they will be projectable. Realists will be quite at home with this picture. Certain concepts are projectable because the categories they represent are held together by real essences, or so our best theory suggests. Boyd suggests that nonrealists accept so much of this picture that they should not demur from any more than the final realist table thumping. Rather than saying that scientific progress depends on making our concepts correspond to the real structure of the world the empiricist will say that empirically adequate background theories provide information which allows us to construct projectable concepts. Philip Kitcher's "Kantian Realist" can say that "the natural kinds would be the extensions of the predicates that figured in our explanatory schemata and were counted as projectable in the limit, as our practices developed to embrace more and more phenomena" (1993, 172).

I propose a generalization of Boyd's strategy. It should be generalized in two directions. First, the theory of natural kinds not only gives a good account of certain elements of scientific practice, it captures an important aspect of the formation and use of concepts by humans in general. It is an important theoretical tool in the psychology of concepts. Second, Boyd's rapprochement between realism and empiricism can be extended to a rapprochement between realism and all its rivals. If the theory of natural kinds is a central part of the best scientific account of concept formation and use, then an ability to make sense of this becomes an adequacy condition on any account of how thought and language relate to the world. In the remainder of this chapter I describe some findings in developmental psychology that suggest that a suitably general version of the theory of natural kinds is needed to explain the use and formation of concepts. I conclude by looking at how this general theory of kinds explains the phenomena of intertheoretic identity of concepts and of conceptual revision. Finally, I consider the implications for the theory of natural kinds of work on the social construction of categories. I argue that this work enriches the theory of natural kinds rather than refuting it.

In what follows I make extensive use of the terms *category* and *concept*. Michael Devitt (personal communication) has pointed out to me the extreme ambiguity of these terms in the existing literature and the confusions which ensue from this. I try to consistently use *category* to refer to the aspect of reality to which some concept is supposed to correspond. I use *concept* to refer to a psychological entity. Kind concepts have categories as their referents.

7.3 Theories of Concepts

According to the "classical" theory a concept is defined by a set of necessary and sufficient conditions. Philosophers are familiar with two serious shortcomings of the classical view. First, convincing lists of defining features are extraordinarily hard to construct for most concepts. Second, most categories seem to have an essential vagueness about their boundaries that is inconsistent with the classical view. Psychologists are familiar with a third shortcoming. The classical view fails to account for the "typicality" structure of concepts. Some objects are "better instances" of a concept that others. They are recalled faster and with less error than atypical instances. For these reasons, the classical view has been generally rejected in psychology.[1]

Prototype theories of concepts were proposed as an alternative to "classical" views in the 1970s (Rosch 1975, 1978; Rosch and Mervis 1975). Psychologists like Eleanor Rosch were inspired by Wittgenstein's idea that concepts are defined by a pattern of "family resemblance." Prototype theories are one version of the family resemblance or "probabilistic" approach to concepts. According to family resemblance theories there is no set of properties which is possessed by all and only the instances of a concept. Instead, each instance has a sufficient number of the features characteristic of that category to make it a member. The family resemblance view meets the three objections to the classical view. First, there is no list of necessary and sufficient conditions for category membership, so the failure to find these lists is unsurprising. Second, a region of vagueness will tend to exist between the number of features clearly sufficient for category membership and the number which is clearly insufficient. Finally, typicality can be defined in any number of ways. Typical instances might, for example, be those instances with many of the features which are most widespread in the whole set of instances. The specific form of family resemblance theory proposed by Rosch and others claimed that a concept con-

---

1. But see Armstrong, Gleitman, and Gleitman (1983) on the idea that typicality tells against the classical view, and Sutcliffe (1993) for a general defense of the classical view.

sists of a "prototype" constructed out of previously experienced instances. This prototype has the full set of features which define the concept. A new instance is a member of the category if it is sufficiently similar to the prototype. A typical similarity metric would sum the weighted features possessed by the new instance.

Research in the 1970s and 1980s led to several new developments within the family resemblance or probabilistic approach.[2] Several studies showed that people are sensitive to information which would have been discarded in the formation of a prototype. They seem to store information about the size of the category, about the degree of variation between instances, and about correlations of attributes within the set of experienced instances. Some of these problems can be overcome by "exemplar" theories in which a concept is represented by several relatively concrete exemplars rather than by a single abstract prototype. A set of exemplars will retain the sort of frequency and correlation information that shows up in empirical studies of concepts. The exemplar approach also creates the possibility of calling up a different subset of exemplars to represent the concept in different contexts. This allows it to tackle a body of results suggesting that typicality effects are context sensitive (tea is treated as a more typical drink than milk when described in one social setting, but not in another). Fortunately, there is no need to adjudicate these disputes here. I am primarily interested in arguments which suggest that no version of the probabilistic approach can be correct.

Prototype and exemplar theories are both "formal" theories of concepts. According to these theories, concepts are constructed by applying a formal rule to a set of features. The rule clusters particulars according to the features they possess. Formal theories see the main intellectual task as specifying the precise form of this rule—the similarity metric or metrics. Unfortunately, choosing a similarity metric will not even begin to cluster particulars. The philosophical difficulties with the notion of similarity are well known (Goodman 1972). Objects have indefinitely many properties. There is no such thing as overall similarity, only similarity with respect to a particular set of properties. Choosing different properties to make up the feature set will result in the production of different clusters. The properties also need to be weighted. A clustering rule that weights all features

---

2. See Medin (1989) for a fuller review.

equally may look theory free, but this is a confusion. Equal weightings are appropriate when there is some theoretical ground for supposing that each character represents the same amount of information (e.g., counting each base pair in a DNA sequence equally in determining phylogeny). But most features are not like this. Giving equal weight to the fact that an organism has legs and the fact that it has stripes is a substantial theoretical decision. Stepping back a little it can be seen that the problem of weighting is not really distinct from the problem of choosing a feature set. In the same way that the feature set is not delimited in any a priori way, it is not subdivided in any a priori way. In the absence of some theory of the domain, the feature set is simply not well defined.

The problem with similarity is not an abstract philosophical worry. The recent history of biological taxonomy is the history of the slow, empirical realization of the logical impossibility of a theory-free measure of similarity (Hull 1988). The early numerical taxonomists, or *pheneticists,* hoped to cluster organisms in terms of overall similarity. Their feature sets were not entirely theory free, but they were intended to include any legitimate biological feature of an organism. The general aim of phenetic taxonomy was to classify without appeal to the substance of biological theory. Organisms were to be clustered according to overall similarity, not similarity in any particular respect. Unfortunately, clustering algorithms constructed on these principles show no tendency to discover any structure in nature. Different data about a group of organisms produce different clusters. These clusters do not stabilize as more data are added, but continue to drift about indefinitely. These problems, among others, have caused this research program to be abandoned in favor of one explicitly based on the theory of evolution. *Cladistic* clustering algorithms selectively utilize data that are likely to pick out the pattern of evolutionary relationship among the organisms under study. Characters which originated in the ancestors of the whole group being studied are discarded in favor of characters that are likely to have originated within the group. These characters are used once only to produce a bifurcating tree structure. Any characters that do not fit this pattern are rejected as noise. These algorithms produce stable groupings. The groupings produced from one data set tend to be highly congruent with those from other data sets. Groupings tend to stabilize further as more data are collected. The explanation for this success is simply that organisms *have* evolved through successive speciation events, and these methods locate the traces left by that process. The success of cladistic methods in biological taxonomy is a classic example of the role of theory in constructing categories. The theory of evolution suggests what sort of pattern is to be found in the data and how to find it. It allows the investigator to distinguish the resemblances that reflect that pattern from those that obscure it.

A new approach to concept formation known as the *theory view* takes these lessons seriously. It argues that formal approaches have simply assumed a solution to the most difficult problems involved in concept acquisition. This is the problem of feature selection. Our background knowledge tells us that in particular domains, certain features are likely to be part of genuinely informative patterns and others are not. If concept acquisition is to be successful, this knowledge must be used to constrain the list of features which are used to assess similarity. Murphy (1993) gives a number of simple examples. People forming a concept of a new animal will not consider the sex and age of the exemplars, or the fact that the organism is in a cage, when constructing a list of defining features and comparing and contrasting these organisms with other known species. Their biological beliefs suggest that these attributes will not be relevant. People forming a concept of a new human artifact will ignore superficial perceptual properties in favor of properties relevant to the artifact's function. Their background theory tells them that function is more central to the processes which give rise to artifacts. The formal approach has only the crudest resources, such as the degree of correlation in the set of experienced instances, to account for either feature selection or feature weighting.

The formal approach has given rise to a large research effort in machine learning. Murphy points out how much conceptual work goes into constructing the supposedly "raw" data from which machine learning programs form concepts. A medical expert system, for example, might learn to recognize a new disease, but it will do so from a list of *symptoms*. Symptoms are the products of medical theory in at least two ways. First, they are a small selection of the possible measurements of a person's physical condition. They are chosen for their likely relevance in the light of current medical knowledge. Second, symptoms are complex physical properties. The way in which the phenomena are divided up and grouped together to form these units is informed by medical theory.

The theory view argues that the feature list and similarity metric used in a particular domain will be a function of people's background knowledge about (theory of) the domain. The clustering of objects on the basis of similarity is a function of previous understanding, not a neutral basis from which understanding is achieved. Surprisingly, the most important body of evidence for this view comes from the study of concept acquisition in children—precisely the area where "theory" might be expected to have the least influence.

7.4 Developmental Evidence for the "Theory View" of Concepts

Frank C. Keil and his collaborators have carried out a large number of experiments on the development of concepts in children. In his book *Concepts, Kinds and Cognitive Development* (1989) Keil relates some of this work to Quine's (1977) discussion of natural kinds. Quine asks how, if similarity is arbitrary, we are able to group instances together in a way that lets us cope with the challenges of the world. He suggests that humans have evolved to make raw similarity judgments in infancy that have a better than random chance of being useful. In later life these judgments are refined in the light of our developing theory of the world. In highly developed scientific domains we may place almost no reliance on raw perceptual similarity when grouping instances together. Keil uses these ideas to interpret the traditional idea in developmental psychology that children move from a view of the world dominated by perceptual similarity to one dominated by more structural concepts of causation and underlying essences. Keil's own development of these themes introduces two important amendments. First, he suggests that the Quinean view underestimates the role of implicit theory in the similarity judgments made by even the youngest children. Second, he moves from a traditional global view of cognitive development, like that of Piaget, to one which stresses the relative independence of different cognitive domains. These two amendments are obviously mutually supportive.

Keil and Batterman (1984) looked at the development of "nominal kind" terms in young children to see if they could detect the shift from raw similarity to more theoretical definitions of terms. Nominal kinds are those which most closely approximate the "classical view" of concepts. Obvious examples are kinship terms like *uncle*. The condition that an uncle is a parent's brother is as close to a necessary and sufficient condition as can be found in natural language. Keil and Batterman constructed pairs of different descriptions for a set of nominal kind terms. The "characteristic" descriptions included highly characteristic properties, such as the fact that uncles are adults, are friendly to one's parents, and bring presents, but excluded the defining condition of being a parent's brother. The defining descriptions included this defining condition but were otherwise highly uncharacteristic. Keil and Batterman found the predicted *characteristic to defining shift* for all the terms they studied. Younger children affirmed the characteristic descriptions as instances of the concept and rejected the uncharacteristic but correctly defined instances. Older children showed the reverse pattern. The characteristic to defining shift occurred at substantially different times for different classes of term, suggesting that the shift is a function of growing understanding of particular conceptual domains rather than some general change in cognitive abilities or the preferred use of those abilities.

A later study investigated domain specificity in more detail (Kelly and Keil 1987). This study looked at the shift within five domains: terms for moral acts (e.g., teasing, stealing), meals (e.g., breakfast, dinner), hand tools (e.g., hammer, drill), kinship (e.g., uncle, sister), and cooking (e.g., frying, baking). The study found that the characteristic to defining shift for a particular domain can occur at different ages, ranging from preschool to puberty. Once it occurs for one term in a domain, however, it will occur very rapidly throughout the domain. The exact degree of correlation between making the shift for one term and making it for others in the domain depends on how tightly conceptually integrated the domain is. Hand tools showed the weakest correlation, since their functions are diverse and relate to many different human practices. The domain is integrated only by the general relevance of design and intended function. Kinship terms were much more tightly correlated, presumably because they tend to be defined in terms of one another.

Other aspects of these results further disconfirmed the idea that the shift results from a general development in cognitive abilities. First, there was no obvious relationship between the "perceptual" nature of defining features and how early they were recognized as being defining features. This makes it harder to argue that the shift occurs because young children are limited to perceptual concepts. Second, the kinds of definitions used in different domains were very different from one another. The procedure used in production is central to the definition of various cooking terms. This has very little in common with the fact that tools are defined by their intended functions. These differences do not fit easily with the idea that the shift represents a generalized improvement in cognitive skills. However, both these patterns in the data are consistent with the idea that the shift is the effect of the child's growing understanding of the central organizing principles of certain domains of concepts.

Keil (1989) discusses the significance of the characteristic to defining shift for understanding the structure of adult concepts. The older formal approaches to concepts all accept that concepts develop over time. This can happen if features are added to or discarded from the representation from which similarity is judged or if the weightings of different features are changed. But if formal theories are to explain the characteristic to defining shift, they must do so in terms of some global, probabilistic property of the features which change their significance. They might suggest that less well correlated features are discarded as time goes by or that a small, efficient set of predictive features is chosen, with redundant features being discarded. But hypotheses of this sort seem at odds with the data. Children distinguish defining from diagnostic features even when the diagnostic features are as well correlated as the defining ones. When there is redundancy in the set of characteristic features, they all choose to keep the same features, rather than discarding characteristics at random. What is striking about the defining features they choose is that they are central to the folk theory of why those objects form a class of things which resemble one another.

Other experiments by Keil and his collaborators looked at the development of terms for the traditional "natural kinds." Good examples include the species of plants and animals and the various physical elements—gold, iron, water, and so forth. People treat these kinds as if they represent the most fundamental identity of each object that falls under them. An initial series of experiments used the idea of scientific discoveries to test children's ideas about natural kinds. Children were told about a group of organisms that scientists had supposedly studied. These organisms had the appearance and behavior of one kind of animal, dogs for example, but the scientists discovered that they had the inside organs and blood of another kind of animal, in this case cats. They were also told that the "dogs" were born from cats and themselves gave birth to cats. The children were asked whether the organisms were really cats or really dogs. These discovery scenarios were contrasted with scenarios in which scientists make the same discoveries about human artifacts. The children were told that scientists studied some things that look just like keys and which could be used to open doors. But the "keys" were found to be made from the same materials as pennies, to have been made by melting pennies, and were able to be melted down and turned back into pennies. The children were asked whether these things were really keys or really pennies. Kindergarten children said that the "keys" were really keys and the "dogs" were really dogs. Groups of eight- and ten-year-old children agreed with the younger children that the artifacts were whatever they appeared to be at the moment. They were strongly inclined, however, to think that animals and plants could not change their species status merely because they looked and behaved like members of another species. Their internal structure and their reproductive relationships were the real determinants of their species identity. The "dogs" were really cats. They merely looked and behaved like dogs.

The results of the "discovery" experiment were replicated in a second study using different organisms and artifacts and extending the class of natural kinds to include minerals. These examples were then used in a complementary "transformation" experiment. In the transformation experiment the objects were described using the sorts of typical features preferred in prototype analyses of concepts. The children were then told about operations in which an object was transformed until it had the typical properties of another kind. For example, they were told of a series of operations on a raccoon which gave it the typical properties of a skunk. They were also told of operations on artifacts, transforming, for example, a coffeepot into a bird feeder (figure 7.1). In each case the children were asked to say what the object was after the transformations had been effected. As in the discovery paradigm, children of kindergarten age were happy to allow raccoons to be transformed into skunks and lead into gold. This seemed no more difficult to them than transforming coffeepots into bird feeders or playing cards into toilet paper. Older children, however, became progressively skeptical of the possibility of changing the true nature of natural kinds. They were most skeptical of changing biological specieshood through transformations of typical surface features and slightly less skeptical of changing one mineral into another by changing its typical surface

Natural Kind

Raccoon/Skunk

Artifact

Coffeepot/Birdfeeder

7.1. Examples of drawings that accompanied descriptions used in Keil's second discoveries study. From Keil (1989). © 1989, The MIT Press.

features. A further interesting result was that although the older children saw no problem with changing one artifact into another, their explanations of how change was possible now tended to stress the changed function of the artifact. Kindergarten children had tended to stress changes in its appearance.

The discovery and transformation experiments strongly suggest that as children develop, they come to see natural kinds as characterized by some sort of inner essence, distinct from their typical properties. They are unwilling to allow objects to change their type identity merely because their properties have changed. They seem to have acquired the belief that both internal structure and genealogical properties are more important in determining the identity of biological species than appearance and that function is a central defining property of human artifacts. Very similar results were obtained cross-culturally in a study involving the Yoruba people of Nigeria (Jeyifous 1986).

All these experiments showed that younger children seem to assign a greater weight to typical properties in determining category membership. But Keil warns against assuming that even the youngest children are relying on overall similarity in a single feature space to determine their category judgments. In a further set of studies, he examined the effect of inter-category distance on children's willingness to allow an object to change from one kind to another. In previous experiments kindergarten children had been happy to allow transformations from plant to plant and animal to animal, as well as from artifact to artifact. The new experiment added transformations between radically different ontological categories. Examples included transforming a fish into a stone, making some worms into a piece of silver, and making a toy mouse into a real mouse. Once again, the children were asked what category the object fell into after the transformation. In this experiment the artifact to artifact and natural kind to related natural kind transformations showed the same pattern as before. Kindergarten children accepted all the transformations. Older children were increasingly unwilling to allow transformations of natural kinds. But on the cross-category tasks kindergarten children maintained that the objects had not really changed kind nearly as often as older children. Keil analyzed these results to see if the reluctance to cross ontological category boundaries could be explained as a result of the overall distance of the transformation in similarity space. On this hypothesis, the degree of reluctance in cases of transformation between very dissimilar kinds in a single ontological category should be somewhere intermediate between that for transformations between similar members of a single category and that for transformations across a category boundary. In fact, the degree of dissimilarity within a category had no appreciable effect. This suggests that the kindergarten children's reluctance to allow cross-category transformations is driven by an appreciation of the categories, not by considerations of similarity.

Keil's results taken as a whole suggest that in addition to developing the evolved similarity metric suggested by Quine, young children draw certain ontological boundaries within their overall domain of concepts. These boundaries override similarity judgments in determining categorization. In later development, characteristic organizing principles emerge for each domain of concepts. Keil has argued that children privilege the intended function of objects in grouping human artifacts. He has also argued that they assume that biological species have unseen properties that guarantee their identity and can survive the transformation of their measurable characteristics. A number of anthropologists have presented evidence for the occurrence of this "essentialist" treatment of species in other cultures (Atran 1990; Berlin 1992). They have further argued that categories for biological species are typically hierarchical, displaying at least four levels of hierarchy. These "folk taxonomic ranks" are interestingly reminiscent of the Linnean hierarchy. Atran argues that they can be used to explain the origin of that formal system.

It is important not to fall into a simple innatist interpretation of these findings. This is particularly tempting because these developmental regularities have many possible adaptive advantages. The fact that the regularities occur across cultures and have probably evolved has led several authors to describe them as innate or genetically programmed. This is unsatisfactory for a number of reasons. First, as I discussed in chapter 5, the idea of a genetic program is not an adequate conceptualization of how evolved traits are reconstructed in each generation. Evolved traits are reconstructed by a whole range of developmental resources. Constant outcomes are explained by the presence of the same range of resources in each generation. Second, the genetic program idea suggests that these regularities in behavior will emerge in every functional individual no matter what other resources are present. This leads to the premature rejection of promising models when this fails to occur. Ellen Markman (1992) has described this problem in the case of principles governing the acquisition of word meanings. A developmental systems approach would regard these developmental regularities as *descriptions* of normal development rather than underlying causes of development. It would anticipate the need for many transgenerational resources to be present if evolved features are to develop reliably. I describe some other unfortunate effects of the innatist approach to developmental regularities at the end of the next section.

Bringing a developmental systems perspective to bear on Keil's work also suggests how to interpret his talk of "theories" that guide young children. It is clear that these are implicit theories. Children do not avow beliefs about the causal structure of nature any more than they avow the principles of logical inference exemplified in their actions. But there is an important difference between children's implicit logic and their implicit causal explanatory theories. The latter are domain specific. It is this which makes it appropriate to talk of the development of theories, rather the development of cognitive ability as earlier developmentalists did. An implicit theory is a domain-specific pattern of reasoning exhibited in children's actions and interpretations. The child's organization presumes that certain portions of the world have a certain structure. From a developmental systems perspective there is no reason to suppose that this theory exists preformed in the genome. Its presence in children's neural organization is a reliable consequence of the interaction of the many developmental resources that construct the psychological phenotype. Later in the development of an individual some of the theory which they relied on as a child may become explicit. It is an open question whether there is a special pathway by which this occurs or if it relies on the individual's reflexively applying the techniques they use to explore other people's beliefs. If the latter, then the move from an implicit theory to an explicit theory may depend entirely on whether an individual is ever called on to reflect on their practices. However this transition occurs, once a theory is made explicit the individual is in a position to subject it to a more systematic program of testing and amendment. Theories which have been made explicit by adults can be expected to exhibit more variation across individuals and groups than the implicit theories of children.

7.5 Natural Kinds and Causal Homeostasis

The function of categorization is to allow extrapolation from observed to unobserved instances. Useful concepts represent projectable categories. Probabilistic theories of concept acquisition suggest that people try to find projectable categories by using concepts to record a summary of the correlations between properties in past instances. But the developmental evidence suggests that people use a much deeper and more intelligent strategy to locate projectable categories. They cluster instances according to their possession of theoretically significant properties in their causal explanatory theory of the domain. In childhood these theories are relatively simple and culturally universal. In later development, however, theories become more complex and more explicit and diverge between cultures and individuals.

Chapter Seven

The phenomenon of conceptual change due to scientific discovery is a continuation of normal human conceptual development.

Boyd and Keil use the idea of *causal homeostasis* (Boyd 1989, 1991; Keil 1989) to capture what makes a category useful. A category brings together a set of objects with correlated properties. The category has causal homeostasis if this set of correlations has some underlying explanation that makes it projectable. A successful category captures what Keil calls a causal homeostatic mechanism—something which means that the correlations can be relied on to hold up in unobserved instances. The search for causal homeostatic mechanisms explains what has been called *psychological essentialism*. People do not simply note the existence of clusters of properties. They postulate a system of underlying causes of the clustering. This postulated "essence" allows the children in Keil's studies to believe that objects retain their identity when the properties that caused them to be assigned that identity are changed.

The problem with the prototype theory is that it suggests that people are operationalists, whereas their behavior suggests that they adopt something much more like realism. The commitment to the unobservable that seems to be implicit in their behavior is reminiscent of Arthur Fine's "natural ontological attitude" (Fine 1984). They manifest every symptom of realism except the desire to turn it into a philosophical theory. This explains why the prototype theory fails to predict the way that concepts change over time. The prototype theory looks at the characteristic properties of an object as a defining description, when the subject is actually interpreting them as symptoms of an underlying causal structure. The prototype theory must account for changes in a concept in terms of local correlations of properties in the observed set of instances. The development of the concept is actually being driven by wider considerations of theoretical coherence. The theoretical entities that are used to express these theoretical considerations can be translated out in a sophisticated empiricist reconstruction of the process, but they cannot be ignored in the construction of psychological and semantic theories.

The concept of causal homeostasis entails a very broad conception of the essence of a category. An essence can be any theoretical structure that accounts for the projectability of a category. The microstructural essences that have received so much attention in discussions of natural kinds are merely one kind of essence. Even the stock examples of natural kinds do not all have microstructural essences. The fundamental kinds of chemistry, such as the elements of the periodic table and categories like alkali and acid, have their properties because of their internal microstructure. But biological taxa, the other classic example of natural kinds, turn out to be united by external forces. Biological taxa at all levels of the taxonomic hierarchy form projectable categories because their members are descended from a common ancestor (Ghiselin 1974; Hull 1976, 1978). The causal homeostatic mechanism is descent. Taxa at the species level have rather more complex homeostatic mechanisms because in their case descent is supplemented by factors such as gene flow, selection, and developmental canalization (Mishler and Donaghue 1982; Mishler and Brandon 1987). In the next chapter I look at the implications of the discovery that biological taxa are "historical entities" for theoretical categories in biology and psychology.

Those who find the notion of *essence* distasteful (Mellor 1977) may wonder why the notion should be retained since its traditional metaphysical basis has been changed so much. I find it useful because it expresses a view about the causes of conceptual revision that is shared by the new causal homeostasis theory and earlier theories of natural kinds. Biological kinds may not have traditional intrinsic essences, but they behave in the ways that cause people to postulate those essences. Discoveries about the underlying causal structure of nature lead people to adjust the extension of biological kinds and to change their minds about which properties of those kinds are essential and which are accidental and should not be extrapolated to unobserved instances. Many of the most famous examples of this kind of change are biological, such as the inclusion of whales and bats in the mammals. Similar striking examples arise with biological and psychological traits. But nothing hangs on the use of the term *essence*. After a short period in which its use provokes reflection on the continuity within the natural kinds tradition, it might be allowed to lapse.

One reason not to use the word *essence* is that it seems so bizarre to extend it to human artifacts. Yet this is what the new theory of kindhood seems to imply. Artifacts display a certain degree of causal homeostasis. They display far less of it than traditional "natural" kinds because the underlying explanation of their unity as a category is a sociological explanation in terms of intention and design (Griffiths 1993). Designing an entity for a particular function does not create a rich cluster of other properties because, as the saying goes, there are many ways to skin a cat. However, Keil is able to point to cases where the extension and intension of categories of artifacts change because of discoveries about their "essence." These cases occur in archaeology and anthropology, when new discoveries about a society cause us to revise hypotheses about the functions of artifacts. The "essences" of artifacts start to look suspiciously like the "nominal essences" (lists of defining properties) with which "real essences" have traditionally been contrasted. Keil suggests that there is a continuum between the traditional natural kinds and the sorts of nominal kinds like *uncle* and *breakfast* that were the subjects of his early studies. Artifacts are towards the nominal end of this continuum. Moving along the continuum away from natural kinds, one sees the nature of the explanation of the unity of categories change in a number of connected ways. Internal properties become less important and origins become more important (but see Keil 1981). There is a decline in the importance of underlying *substance* in defining the category. This last point may explain the fact that as we move away from natural kinds, the intuition that an object cannot change its kind without ceasing to be the same object declines in strength. Most importantly, the richness of the homeostatic clusters tends to decline. The traditional natural kinds are among the richest. The kindhood of a physical element determines almost all its salient properties. Traditional biological kinds are also fairly rich. Cladists have argued that a genealogical classification of organisms is the maximally informative and maximally predictive classification available. In contrast, knowing what sort of thing an artifact is, knowing that it is a bracelet for example, may fix very few of its features. There are just too many ways to skin a cat, or in this case too many ways to decoratively encircle the wrist. I have argued that functionally defined categories in biology are similarly impoverished (Griffiths 1994). They too have something more like "nominal essences."

Some authors object to the idea of natural kinds on the grounds that it implies that there is a single correct way to classify reality (Dupré 1981, 1993). They argue that there are many equally useful cross-cutting taxonomies of the world. The causal homeostasis theory certainly allows that there may be several legitimate taxonomies of a domain. But it denies that all taxonomies are equally legitimate. When there are several legitimate taxonomies of a domain, each must have some underlying causal homeostatic mechanism. There may be a sound ecological explanation for the causal homeostasis of the category of *trees,* even though it is not a legitimate genealogical grouping of organisms (because trees have evolved from several separate ancestors). In that case, there would be two ways to classify certain groups of plants—genealogically and ecologically. But there are some categories without causal homeostatic mechanisms, and these should be rejected. These need not be categories which are entirely useless for explanation and induction. Categories that need to be eliminated are more usually ones whose apparent causal homeostasis results from their approximating some other category with real causal homeostasis. Replacing the crude approximation with the category that is doing the actual work is a pure epistemic gain. Retaining the old category would not be pluralistic, but merely foolish. In a discussion of biodiversity E. O. Wilson recounts how attempts to control the mosquitoes that spread malaria were hampered by bad taxonomy of the *Anopheles* genus. A little later he recounts how the modern recognition of many species of the protozoan *Paramecium* creates "a strong temptation to ignore the biological complexity and stay with the three old, easy species, but the malaria example counsels otherwise. Biologists know in their hearts that there can be no compromise on matters of such importance" (1992, 46).

It is also important to recognize that the legitimacy of kinds other than the traditional natural kinds does not mean that all kinds are equal. John Dupré (1981) notes that many terms from horticulture are not well based in biological theory. *Lily* denotes an extraordinary assortment of taxa. This is an important and widespread phenomenon. It does not, however, show that there is nothing to choose between different taxonomies of nature. In the light of the causal homeostasis theory it is evident that *lily* is a nominal kind, defined by flower form, rather than a natural kind. It may be thought of as a natural kind by those who know nothing about flowers, but a study of people learning gardening would show a defining to characteristic shift in their understanding of *lily* and similar terms (the inverse of the shift found in Keil's studies of children). The folk category of lilies is of extremely limited use for explanation and induction. It collects no cluster of properties beyond a certain vague visual gestalt. Hence no gardener supposes that the delicate drainage requirements of "true lilies" (pretty members of the genus *Lilium*) has any implications for the treatment of day lilies or calla lilies. They might, however, substitute calla lilies for true lilies in a planting plan because the soil in that spot is waterlogged in spring and they will look similar. The causal homeostasis theory gives us the tools we need to understand why different kinds are useful for different purposes and why some traditional "natural kinds" have such impressively widespread utility.

I conclude this examination of the causal homeostasis approach with a further example of the pernicious effects of the innateness concept (which I promised at the end of the last section). Some authors have argued that "psychological essentialism" should be understood as a universal human tendency to presume the existence of microstructural essences. Scott Atran (1990) has argued that this will make it very hard for humans to assimilate the definitions of biological categories derived from evolutionary theory. These definitions, as we have seen, appeal to external forces to unite categories. But this pessimism is unwarranted. The evidence Atran cites is that people in all cultures tend to form a traditional essentialist conception of species. Those who see development as the unfolding of a genetic program will infer that this is an inescapable part of that program: the genes program for traditional taxonomy. But many theorists see development as the unfolding of repeated patterns because of the presence of the same resources in each generation (Oyama 1985; Griffiths and Gray 1994; see also chapter 5). These theorists will expect the availability in the culture of new cognitive resources to enrich the potential of the developmental process. The developing child is able to catch up with the conceptual development of the community to which it belongs. Children striving to construct an explanatory theory of the domain of biological objects may well be able to assimilate common descent as part of their biological theory. This seems likely because genealogy is such a central part of our understanding of the social domain. This strategy may be therefore be readily available in children's thought. This transfer will be even more likely if it is true that the social and biological domains differentiate out of a single explanatory domain in early childhood (Carey 1985).

7.6 Intertheoretic Identities and Conceptual Revision

Description theories of meaning fail to explain two important phenomena in science. First, the intension and extension of concepts change as the result of changes in theory. Second, concepts can retain their identity across radical changes in theory. Both these phenomena can be explained by the causal homeostasis theory of concepts.

The extension and intension of concepts change because the core of each concept is an explanation of causal homeostasis in the category corresponding to that concept. In many cases this is an explanation sketch and in some cases a promissory note, but this is quite consistent with the central thrust of the causal homeostasis theory. The use of a concept for explanation and induction commits its user to the *project* of having a category with causal homeostasis. The pursuit of this project is what causes revision of extension and intension. Revision of extension occurs to keep the scope of concepts in line with the scope of the categories which possess explanations of their causal homeostasis. These revisions of extension are necessary because the causal homeostatic mechanism is the warrant for projecting the properties of the category onto new instances. If I want to be able to predict the spread of a disease which is devastating forests, I will revise my tree concepts in the light of new discoveries about evolutionary relationships. This will ensure that I have projectable categories with which to predict susceptibility to the disease.

Revision of the intension of categories can occur simply because features are not as characteristic of the category as previously thought. The inclusion of the Monotremata in Mammalia means that giving birth to live young is no longer a universal feature of mammals. The discovery of the platypus changed ideas about the common ancestor of the mammals and thus about the "essence" of Mammalia. But intension can also change in another way. Changes in the underlying theory can show that a universal feature is not projectable. The child who realizes that categories like *uncle* are genealogical no longer expects to be able to project predicates about the age of uncles. The fact that all uncles are adults in the child's experience ceases to be a good basis for induction, because the underlying theory does not entrench this sort of link. The age of uncles is an accidental property.

The second phenomenon to be explained is the intertheoretic status of terms. Here I need to distinguish two classes of terms which occur intertheoretically. First, there are phenomenological terms like *gold* or *Aves,* which refer to ways of grouping phenomena. Aves can occur in both creationist and evolutionary taxonomies. It clearly refers to the same group— the birds—even if the two theories disagree about its exact boundaries. Causal theories say this is because both creationists and evolutionists are in causal contact with the same ultimate reality. The causal homeostatic theory gets at the same idea in a less metaphysical form. There is a correlation between certain properties that both creationists and evolutionists attribute to an underlying homeostatic mechanism. Having feathers correlates with many other features: being bipedal, laying cleidoic eggs, and having modified tetrapod forelimbs or wings, a furcula or wishbone, and a beak. Creationists and evolutionists have conflicting explanations of the causal homeostasis of this set of feature correlations. One theory says that all birds are descended from a common ancestor and that the correlated features reflect the common inheritance of the group. The other theory says that God intends all these creatures to be alike in these respects. The set of correlated features which the two groups identify are sufficiently similar for us to say that they offer conflicting explanations of the same set of correlations. Hence they are both referring to the same phenomenological category. This explanation of intertheoretic reference assumes that adherents of the two theories can identify the same features. But this is an empirical, not a metaphysical, claim. The claim that the same concept is used in two theories is a claim in the psychology of concepts. The creationists and evolutionists are both objects of study in the cognitive psychologist's theory. This psychological theory of concepts claims that the two groups create the category *Aves* in response to the same feature correlations. No commitment to strong metaphysical realism is required. The idea that both groups are affected by the same ultimate reality is replaced by the claim that they are both affected by certain entities recognized in our best theory of concept formation.

The second class of terms which occur intertheoretically are the terms which refer to the postulated causal homeostatic mechanisms which underlie phenomenological categories. My account here owes much to Frederick Kroon (1985). Kroon describes a phenomenon which he calls the *overdetermination of reference by theory*. There seem to be conditions on the identity of theoretical terms which offer more hostages to fortune than is necessary on a strictly causal account of reference. The causal theory says that the reference of theoretical terms is determined by the real kinds with which a scientist interacts during the construction of a theory. This means that scientists could maximize their chance of achieving reference by using a theoretical term with the cognitive content "whatever is responsible for such and such phenomena." But scientists don't seem to follow this safe course. For example, early chemists could have used *phlogiston* with the cognitive content "whatever substance accounts for combustion and calcination." In that case, phlogiston would have turned out to be oxygen. But in actual fact, early chemists used *phlogiston* with a cognitive content something like "whatever substance accounts for combustion and calcination by being lost from substances during these processes and whose presence or absence explains the difference in the properties of substances before and after these processes." Because they placed these additional descriptive conditions on phlogiston's identity, they were unable to identify it with oxygen. Kroon's response to the overdetermination of reference by theory is a causal descriptive theory of reference for theoretical terms. Theoretical terms refer to the underlying natural kind (if any) that plays a particular theoretical role. Kroon argues that there is a particular emphasis on causal explanatory mechanisms in these theoretical roles. The descriptive identity conditions for a theoretical term typically consist of a sketch of how the underlying kind determines the observable properties that led to its postulation. Other potential properties of the underlying kind are regarded as inessential to its identity. Kroon explains what he calls the "selective stress" on causal explanatory mechanisms in terms of the scientists' "epistemic warrant" for the introduction of the term. Only if a scientist has some idea about the causal mechanism responsible for the phenomenon will there be any possibility of investigating the postulated kind. Other kinds of term introduction may fix reference according to the causal theory but are frivolous from the point of view of starting a research program.

I interpret Kroon's picture as a contribution to the psychology of concepts. His explanation of the selective stress on causal mechanism is a special case of a more general explanation of how concepts are constructed. Theoretical concepts are introduced to refer to the mechanisms responsible for causal homeostasis in certain phenomenological categories. The cognitive content of a theoretical term is a sketch of the way in which causal homeostasis is produced. So two theoretical concepts are coreferential if they explain (roughly) the same clusters of features using (roughly) the same causal structure. If extensionally similar phenomenological concepts are associated with theoretical concepts which propose very different causal structures, then the similar extensions of the related phenomenological concepts will not be sufficient to make the theoretical terms coreferential. Evolutionists can identify many of their taxonomic groupings with the groups named by preevolutionary biologists, but evolutionists reject theoretical identities between their notion of a common ancestor and the notions that previously explained these groupings, such as ideal morphotypes. Common ancestors explain the patterns of resemblance among taxa by descent with modification. Morphotypes explain the resemblance by participation in a common platonic form (Agassiz) or independent possession of the same stock of developmental potentials (Kant). These causal mechanisms are too different to allow the identification of common ancestors with ideal morphotypes. It may be possible, however, to identify the common ancestors postulated by evolutionists with the ancestral forms postulated by Buffon. According to Buffon, the species in a genus resemble one another because they all *degenerate* from a single ancestral species. The causal homeostatic mechanism for Buffon is heredity, just as it is for the evolutionist.

7.7 Social Construction and Causal Homeostasis

Ian Hacking has drawn attention to aspects of the process of concept formation that I have so far ignored. Concepts are used not only for the "spectator sports" of explanation and induction (Hacking 1991b). Placing an occurrence under a concept like *murder* or *child abuse* has implications for what should be done about it, as well as for what can be predicted about it. Some of Hacking's work documents the changing extension and intension of the concept of child abuse and relates these changes to the social and political agendas of groups using the concept (Hacking 1991c, 1995). A concept originally applied to small babies with broken bones has come to apply to preteens exposed to parental sexual activity. This has not happened because sociology or developmental psychology provides a theoretical warrant for supposing that discoveries about small babies subjected to violence will be projectable to preteens exposed to parental sexual behavior. The concept has been extended as an increasingly wide range of child-care practices have been called into question. Child abuse is a concept which functions in programs of social action rather than as part of a search for scientific explanation and prediction.

Hacking's work includes another challenge to the theory of concepts and categories that I have outlined. This is Hacking's *dynamic nominalism*. The causal homeostasis theory says that categories are useful if there is some underlying mechanism that maintains resemblances between the members of the category. Dynamic nominalism raises the possibility that the causal homeostatic mechanism for a category might be the existence of the concept of that category and the broader sociolinguistic practices in which the concept is used. For example, a robust set of generalizations about the psychological effects of child abuse might exist precisely because of the practice of regarding that range of actions as abusive. The psychological effects of corporal punishment may be very different, depending on whether or not the child has learned to classify this experience under the same concept as sexual contact between an adult and a child (i.e., abuse). In his study of multiple personality syndrome (MPS) Hacking (1995) suggests that the diagnostic categories associated with the modern MPS epidemic may have this self-validating quality. The dissemination of the modern theory of the disassociative personality has the effect on the psychological development of distressed individuals of making them conform to the theory. Hacking claims that the same phenomena occurred on a smaller scale in C19 France, where an earlier wave of multiple personality patients produced the extraordinary psychosomatic symptoms predicted in contemporary theories of hysteria.

The causal homeostasis view of concepts needs to respond to Hacking's challenge in two main ways. First, it needs to acknowledge the possibility that some categories may have causal homeostasis through the sort of reflexive mechanism described by Hacking's dynamic nominalism. Second, it needs to acknowledge that there are other dynamics at work in conceptual change over and above those captured in the causal homeostatic model. I have partly anticipated the first of these two responses in my discussion of the social construction of emotion. I introduced in chapter 6 the idea of "substantially socially constructed" categories of emotion. The existence of a particular emotion in individuals may be the result of the existence of the corresponding emotion concept in the local culture. Prevalent beliefs about emotion may be an important developmental resource for individuals. These beliefs determine how certain behaviors are received by the community and may thus contribute to the development of the psychological phenotype. The result may be that the prevalent beliefs about emotion accurately describe the emotional phenotype in that locale. In this process, the existence of a nonarbitrary *category* (the fact that a set of instances share various common features) is dependent on a sociolinguistic process involving the *concept* of that category. Such categories are "substantially" socially constructed. I sharply distinguished this possibility from the trivial thesis that emotion *concepts* are the product of a sociolinguistic process. I showed that this is all that some authors mean when they say that "emotions are social constructions."

Richard Boyd draws a similar distinction between trivial and substantial constructionist theses with his principle of the "metaphysical innocence of theory construction" (Boyd 1991). The principle states that if our conceptual frameworks affect the structure of the world, they do so by some natural causal mechanism. Social constructionism is a substantial hypothesis when it alleges that the introduction of some concept has an affect on the world via some causal mechanism. For example, the concept of a psychological or spiritual disorder may be internalized by individuals and provide a model for the "disclaimed actions" described in chapter 6. A disorder which did not previously exist has been brought into being by the concept of that disorder. Social constructionism is either trivial or false when it alleges that the introduction of a concept in and of itself changes the world to which the concept is applied. The claim is trivial if it means that things that were not previously brought under that concept are now brought under it. The claim is false if it means that simply putting instances together under a concept makes them similar in ways that they were not similar before. The decision to classify certain events fifty years ago as child abuse has no effect on those events because no natural causal mechanism can reach them from the present.[3]

The second way in which the causal homeostatic theory of concepts needs to respond to Hacking is to recognize the full range of dynamics at work in conceptual change. The causal homeostatic view derives from the fact that concepts are used for explanation and induction. It predicts that concepts will evolve to maintain and increase the causal homeostasis of the categories to which they refer. Hacking reminds us that concepts are also used for social and political ends. They are used to condemn things, to promote attention to one aspect of a situation rather than another, and to induce conformity with certain norms of behavior. The use of different concepts promotes different agendas. Concepts may be contested on political grounds, not because of different views about the basis of causal homeostasis. Introducing the concept of love may have served to create more

---

3. But Hacking (1995) suggests that the new classification can have a real effect on what a person can (truthfully) say that they remember about those events.

humane relations between the sexes in medieval society, but it need not have promoted understanding of the medieval mind. In fact, it may have achieved its purpose precisely by misrepresenting to medieval people how their minds worked. Similarly, extending the concept of child abuse may have drawn society's attention to some social injustices but not improved our ability to understand the psychological disorders resulting from those injustices.

The need to recognize these nonepistemic dynamics in conceptual change should be clearly distinguished from the need to recognize multiple epistemic projects and the consequent need for multiple conceptualizations of the same subject matter. Many of the objects that can be classified as money can also be classified as lumps of matter. Classifying these objects as money recognizes a cluster of economic and social properties that are correlated in instances ranging from cowrie shells to silver denarii. Classifying some of the same objects as samples of gold recognizes another cluster of properties which are correlated in all samples of that element. The existence of many different epistemic projects leads to the recognition, within a narrowly causal homeostatic account, of many alternative schemes of classification. The various cross-cutting taxonomies of the same subject matter which are characteristic of the life sciences, and the different theoretical purposes which these serve, are the subject of the next chapter. But these taxonomies are not in competition with one another. All of them can and should be adopted. The more that are adopted, the greater will be our capacity for explanation and induction. It is true that there can be real conflicts over which scheme of classification to adopt within the realm of the purely epistemic. I deal with some such conflicts in the next two chapters. But when one epistemically oriented scheme of classification threatens to displace another, it subsumes the goals of the other scheme of classification. The new classificatory scheme offers to fulfill all the explanatory and inductive promise of the other and some more besides. When it can be shown that the explanatory and inductive potential of two schemes overlap, so that neither can subsume the other, then both must be retained and they are not in genuine competition (Hacking [1983] describes how this occurs with the two standard definitions of an acid). The conflicts between different schemes of classification which Hacking describes are quite unlike these "conflicts" between multiple epistemic projects. The projects which Hacking's socially involved concepts are designed to further are not primarily epistemic. The adoption of these concepts may or may not facilitate explanation and induction. Concepts which serve these nonepistemic purposes are frequently in profound competition with one another. Different definitions of indigeneity or of aboriginality may serve different political agendas (G. Griffiths 1995). Since alternative definitions of indigeneity seek to define the limits of the legitimacy conferred by the notion of indigeneity, they cannot all be successfully adopted. One concept of indigeneity excludes New Zealand Maori in certain regions on the grounds that they displaced an earlier wave of Polynesian settlement. This concept seeks to undermine land claims by those peoples. In the same way, different definitions of child abuse or of sexual harassment suggest different visions of society. The different projects in which these definitions are embedded often cannot subsume one another or be pursued in a complementary manner (although on some occasions two groups each urging a conceptual shift find that they can unite behind one of their original proposals).

The existence of these nonepistemic dynamics in conceptual change means that the causal homeostasis theory will not adequately predict conceptual change in vernacular concepts. To the extent that science is driven by nonepistemic agendas, it will not predict conceptual change in science either. Nevertheless, in the final chapters of this book I will concentrate on asking which emotion categories have genuine causal homeostasis and will therefore serve the goals of explanation and induction. My claim is that these are the categories that *should* be adopted by a scientific psychology of emotion, since the goals of such a psychology are explanation and induction. The causal homeostatic theory can be thought of as a "censored model" of the dynamics of conceptual change (Orzack and Sober 1994). It describes how concepts would evolve if the only aim of those using them were scientific understanding. I am also inclined to agree with Hull (1988) that the distinctive character of science as a social enterprise is that individuals are rewarded for furthering epistemic goals. The conceptual dynamics described by the causal homeostatic theory might therefore be expected to dominate within scientific thought. The censored model may be a useful idealization.

These expectations cannot be extended to everyday thought about the emotions. Although vernacular concepts are used for explanation and induction, they are also used in the service of many other projects. This creates a whole alternative field of inquiry concerning emotion concepts. We might try to uncover the other social projects in which emotion concepts are involved. The task of discerning the nonepistemic functions of concepts like love and anger would be a far larger task than that which I have set myself in this book. Some previous research into the history of emotions can be interpreted as attempting this task (e.g., Hunt 1959). If successful, such research would reveal other dynamics governing the historical development of vernacular emotion concepts. These will determine the future relationship between the emotion concepts of psychology and those used in everyday social interactions. It would be a positive development if philosophers who are interested in projects other than commenting on the science of emotion modified their approach in the light of the theory of kinds discussed in this chapter. At present these philosophers suppose that they are uncovering the true nature of emotion as revealed a priori in vernacular emotion concepts. In fact they are picking apart the beliefs about emotion that have become prevalent through the interaction of the various dynamics which affect emotion concepts. This places the philosopher in the unsatisfactory position of trying to understand emotion by looking at a picture of emotions which often deliberately misrepresents them. The same can be said of recent attempts to understand the nature of desire via conceptual analysis (Marks 1984). People use concepts like emotion and desire not just to describe their actual psychological workings but also to construct the psychology of the young and to set up norms of behavior for adults (some of them highly unrealistic norms). Using these concepts as a guide to the emotions is like studying female sexuality by reading pornography. If the conceptual analytic activities of these philosophers were coupled with a sociological and historical examination of the role of emotion concepts, they would be in a better position to contribute to an understanding of emotion.

8

Natural Kinds in Biology
and Psychology

8.1 Natural Kinds in Biology

Biological species are one of the most frequently cited examples of natural kinds. Species are the lowest level of the traditional hierarchical taxonomy of living forms—species, genera, families, orders, classes, and phyla. Most philosophical considerations about the nature of species apply equally to all levels of this hierarchy. In discussing the nature of species we are really discussing the nature of biological taxa in general (even the common philosophical examples of "species" like tigers, swans, and ravens are actually names of higher taxa like genera or families). Biological taxa and chemical elements have been the twin paradigms of natural kinds, and it has often been assumed that the kindhood of biological taxa must be just like the kindhood of chemical elements. Each member of the kind must have some underlying microstructural property that explains all its other projectable properties. This microstructure is the "essence" of the kind. But in the last few decades a consensus has emerged in theoretical biology and the philosophy of biology that this is not the case. The kindhood of biological taxa is very different from the kindhood of chemical elements. Biological taxa are historical entities. They are groups of organisms held together by their common history rather than any intrinsic resemblance to one another. This view of biological taxa is associated with Michael Ghiselin (1974) and David Hull (1976, 1978, 1984). Hull and Ghiselin call their view *individualism* about species. They use the label *essentialism* for their opponents' view—the view that all members of a biological species share some set of intrinsic properties. I argue below that individualism can be interpreted as the view that species have historical, rather than intrinsic, essences. This makes it potentially confusing to think of Ghiselin and Hull as opponents of essentialism. I also place very little emphasis on the parallels they draw between species and classic ontological individuals like persons and organisms. I am concerned with the more general view that species and other taxa are historically defined (Hull claims that all taxa are historical entities but only some are full-blooded ontological individuals). In what follows I replace "individualism" by the phrase "the historical view" and call the opposing view "intrinsic essentialism."

The simplest intrinsic essentialist theories are not viable for obvious empirical reasons. Species typically show variation not in some peripheral subset of their features but in all of them. No character, however central to our stereotype of that species, to its morphology, or to its genotype, is essential for an individual organism to be a member of the species. There are unstriped tigers, there are calves with two heads, and there are individuals with highly abnormal genomes (sufferers of Down's syndrome are human despite an additional chromosome). A more sophisticated intrinsic essentialism can attempt to cope with the facts of variation by making use of statistical essences. On this view an individual is a member of a species if it has a sufficient number of appropriately weighted properties from the defining set. But statistical intrinsic essentialism is just as mistaken as its simplistic predecessor. A number of major problems are apparent at a glance. The first involves a trade-off. An essentialist definition can be either practical, with some chance of being applied, or impractical, requiring a vast knowledge of the distribution of all sorts of minor variations. Insofar as a definition is practical, it will either fail by missing the more unusual members of the species or fail by picking up unusual members of related species. A second problem is that even a successful intrinsic essentialist definition will not stay successful. The conventional view is that species undergo continuous and potentially unlimited change. Unless statistical intrinsic essentialism is advanced in conjunction with a very radically "punctuated" view of evolution, it will define indefinitely many overlapping "chrono-species" within each evolutionary lineage. The idea of speciation events—a critical category in any account of evolution—would be confounded with gradual changes in the character of a single species and even with fluctuations in the proportions of polymorphic traits in a population.

These problems arise because intrinsic essentialism tries to combine a Darwinian view of the evolutionary process with an Aristotelian view of its products. The process consists of a large number of individuals who randomly explore the space of possible forms. Individuals survive differentially as a result of these explorations and some of these individuals exchange genetic material. Most of the resemblance among these individuals can be explained by common descent. The clustering of surviving individuals into types can be explained by the differential survival of these types, by patterns of gene exchange and by the phenomenon of developmental canalization (see section 5.5). The essentialist proposal is to regard the range of individuals produced by this process as falling into a number of eternal types. Species are not an actual element in the evolutionary process, but a set of abstract types into which the products of that process coincidentally fall. It is not surprising that the intrinsic essentialist notion of species is not one which fits the role played by the species concept in conventional accounts of evolution. The only way to forge some connection between intrinsic essentialist species and evolution is with the aid of empirically controversial additions to evolutionary theory. I have already remarked that a very strong punctuationism might do the job. The related idea that species occur because only a few regions of the space which lineages explore are compatible with the laws of biological form has surfaced from time to time in evolutionary theory, but currently has little empirical support.[1] As long as the theory of evolution remains fundamentally Darwinian, intrinsic essentialism will fail to meet the first requirement for a theory of natural kinds. Its essences do not explain why the members of its categories resemble one another. They fail to identify the causal homeostatic mechanism of each category. This means that the predicates it produces are not projectable.

Ghiselin and Hull's alternative was to suggest that species are not kinds defined by shared intrinsic properties but spatiotemporally located particulars like New Zealand or the Swiss Family Robinson. An organism's membership of a species is like membership of a family, resting on the fact that is united in a pattern of common descent with its conspecifics, not that it resembles them in its intrinsic properties. No organism descended from different ancestors can be a member of the species, however closely it may resemble the organisms that are members. This genealogical or historical

1. For these highly controversial "process structuralist" views of evolution, see Goodwin (1994), Goodwin and Saunders (1989), and Goodwin and Webster (n.d.). Philosophical analyses of these views can be found in Smith (1992), van der Weele (1995), and Griffiths (1996).

view of species fits far better with our understanding of the evolutionary process. It is a process whose outcomes are influenced as much by its initial and background conditions as by any underlying laws, and it has a large stochastic element. Adaptive forces are the results of local circumstances. The product of any particular set of adaptive forces will be affected by the range of existing organisms available for them to act on, by the occurrence and order of the relevant mutations, and by purely stochastic effects (or "drift"). All of this implies that similarity and difference among organisms are very largely to be explained as the result of history. Mammals and birds are endotherms and snakes are ectotherms because mammals and birds are descended from common ancestors which developed this feature in response to some local selective factors and the vagaries of mutation and snakes are not descended from such ancestors. If taxa have historical explanations, then historical essences for taxa are the appropriate ones. Historical essences correctly identify the causal homeostatic mechanism that makes taxa into projectable categories. That mechanism is common descent.

The historical nature of species and higher taxa is reflected in the actual principles of classification which have been adopted by systematists. These are strictly genealogical or historical. No matter how closely certain features of a marsupial "rat" resemble some species of rodent, they will not be counted by systematists as grounds for classifying the two species together. The shared features are *homoplastic*—produced by parallel evolution—and not *homologous*—derived from a common origin. This is as true for parallel genetic evolution as for the better-known phenomena of morphological parallelism. These principles are not arbitrary but are the outcome of competition between alternative systematic schools. The approach recommended by statistical intrinsic essentialism is very similar to an approach which has been tried and abandoned by actual systematists. The "pheneticist" program in taxonomy tried to produce classifications of the sort called for by statistical intrinsic essentialism.[2] The pheneticists proposed to classify organisms using something like a metric of overall similarity. All the organism's characters are compared to produce a phenetic classification. No distinction is made between homologous and ho-

---

2. Although the pheneticists did not intend to achieve this result. They took a highly operationalist view of the categories produced by their methods.

moplastic characters.[3] This program was a practical failure because it failed to yield a unique, stable classification. Different data sets yield different classifications, and despite speculations to the contrary there is little or no tendency for fluctuations to disappear as more and more characters are taken into consideration (de Queiroz and Goode n.d.). Phenetic methods thus failed to accomplish the fundamental aim of taxonomy—the discovery of an underlying structure to biological diversity. Genealogical or historical methods, on the other hand, seem to achieve just this and have been widely accepted on this basis.

It is perhaps difficult for philosophers to appreciate just how wrong intrinsic essentialism is, because it is not *necessarily* wrong. There are possible worlds with radically different biologies and histories in which intrinsic essentialist classifications of species are scientifically productive! If identical organisms regularly reevolved to fill recurring ecological niches, in the manner envisaged by Charles Lyell (1830; cited in Hull 1988, 36), then an essentialist classification would be useful. It is the contingent fact that the complexity of the genetic material, among other things, makes "reevolution" statistically impossible that makes essentialist taxonomy useless. Another possible world which would favor essentialism is one where a form of creation science is true and species are immutable types pursuing divine destinies. In the actual world, however, species are clusters of organisms with a common history. Members of clusters resemble one another because of their common history, gene flow, developmental canalization, and the selective regimes in which populations live. Real-world biology has found scientifically productive ways to classify these clusters of organisms and it is possible to spell out the principles of these classifications by paying attention to real-world biology.

There is an obvious line of thought that might lead someone to dispute this conclusion. The effects of convergent evolution, as exemplified in the similarities between bats and birds or between placental wolves and marsupial "wolves" are striking. These effects are often explained as the result of similar selection pressures. This suggests a way to save the essentialist approach to taxonomy. If similar selective pressures gave rise to similar organisms, there would be an ahistorical basis for classification. Different

---

3. Or between "primitive" and "derived" characters, a distinction which is explained in the next section.

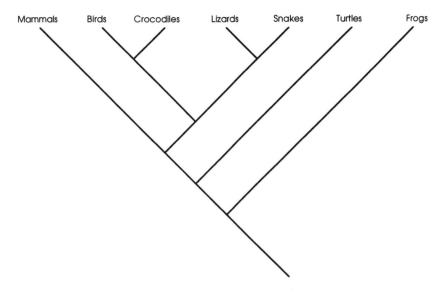

| Mammals | Birds | Crocodiles | Lizards | Snakes | Turtles | Frogs |

8.1. A hypothetical cladogram.

organisms placed in the same type of environment would come to share sufficient characteristics to make them an interesting type. Organisms could be divided into these ecological categories rather than into genealogical categories. I will return to this idea after outlining in more detail how the historical approach works in practice. Ecological classifications turn out to be a supplement, not a rival, to phylogenetic classifications.

8.2 Cladistic Systematics

The school of systematics that uses purely genealogical or historical principles is known as *cladistics* (or *phylogenetic systematics*). The burden of my discussion in the last section was that the taxonomic categories in biology are cladistic categories.

Cladistic systematics classifies organisms in a hierarchy of strictly nested groups called *clades* (figure 8.1). Cladists maintain that there is a uniquely correct ordering of all organisms which has this form. Systematics is not an exercise in producing classifications convenient for human purposes, but an attempt to discover the underlying structure of nature. The belief that there is such a unique real structure, and that it has the branching form just mentioned, is based on views about the mechanism of evolution. If species are produced by the modification of existing organisms, leading to speciation events in which some subset of an existing species comes to function as a separate evolutionary unit, then the pattern of relationships among organisms must have this structure. This fact was evident to Darwin himself, and the only figure in *The Origin of Species* (Darwin 1859) has this form. Diagrams conforming more or less strictly to cladistic principles are found in many bodies of literature after that time (Craw 1992). These principles were definitively formulated by the German systematist Willi Hennig (1966).

According to strict cladistic principles a species goes extinct whenever it speciates, giving rise to two new species. Each species thus represents the segment of a lineage between two speciation events (Ridley 1989). Of course, when a small segment of an existing species forms a new species, nothing of actual biological significance happens to the existing species. The "extinction" of this "stem species" after the speciation event is a naming convention required to produce an unequivocal representation of the evolutionary process. Speciation by the division of one species into two separate evolutionary units is known as *cladogenesis*. Cladogenesis is often contrasted with *anagenesis* or *anagenetic speciation*, which is the transformation of a single, continuous lineage from one species into another. Such events are not recognized by cladistics, which merely regards this as a change in the characteristics of an existing species. Anagenic speciation is best regarded as a pragmatic device of paleontology. Events of cladogenesis in which one segment of the stem species remains largely unaffected are undetectable by paleontological means. Paleontologists must treat such sequences of cladistic species as a single species. This practice creates difficulties when a single lineage undergoes a great deal of change during its history. Paleontologists resolve this by treating different stages of this continuous record as different species. There are probably plenty of real cladistic species within this continuous record, but they cannot be identified. The divisions which are made instead are made to mark discontinuities between the forms found in strata of one period and those found in another. Anagenic speciation is a device for classifying fossils, not a type of evolutionary event.[4]

---

4. This conclusion is not merely the result of a dogmatic adherence to cladism. E. O. Wilson, who takes a traditional, and only minimally cladist, approach to species, compares divisions made within a single lineage on the basis of paleontological evidence to "a scientist's koan, the equivalent of the sound of one hand clapping, the length of a string. Yet paleontolo-

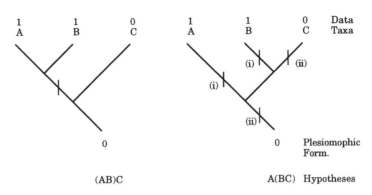

8.2. Resolving a cladogram by character analysis. A simple one-character example. Redrawn from Sober (1988a).

A cladistic tree is "resolved" by character analysis. The patterns of shared characters among the different taxa are used to generate hypotheses about the branching structure of evolution. For this purpose, characters found in a group of taxa must be divided into *primitive* and *derived*. Primitive characters are those possessed by the common ancestor of the group as a whole. Agreement in a primitive character (plesiomorphy) is evidentially irrelevant. Agreement in a derived character which has arisen within the group being classified (synapomorphy) suggests that the organisms which share that character have a common ancestor. Suppose, for example, that we are classifying New Zealand native birds. The New Zealand pigeon and the kea should not be placed together because they can both fly, even though this differentiates them from other New Zealand natives. On the other hand, the kiwi should be placed with certain extinct species because it *cannot* fly. Flying is a primitive characteristic of the whole order Aves, and individuals who share it do so simply by virtue of membership of this order. Flightlessness is a derived character, suggesting a particular evolutionary event in the history of New Zealand natives. In a sense, cladistics rules out "double-counting" of traits. If a trait has been used to differentiate two groups, then it cannot be used to differentiate subgroups nested within those groups.

Organisms are tested for agreement or disagreement in derived characters and grouped accordingly. In the elementary case shown in figure 8.2,

gists, driven by practical necessity, go on distinguishing and naming chronospecies. They are right to do so" (Wilson 1992, 48–49).

two hypotheses are suggested: either A and B are closely related and C is the out-group, or B and C are closely related and A is the out-group. The 110 distribution of the character state can be explained by either tree. The left-hand tree, however, can explain it with a single change of state. The right-hand tree can explain it in two ways, but each requires two changes of state. The left-hand tree is preferred, as it is more parsimonious. In more sophisticated cases, where many characters are involved, clustering algorithms operate on the general principle of minimizing the number of separate evolutionary events. All other things being equal, a tree in which a character has evolved independently $n - 1$ times is preferred to a tree in which it has evolved n times. Clearly, this general principle rests on substantial assumptions about the dynamics of evolution (Sober 1988b).

Each clade is a *monophyletic* group: every organism in the group has a common ancestor with any other member more recently than it has a common ancestor with any organism outside the group. In other words, the group contains all and only the descendants of some ancestral group. Alternatively and equivalently, clades form a strictly nested hierarchy. Monophyletic groups (or "natural groups") are contrasted to *paraphyletic* groups, which include a common ancestor of all members of the group but omit some of its descendants, and *polyphyletic* groups, which include a number of organisms but no common ancestor for them. The monophyletic groups, or clades, are the natural kinds of organisms.

All monophyletic groups are natural kinds. Every organism therefore belongs to a hierarchy of cladistic taxa (see figure 8.1). However, cladistics denies the reality of the traditional taxonomic "ranks." There is no real fact in the world that corresponds to the traditional ranking of higher taxa into genera, families, orders, classes, and phyla. This is because there is no basis for making "horizontal" comparisons of nonoverlapping segments of the phylogenetic tree. Higher taxa are therefore strictly incomparable. It has been found useful in many cases to retain notions of rank for classificatory convenience, but such notions are mere artifacts of a system of classification. Many authors have argued that species (or "basal taxa") have a more substantial ontological status than higher taxonomic groupings. Species are held together by current causal processes, such as gene flow or the requirements of their niche, whereas higher taxa are held together only by the past genealogical event which defines them. Ghiselin and Hull have both argued that species are akin to paradigm individuals like organisms in that their parts interact and that they are causal actors in the evolutionary process. Hull has marked this distinction by claiming that species are ontological individuals whereas higher taxa are merely "historical entities." The contrast is between objects like a human individual, which seem to act as integrated wholes, and objects like a human family, which typically do not. These debates, while of the first importance, do not bear on any of the issues in this book. My main concern will be with cladistic traits (homologues), which are defined by higher taxa as well as by individual species.

8.3 Clades as Natural Kinds

In some respects cladistics might have been invented as an example to support the philosophical theory of natural kinds. According to cladistics the true phylogeny represents a set of real distinctions in the biological world, which systematics does its best to estimate. Cladistic orthodoxy insists that classifications are always provisional. A current description of a taxon is not a definition, but a hypothesis about the structure of an underlying reality (a view expressed in the slogan "homology is an inferential concept"). The cladistic literature stresses the way in which older classifications can be seen to dimly grasp real divisions in nature in the context of an inadequate theory about their basis. The exact boundaries and the real basis of these divisions is revealed by evolutionary theory and modern systematics. There are examples of reference failure, as when a species name turns out to refer to a seasonal or geographic variant of a species already named. The names given to groups of so-called cryptic species, which are morphologically identical but evolutionarily distinct, provide examples of "partial reference." The name is attached to a cluster of properties that has a causal homeostatic mechanism underlying it, but it is equally attached to more than one category.

In another respect, however, biology has confounded philosophical expectations. Biological taxa are not unified by a shared microstructure which explains their other properties. Ghiselin and Hull took microstructural essences to be a core element of the theory of natural kinds (see also Dupré 1981). A natural kind must be defined by an essence of intrinsic properties. They found support for this view in another traditional view, namely, that the definition of a natural kind cannot restrict it to one place or time. Anything that shares the essence of the kind is a member of the kind, no matter where or when it occurs. This led them to deny that biological taxa are kinds or categories at all, because they are defined in terms of unique historical events. They suggested instead that taxa are individual objects. They compared taxonomic names like "royal albatross" and "Aves" to proper names like "Alpha Centauri" and "the Milky Way." Proper names are supposedly very different from natural kind terms. The essence of a natural kind is its microstructural constitution. Gold can arise independently at many different locations in the universe, provided only that what arises has atomic number 79. The essence of an individual is given by its historical origins. A human individual, according to Kripke (1980), is essentially the product of its actual parents and a human family of its actual ancestors. If Hull and Ghiselin are right, a species is like a human individual or family. It is essentially a product of the actual historical event from which it arose.

I believe that Hull and Ghiselin are right about the "individuality" of biological taxa, but that they are wrong about natural kinds. The causal homeostasis theory of natural kinds provides a much broader conception of "essence." The essence of a kind is its causal homeostatic mechanism—whatever it is that explains the projectability of that category. A microstructural essence is only one kind of causal homeostatic mechanism. Other possibilities include external forces like those produced by the ecological niche of a species and the "design niche" of an artifact. Yet another possibility is the shared history that holds together the members of a biological taxon. Within the general framework of causal homeostasis the nature of kindhood is open to revision in the light of scientific advance. In the case of biological taxa, evolutionary theory reveals that a category can be uniquely localized in space and time but still useful in explanation and induction. Despite being localized, it can fulfill the traditional role of natural kinds of being the subject of true, counterfactual supporting empirical generalizations.

The traditional conception of a natural kind supposed that natural kinds would enter into exceptionless empirical generalizations or "natural laws." This conception reflects a philosophy of science in which the sciences that do not yield exceptionless laws are seen as inadequate and awaiting replacement by some more exact science. The logical empiricist philosophy of science of the first half of this century assumed that physics gave a privileged description of reality and looked forward to the day in which science could be "unified" on the foundations provided by physics

(Oppenheim and Putnam 1958). The last half century has seen the abandonment of this dream. The "unity of science" has dwindled to a minimal notion of supervenience—the world studied by economics or population biology does not change independently of the world studied by molecular biology or by microphysics. In this new philosophy of science the exception-ridden generalizations of many life and social sciences are seen as the only way to uncover some of the regularity inherent in natural processes (Fodor 1974; Lycan 1990). To reduce these sciences to their physical substrate is to eschew some epistemic access to that regularity. It is to know less about reality. This new philosophy of science has given rise to an "enthusiasm for natural kinds" in many special sciences (Boyd 1991; Hacking 1991a and 1991b). Natural kinds are no longer conceived as the subjects of the fundamental laws of nature. They are simply nonarbitrary ways of grouping natural phenomena. These kinds are nonarbitrary (or "natural") because they have some degree of projectability. Observations about them can be projected onto new instances with better than chance results. Cladistic categories are remarkably projectable. A cladistic taxon represents a strong probabilistic cluster of properties from the molecular to the behavioral. Knowing that something is a member of Aves allows us to predict better than chance both how it will metabolize certain toxins and what learning algorithms it will use. Some taxonomists have claimed that cladistic classifications are "maximally predictive" (Fink 1979). A cladistic classification of an organism makes more correct predictions about its unobserved properties than any other available classification. Cladistic kinds, like other natural kinds in the special sciences, are the subjects of true, counterfactual supporting, empirical generalizations, even if these generalizations do not conform to the traditional ideal of a natural law.

8.4 A Cladistic Approach to Biological Traits

If the natural kinds of organisms are cladistic taxa, it would seem to follow that the natural kinds of traits are cladistic homologues. A homologue is a trait uniting a clade. Every species in the clade either has the trait or is descended from a species that had the trait. It is a trait all of whose bearers have it in virtue of their descent from a single ancestral population in which it originated. Homologous traits are contrasted with analogous (or homoplastic) traits, which have arisen independently on more than one occasion. Human limbs are homologous with avian limbs because both are derived from the same distant, ancestral tetrapod body plan. Human and avian thermoregulatory capacities are homoplastic because they arose independently in these two lineages. Cladistic homologues, like cladistic taxa, can be seen as the natural kinds for which biology has been searching. Traditional morphologists divided resemblances among individual traits into homologies and analogies. Homologous traits were "really the same" in some sense, although they might be physically very different in different species. Analogous traits appeared to be the same but were not really so. Human eyes were known to be homologous with those of other vertebrates but merely analogous with those of squid and octopuses. In previous eras the notion of homology was basically mysterious. It reflected the true order of nature, whatever that was. Since Darwin, however, homology can be identified with resemblance due to descent from a common ancestor. Analogy is identified with resemblance (homoplasy) due to parallel evolution.

It is striking how closely the identification of homologues with characters uniting monophyletic groups conforms to the model of conceptual revision outlined in the last chapter. The criteria by which homologues were originally recognized are explained and shown to be inessential by the new evolutionary account of homology. Traditional morphologists thought it important that homologues had "special qualities." These can be identified with the nonadaptive features that are transmitted in lineages. Thus, the vertebrate eye has the blood vessels on top of the retina, while the cephalopod eye has them behind the retina. This feature of the vertebrate eye is a historical accident, and its distribution among the vertebrates can be explained only by their common descent (see section 3.3). "Special qualities" are thus important to diagnosing homologies, but they do not form part of the definition of a homology. Traditional morphologists also thought the position of a structure in the fundamental layout of the organism important in diagnosing homology. This reflects the importance of relative position in the development of the embryo and the difficulty of altering relative position without disrupting development. These facts make relative position phylogenetically stable and hence good for diagnosing evolutionary relationships. Once again, the evolutionary definition of homology makes the old diagnostic property important and informative but not actually essential.

In proposing that biological classifications of traits are cladistic I find myself aligned with a number of biologists and philosophers of biology but directly opposed to many psychologists and philosophers of psychology who take themselves to be inspired by evolutionary biology (McNaughton 1989; Plutchik 1970, 1980; Neander 1991a and 1991b; Millikan 1986; Sterelny 1990). These authors claim that biological cate- gories are primarily functional. Homologous traits should be classified together only if they have performed similar functions in recent evolutionary history, and homoplastic traits should be freely grouped together if they meet this condition. These authors all stress the importance of grouping traits together because they are adaptations for the same end, rather than because they are descended from a common ancestor. Neil McNaughton claims that psychological characters should be categorized on the basis of their *teleonomy,* or adaptive purpose. Karen Neander claims that "a great proportion of biological categories are functionally defined" (1991b, 467). Kim Sterelny claims that certain famous biological models make psychological attributions to animals that are "implementation neutral" (1990, 101) and so require an "ecological level" classification of psychological traits that applies equally to many diverse organisms.

Neander's argument for the existence and importance of a functional classification is simple:

> Take the heart, for instance. Biologists need and have a category that ranges across species, but hearts are morphologically diverse across different species . . . Hearts are also morphologically diverse within a species, because of pathological deviations from the norm, due to disease, injury and deformity. They are all, however, *organs for pumping blood.* (Neander 1991b, 467; italics in original)

I take this to be the main argument which inclines philosophers to believe that biology uses functional categories. An almost identical argument is given by Ruth Millikan (1984, 24). Neander's argument makes two claims for proper functional taxonomies. First, she claims that they are needed for certain cross-species generalizations. This is the real basis of the importance of functional classifications. Second, Neander claims that only a proper functional taxonomy will allow us to classify malformed and diseased organs with their well-formed equivalents. This is a red herring. Neander is correct to say that a proper functional taxonomy will allow type identities between malfunctioning and well-functioning traits. An item has its biological proper function in virtue of its selective history.

This implies that it retains its function no matter how damaged or diseased it is and whether or not it can perform its function. But functional kinds derive this ability from their logical relationship with cladistic kinds. Biological functions attach to items in virtue of their evolutionary history. So in order to ascribe a function to an item, it is necessary to establish that it is a member of a lineage with a unique evolutionary history, or, in other words, a clade. Functional kinds are therefore either coextensive with cladistic kinds or with disjunctions of cladistic kinds. This is a substantial conclusion and one that has not been sufficiently stressed, but it does not defeat the claim that biology needs functional classifications. That claim rests on Neander's other proposed advantage for functional classifications, the ability to classify traits across a wide range of species. If functional classifications are to be of value in biology, it must be because of their superior generality—the fact that they unite disjunctions of cladistic homologues.

8.5 A "Two-Level" Theory of Biological Traits

The argument that functional classifications are needed in order to express ecological generalizations that apply across taxonomic boundaries is an old one. In its most traditional version it is combined with progressive views of evolution. The histories of several different lineages are interpreted as those different lineages passing through the same series of "grades" of complexity or adaptedness (Lovejoy 1936; Gould 1985 [esp. sec. 5], 1989). But it is not difficult to break the association between functional classifications and progressivism. Parallels between unrelated organisms can be attributed to common adaptive pressures on those organisms in a more piecemeal fashion. From time to time, different organisms find themselves in similar ecological situations, and this creates resemblances between them as they seek solutions to the same problems. The vertebrates and the invertebrate cephalopods both evolved a focusing eye with a lens and retina, mammalian tigers and marsupial "tigers" both developed striped camouflage. Since ecological problems need not occur in any particular order, this idea does not imply a commitment to progression. The next change in the environment might produce an ecology that favors the rudimentation of a trait rather than its progression to the next "grade."

Traditional, intuitive taxonomy was often criticized for "mixing grades and clades." Organisms were assigned to a single set of categories, sometimes on the basis of hypothesized common descent and sometimes on the basis of functional parallelism. This procedure seems fundamentally confused, and it is hard to see what theoretical role there is for such bastard categories. But it is possible to introduce functional classifications in a far more sensible way. Functional classifications can be used to group cladistic units together in a way that allows the theorist to express generalizations about the evolutionary process that apply to many different lineages. In Hull's neat phrase, evolution can be seen as a matter of "genealogical actors in ecological roles" (Hull 1987). The actors are the characters in natural historical narratives and the roles are the characters in ecological narratives. These narratives are complementary rather than competing. An example of such an ecological role might be "top-rank freshwater predator." The crocodile and the anaconda could be seen as two genealogical actors that fill this role using very different equipment. The ecological role is multiply realized by different phyla.

The idea that biology involves multiple explanatory levels, each with a proprietary way of classifying organisms and their traits, is a compelling one. I have suggested elsewhere (Griffiths 1994; Goode and Griffiths 1995) that there are at least four such levels, each allowing access to a different body of generalizations about evolution. At the most abstract level of biological explanation, evolutionary outcomes are explained by the generalizations of population genetics and evolutionary games theory.[5] The main point to grasp about this "population dynamic level" is that traits are described solely by their relative fitness functions. Generalizations at this level can be applied indifferently to a set of political strategies in chimpanzees or to a set of life-history strategies in beetles. Population dynamic models like Maynard Smith's "hawk-dove" game and "mouse/haystack" model are often misinterpreted because they are developed using the illustrative examples from which they take their names. In fact, such models require no assumptions about the situations they describe except genetics (or in game theory a simple heritability assumption) and the existence of fitness differences. Theories at the population dynamic level contain the "consequence laws" (Sober 1984a) which explain the traits found in actual popu-

---

5. It now seems to be widely agreed that these fundamental dynamic equations of the evolutionary process are irreducible to any lower level. See Mills and Beatty (1979) and Rosenberg (1978). See also Rosenberg (1982, 1983) and Rosenberg and Williams (1985) for an alternative view, and Sober (1984b) and Brandon and Beatty (1984) for discussion.

lations as the consequences of the relative fitness of those traits. Given the relative fitness functions of the alternatives and the starting frequencies, population dynamic theories compute the frequency of each alternative after any given number of generations.[6]

In theories at the "general ecological level," traits are classified according to the adaptive purpose which they serve. These are the functional, or ecological or adaptive, classifications which might be thought of as alternatives to the cladistic classifications I have been advocating. General ecological theories aim to provide "source laws" (Sober 1984a) describing the sources of the relative fitnesses that enter into population dynamic explanations. The optimality models which have been so prominent and controversial in recent biology are models at the general ecological level. One example popularized among philosophers by Peter Godfrey-Smith (1991) is signal detection theory. This theory predicts that internal states which coordinate sensory data with adaptive responses will have their fitness determined by how well they trade off the probabilities of correct, false-positive, and false-negative responses (given the values of these various responses to the organism). Ecological explanations of this kind are less abstract than explanations at the population dynamic level. But they are still very far from the history of any particular species. They purport to apply to any organism from any lineage facing a particular type of adaptive problem.

General ecological descriptions are realized in particular cases by particular lineages of organisms or traits. These are the cladistic groups which have been discussed in the first part of this chapter. We might call this the "natural historical level." The flukes of whales, the tails of fish, the feet of seals, and the wings of penguins are different lineages' solutions to the problem of exerting muscular force on a liquid medium. They are cladistically distinct, but functionally identical. Kinds at the natural historical level enter into natural historical narratives about the evolution of particular lineages. Source laws and consequence laws concerning relative fitness figure in these narratives, but so do particular historical facts that affect the outcome of the process.

6. The fitness of an item will, of course, be relativized to a class of environments, and very often be frequency dependent, so that each item is associated not with a simple value, but with a function taking a set of alternatives and their frequencies to fitness values. In many cases details of the genetically stable combinations of traits in the population and of mutation rates may also be needed.

The lowest level of explanation is that of the cluster of anatomical and physiological disciplines which describe the actual physical capacities of biological traits (Amundson and Lauder 1995; Wouters 1995). Cladistic categories are multiply realized at the "anatomical level" because of individual variation.

Cladists have traditionally rejected functional classifications of organisms because they are less informative than cladistic classifications. Resemblances among organisms in genetic structure, morphology, and even behavior owe more to common descent than to adaptation to the recent environment. The New Zealand kiwi is supposed to occupy a similar niche to nocturnal mammals like hedgehogs or badgers that feed on invertebrates in leaf litter. It is said to be a remarkable example of parallel evolution. It is nevertheless a great deal more like other birds than like a hedgehog! Cladistic classifications are also "maximally predictive" classifications. They group organisms in a way that best predicts previously unnoticed patterns of resemblance. William Fink (1979) provides a striking example. Crocodiles are archosaurs, closely allied to the birds. As Fink points out, they have a remarkable cluster of birdlike characters, including "complex vocalisation patterns (including peeping by hatchlings and chirping), nest building, and brood care, none of which are found in other 'reptiles' " (1979, 373). Fink predicts that closer attention to crocodile behavior from this perspective will reveal other unnoticed parallels. Such are the usual arguments for favoring cladistic over functional (grade) classifications. But the multilevel picture of biological explanation looks set to render these arguments irrelevant. Functional classifications need not be seen as competing with cladistic ones. They are a supplement to them. Organisms can be grouped into clades, but these clades can be grouped again, at a higher level, into functional categories. The more abstract classification allows us to discern broad patterns of adaptation. This in no way impugns the cladistic classification of the same organisms.

Seeing the relation between ecological and phylogenetic categories in this way can help explain the relative lack of detail and predictive power provided by functional classifications. Specifying an adaptive problem tells us very little about the detail of the mechanism that solves that problem. There are many ways, for example, to break down prey into digestible form. But knowing what means are available for modification to solve the problem places much tighter constraints on the possible solutions. The anaconda and crocodile use very different solutions to the problem of breaking down prey, but they both use solutions that are similar to those used by their relatives. Because of the peculiar jaw found in snakes, the anaconda is able to swallow its prey whole and relies on digestive juices to reduce them. But if this is why functional classifications are uninformative, then being uninformative is no great criticism. As long as there are *some* generalizations about functional categories, then introducing a functional classification will add to our understanding of the dynamics of evolution. The fact that these generalizations are relatively sparse is not a problem, because they are a supplement to, rather than a replacement for, their cladistic cousins.

8.6 Explanatory Levels in Biology and Psychology

I have suggested that there are a number of levels of explanation in biology and that there are natural kinds at more than one level. Since emotions have an evolutionary history, these kinds seem likely candidates for the referents of emotion terms. But emotions are also psychological phenomena, and it has long been a truism that psychological processes can be described at a number of theoretical levels, each of which has its own explanatory categories (figure 8.3). In this section I address the relationship between the explanatory levels and natural kinds of the two disciplines.

Perhaps the most famous characterization of the levels of explanation in psychology is that proposed by David Marr in *Vision* (1982). This model of psychological explanation forms part of the official methodology of evolutionary psychology (see chapter 5). Marr proposed that an adequate approach to vision must make use of three levels of description. The highest level describes the task which the psychological system accomplishes. In the case of vision, Marr claims that the system produces an interpretation of the world in terms of moving, three-dimensional objects with color from patterns of stimulation of the retina. The intermediate level describes how the system processes information in order to accomplish this task. It details the algorithms by which retinal patterns are transformed into representations of the world. The lowest level describes how these computational processes are implemented in the brain.

Another attempt to differentiate among levels of explanation in psychology was made by the early functionalists (Putnam 1967; Lewis 1980).

Population Dynamic Level	
Traits classified solely by relative fitness functions. Explanation by "consequence laws."	
General Ecological Level	Ecological Level
	(Level of Task Description)
Traits classified by the adaptive problem that they solve. Explanation involves "source laws."	What does the trait do for the organism?
Natural Historical Level	Computational Level
Traits classified by homology. Explanation by historical narratives.	How is information processed to accomplish the task?
Anatomical Level	
Traits classified by their physical capacities.	Implementation Level
	How are computations physically implemented?

8.3. Levels of explanation in biology and psychology. See text for explanation.

Classic functionalism has just one level distinction, between the so-called "functional" and the so-called "physical" levels. The neurosciences are located at the physical level and psychology at the functional level. The neurosciences describe one physical implementation of a computational structure. Psychology describes the computational structure itself. Psychological states are identified with particular roles in the computational structure, and the aim of the neurosciences is to find the occupants of those roles in normal humans. The later school of "homuncular" functionalism generalizes the functionalist role/occupant distinction to create a multiplicity of levels of description which successively realize one another (Cummins 1983; Lycan 1987, 1990). This theory emphasizes the hierarchical nature of descriptions of information-processing systems and suggests that there is a whole series of computational levels. Homuncular functionalism also argues that the categories of the neurosciences are themselves functional, creating a whole series of "neural" levels. The physical/functional distinction is thus replaced by a continuum. But the fundamental insight of both traditional and homuncular functionalism is the same. The full range of true generalizations about psychological systems is available only if a series of different theoretical vocabularies is utilized. Each vocabulary abstracts further from the details of physical implementation and is applicable to a wider range of systems.

Kim Sterelny's recent account of levels of psychological explanation draws on both Marr and the philosophers (Sterelny 1990). He proposes three levels similar to Marr's. He rechristens the highest level the "ecological level." Sterelny argues that it is in the study of the interaction between organisms and their environment that this level of description finds its real explanatory role (1990, 44–46). Sterelny refers to the intermediate level as the "computational level." Homuncular functionalists like William Lycan emphasize the possibility of large numbers of such levels between the superficial "task description" and any obviously physical level. Sterelny plays down this possibility and argues for a single "computational level" (1990, 59–60). Sterelny is closer to Lycan in his treatment of the "implementation level." Lycan argues that the vocabulary of the neurosciences is itself multiply realizable at lower levels. There is, for example, more than one biochemical way to build a neuron. Sterelny agrees that conventional neural descriptions are themselves at some level of abstraction from any ultimate physical description. There may, therefore, be more than one distinct implementation level. In what follows I shall largely conform to Sterelny's terminology. I want to stress the relationship between psychological and biological explanations, and so the term *ecological level* is useful. The issue of the number of computational levels can be sidestepped for my purposes, and I refer to the *computational level* without deciding whether it is one or many. It is also unimportant to me how many distinct levels are required by the neurosciences. I require merely that the computational level(s) be higher than the implementation level(s) and multiply realizable therein.

Sterelny's observation that the level of task description in psychology is an ecological level is an important one. Ecology is the study of the interaction of the organism with its environment (including other organisms). Part of this project is what we might call "cognitive ecology"—the study of that part of an organism's interaction with the environment which is mediated by information-processing mechanisms. The emerging discipline of "cognitive ethology" (Bekoff and Jamieson 1990) is part of cognitive ecology, as is most current work in "evolutionary psychology" (see chapter 5). Cognitive ecology aims to discover what the cognitive capacities of a particular species allowed it to achieve in its evolutionary environment.

The descriptions that cognitive ecology is trying to produce are precisely psychological "task descriptions" in Marr's sense—specifications of what a particular cognitive system is able to achieve in relation to its surroundings.

There is a close connection between this descriptive task and attempts to provide evolutionary explanations at the general ecological level. General ecology attempts to explain why organisms have mechanisms that are able to accomplish certain tasks. These explanations are not concerned with the particular mechanisms organisms use to perform the tasks. Instead, they explain why it is one task rather than another which is performed. This is explained in terms of the relative adaptive value of those tasks. When dealing with cognitive systems, explanations at this level would specify the adaptive advantages of satisfying a particular task description rather than various alternative task descriptions. For example, Shepard (1992) argues that our system of color representation, which uses just three axes to define the space of possible colors, is an adaptation to the presence of three main types of variation in the illumination of natural scenes. A system which represents information about surface reflectances in just this way will best achieve the ecologically important goal of giving constant representations of objects under varying illumination.

Natural kinds produced by investigating the evolution of cognitive systems at the "general ecological" level will be kinds at the level of task description (ecological level) in psychology. Sterelny has also argued that the reverse is the case. Psychologically interesting task descriptions will tend to be descriptions of ecologically meaningful tasks. Psychology needs a level of task description which generalizes away from the specifics of organisms' computational arrangements because there are resemblances between organisms (and artificial systems) which are radically different at the physical and computational levels. The reason that these diverse organisms resemble one another at this more abstract level is that they must all solve the same adaptive problems in order to cope with the world. Vertebrate and invertebrate cognition may be radically different at the computational level, having been constructed in complete isolation, but the fact that both systems have to cope with the same world of three-dimensional objects and perform many of the same tasks on those objects (ingesting them, avoiding them, etc.) will lead to resemblances at the level of task description.

Another obvious point of contact is between the neural or implementation level in psychology and the physiological-anatomical level in evolutionary theory. Both are concerned with the actual physical capacities of the nervous system. The relation between the computational level and the various levels of explanation in biology is less clear. I suspect that the adoption of one computational solution rather than another will reflect lineage in the same way as anatomical characters.[7] If the balance system of an octopus species uses algorithm A and humans use algorithm B, we would expect other cephalopods to use algorithms related to A and many vertebrates to use algorithms related to B. But this suggestion does not license any identification of the computational level of analysis in psychology with the cladistic or natural historical level in biology. The idea of a cladistic classification seems to have a far wider application in psychology. For example, particular implementations of a computational process may be associated with particular lineages.

The links to be drawn between levels in biology and psychology appear to be threefold. Kinds at the general ecological (functional, adaptive) level in biology will be kinds at the ecological level (level of task description) in psychology. Kinds at the natural historical level in biology may be either computational level kinds or implementation level kinds in psychology. Kinds at the anatomical level in biology will be kinds at the implementation level in psychology.

8.7 Explanatory Levels and Conceptual Revision

In chapter 7, I outlined the consequences of the causal homeostasis theory of natural kinds for intertheoretic identities and conceptual revision. I made four main claims:

1. Revisions of the extension of concepts will aim to pick out categories that have causal homeostasis. Current theory predicts which categories will exhibit this desirable property.

2. Revisions of intension will occur to reflect not only discoveries about which features are *actually* reliably present in the category but also discoveries about which features *must be* reliably present. These counter-

---

7. Lauder (1990) argues that evolution can preserve function independently of the structure underlying that function.

factual claims follow from current theories about the category's causal homeostatic mechanism.

3. Phenomenological concepts from two different theories will be identified if both concepts were introduced to refer to a kind marked by roughly the same cluster of features.

4. Theoretical concepts from two different theories will be identified if they explain the causal homeostasis of roughly the same clusters of features using analogous schemes of causal explanation.

My aim in this second part of the book is to apply this theory to emotion concepts. The theory of natural kinds should prescribe how to revise emotion concepts in the light of current science. It should also prescribe which current theoretical concepts should be identified with older emotion concepts. It should tell us, in other words, what emotions really are. I have already noted that these prescriptions need not be followed in practice. They prescribe how concepts *should* evolve *if* the only aim of their evolution is increased scientific understanding.

The recognition that the life sciences typically utilize different natural kinds at different explanatory levels creates some real difficulties in applying the injunctions of the theory of natural kinds. Different complementary explanatory levels will classify the emotions in different ways. All of these classifications represent natural kinds. The injunction to revise the intension and extension of the concept of fear so as to fit the causal homeostatic mechanism underlying fear becomes ambiguous. The paradigm cases of fear in humans may all be examples of an ecological level kind "response to danger" and of a computational level or neural level kind unique to humans and their close evolutionary relatives. The identification of the pretheoretic concept of fear with some theoretical concept is equally problematic. Which of these two theoretical concepts (if either) should be identified with the concept of fear?

There is an obvious way to try to resolve this ambiguity in the injunctions of the theory of natural kinds. Although an individual organism may be subject to explanations at several different explanatory levels, each of these explanations will classify that organism with a different group of "similar" organisms. Higher levels will abstract away from various differences and regard a broader range of systems as type-identical to the system under study. Kinds at the implementation (neural) level, for example, can be used only to characterize systems with similar physical constitutions. Kinds at the ecological level can be used to characterize any system which interacts with the environment in an appropriate fashion. This suggests that the range of systems to which the existing concept applies can be used to determine the explanatory level at which the kind is meant to be located. Concepts which apply to any system which interacts with the environment in a goal-directed manner are intended for ecological level kinds. Concepts whose application is restricted to humans are perhaps intended for implementation level kinds. In general, the best theoretical concept with which to identify an existing concept is one which can be applied to the range of systems to which people apply the existing concept.

The shortcoming of this suggestion may be seen through an example. Consider pain. There is a neural system, homologous in a large group of vertebrates, that is the neural basis of pain in humans (Melzack 1973). There may also be an interesting category of "avoidance/withdrawal" responses at the ecological level. Terrestrial species, both vertebrate and nonvertebrate, artificial intelligences, and the silicon-based martians beloved of philosophical science fiction may form a single group for ecological purposes and share states of this kind. Suppose that both of these kinds have a place in a multilevel psychology. The proposal just described asks us to determine whether the pain concept is applied only to the narrow class of systems with the same neurology, or to the wider class which produce behavior that fulfills the same task. This turns out to be difficult to determine. It is difficult because the various pain phenomena *collectively* constitute the existing concept of pain (Dennett 1978). In the paradigm case of normal humans they are coextensive with one another. People are unclear how to apply the concept in the wider range of cases where the different phenomena are not coextensive. Do squid or computers *really* feel pain? The uncertainty of ordinary speakers on this question leaves it unclear which of the theoretical kinds should be identified with pain.

There are considerations other than preservation of extension that may help to resolve the ambiguous injunctions of the theory of natural kinds. One such criterion may be the quality of the explanations offered by the rival theoretical kinds. There are many sorts of causal homeostatic mechanisms, and some produce richer or more projectable categories than others. I discussed in chapter 7 the relatively impoverished nature of artifact kinds, whose causal homeostatic mechanism depends on the sociology of design processes, when compared to kinds from the physical sciences with micro-structural "essences." Artifact kinds allow the projection of very few properties when compared to chemical elements. If two candidate kinds are available, it may be preferable to identify the pretheoretic concept with the kind embedded in the most powerful explanatory enterprise. Induction and explanation with this category may be either more productive, or more reliable, or both. I will argue in the next chapter that considerations of this sort can help make choices in emotion theory.

9

What Emotions Really Are

9.1 Introduction

The development of a scientific psychology of emotion requires emotion concepts to be refined or replaced so that the categories corresponding to emotion concepts have strong causal homeostasis. Such categories will be projectable and therefore useful for explanation and induction. The concepts that result from this process are the best available framework for understanding the phenomena associated with vernacular emotion concepts. They are the best available answer to the question "What *are* emotions?" My aim in this chapter is to ask which theoretical concepts explain the phenomena associated with vernacular emotion concepts. The categories to which these concepts refer are what the emotions really are. Of course, scientific understanding is not the sole or main goal of everyday life. Vernacular emotion concepts serve other purposes besides those of explanation and induction. The future development of these vernacular concepts is unlikely to be as simple as their refinement or replacement by the concepts best suited to scientific understanding. But that is exactly what should happen within the conceptual vocabulary of psychology, and it is in that vocabulary that the best available answer can be given to the vernacular question, "What *are* emotions?"

In the first part of this chapter I compare two ways of categorizing emotion which might answer the question of what some emotions really are. The first is the set of categories which emerge from the affect program theory. These categories are referred to by some of the names used for vernacular emotion categories. However, these categories contain only a small part of the extension of the original, vernacular emotion concepts.

So they explain only a part of the phenomena associated with those concepts. The second set of categories I consider are derived from an ecological account of the functions of emotion. These ecological categories may come closer to the extension of vernacular emotion concepts. They might therefore explain more of the phenomena associated with the vernacular concepts. There are, however, three serious problems with this second set of categories. First, they do not have the potential to explain facts about emotion at the computational or implementation levels. They could explain facts only at the level of task description. Second, the ecological theories from which they are supposed to emerge do not yet exist and there are reasons to think that if and when these theories are developed, they will not be particularly useful for explanation and induction even at the level of task description. Finally, and most important, current work with categories of this sort proceeds by taking vernacular emotion categories and assuming that they somehow correspond to categories in cognitive ecology. There are no actual grounds for supposing that categories derived from a developed cognitive ecology would correspond closely to the vernacular categories. I suggest that for some emotions, the correct answer to the question of what those emotions really are is that in some instances they are affect programs and that it is not currently known what the other instances are. If no new theory arrives which reintegrates the whole range of instances of these vernacular concepts, then they may come to be identified with the concepts which emerge from affect program theory and their extensions revised accordingly.

In the second part of the chapter I argue against an identification of the general category of emotion with the category of affect program phenomena. The vernacular concept of emotion in general is founded on an analogy between two very different classes of mental phenomena. One of these is the affect program phenomena and the other is the less well understood group of higher cognitive phenomena discussed in chapter 5. The vernacular emotion concept partially refers to both these categories. I consider and reject an attempt to construct a theoretical category on the basis of the similarities between these two classes of phenomena, because this category has no role in any promising explanatory project. The general category of emotion should be replaced by at least two distinct categories in a future psychology of emotion.

9.2 Cladistic versus Ecological Approaches to Emotion

The known affect programs correspond roughly to the occurrent, phenomenologically salient instances of the vernacular concepts of surprise, anger, fear, sadness, joy, and disgust. They are stereotyped responses involving several bodily systems. These responses are exhibited in all human cultures and are homologous to responses in other vertebrates, particularly primates. There are reasons to be cautious about any simple realization of the affect programs as neural programs. There seems no reason, however, to be skeptical about affect programs as stably replicated elements of the human behavioral repertoire. The six affect programs are cladistic kinds of the sort described in chapter 8. The fear affect program in humans can be classified as a homologue of fear in related species or regarded as a uniquely human structure in virtue of the characteristics which mark it as distinct from homologous structures in other primate species (autapomorphies). In this respect it is no different from a trait like the human arm, which has unique features but can be homologized more or less broadly with everything from a chimpanzee arm to a cetacean fin.

The affect program categories of emotion are derived from a theory which explains many of the phenomena which originally drew human attention to these emotions. The details of each affect program are subject to the sort of explanation first offered by Darwin (1872). Ancient functional responses have been retained due to their secondary adaptive role in interspecific communication. More general aspects of these emotions can also be explained. The modularity of the affect program system explains what was traditionally called the "passivity" of these emotions—their independence from long-term planned action. It explains both what "passivity" is and why it exists. The phenomenon itself is the result of the separate information storage and processing that lead to the production of the affect programs. This explains phobias and other conflicts between emotional response and higher cognitive processes. The existence of these information processing arrangements is hypothesized to have an evolutionary explanation (detailed in chapter 4).

The explanatory power of the affect program theory has led some people to treat it as a theory of the emotions of anger, surprise, fear, sadness, joy, and disgust. However, this identification of vernacular emotion concepts with the concepts of the affect programs would involve substantial conceptual revision. The idea that anger is an affect program response, for example, would distinguish genuine anger from many calmer states of disapproval and long-term resolutions to seek redress that currently fall under the vernacular concept of anger. So in fact, the affect program theory can explain only a part of the phenomena associated with these vernacular emotion concepts. The proposal to identify surprise, fear, anger, sadness, joy, and disgust with the affect programs of those names also faces the problem of multiple levels of explanation discussed in the last chapter. Many natural kinds are relevant to explaining the cluster of features that mark out paradigm human emotions. The psychologists Robert Plutchik (1970) and Neil McNaughton (1989) have argued that vernacular concepts of emotion are best identified with theoretical concepts at what I have labeled the "general ecological level" rather than with cladistic categories. In the ecological approach to emotion, responses are classified in terms of their presumed adaptive function. Plutchik begins by describing the basic adaptive pressures which all organisms supposedly face. Emotional responses are then classified according to which of these pressures was influential in their evolution. The taxonomy of emotion types that results might include such things as "imminent danger response," "current danger response," and "copulation opportunity response." These might be identified with fear, panic, and lust respectively.

It is arguable that the ecological proposal would do less violence to pretheoretic emotion concepts than the affect program proposal. The ecological concepts come closer to some conceptual analyses of vernacular emotion concepts. A whole generation of philosophers concluded that emotions can be classified by the objects in the world to which each emotion is an appropriate response. This led them to claim that each emotion involves the thought that its characteristic object is present, a claim that was shown to be problematic in chapter 2. But the idea that each vernacular emotion concept is the concept of the response appropriate to some object need not be expressed in terms of the thoughts that make up the emotion. It can be expressed by the claim that emotions are responses whose ecological function is to react to situations with a particular significance for the organism. Fear is a response to danger, anger to conspecific challenge, and so forth. This idea allows us to pass over the differences between responses mediated by dedicated modules like the affect program system and those mediated by higher cognitive processes. The ecological theorist can hypothesize a single adaptive function for all the psychological processes which ordinary people think of as anger, everything from the affect program response to cold, calculated vengeance. At one end of this spectrum the evaluation is modularized, the functional category is given a simple, operational definition (e.g., such and such body language is a challenge), and the response is stereotyped and inflexible. At the other end of the spectrum all the organism's cognitive resources are brought to bear in evaluating the situation, and the response is flexible. In both cases, however, the procedure has the biological function of determining if the situation has a certain significance, and the response is designed to cope with that class of situation.

The ecological approach to emotions may be able to include modular affect program instances of an emotion and higher cognitive instances in a single theoretical category. It may also be able to accommodate the conceptual analyst's distinction between the causal and intentional objects of emotions. The conceptual analyst's claim is not that fear is always caused by danger, but that it is always directed onto dangers, real or imaginary. Similarly, the ecological theorist does not claim that fear is always produced in response to danger, but that it is the biological function of fear to be produced in response to danger. In malfunctioning organisms, or in abnormal environmental conditions, fear may be tokened in response to something that is not dangerous. This can even happen in a well-functioning organism under normal conditions if the organism has evolved to accept false-positive responses so as to reduce the rate of false negatives. In all these cases it remains true that the occurrence of a fear response has the *function* of meeting a danger. So the ecological theory can make the idea that emotions are type-identified by a particular state of affairs in the external world consistent with the fact that they often occur disassociated from those states of affairs.[1]

Ecological concepts of emotion may also be applicable to the full range of other species to which vernacular emotion concepts are applied. An ecological-level account would ascribe emotion to organisms in whom a response to danger has evolved in parallel to the response in vertebrates. It could ascribe emotion to squid and octopuses for example. The affect program approach would ascribe emotions only to organisms whose psy-

---

1. This approach uses the same resources that Ruth Millikan (1984) used in her attempt at a general account of intentionality.

chology is homologous with our own. Squid and octopuses are excluded. In the last chapter I proposed that the range of application of a term across types of psychological system might be a way to choose between two proposed identifications for a pretheoretic concept. It suggests which level of explanation is most appropriate to the cluster of phenomena that ordinary speakers are trying to capture with the concept. But I also suggested that this criterion will usually be inconclusive, and so it turns out to be in this case. People may agree that an octopus discharges its defensive cloud of black ink "when it is afraid," but the same speakers back off if asked whether the octopus is "really afraid" or if it "experiences emotion." The tendency to disavow these applications or regard them as somehow metaphorical is even stronger in the case of insects and, for some people, artificial intelligences. The application of the concept in its paradigm, human cases, relies on the coincidence of a whole set of features, some at the level of task description, some at lower levels. As some of these features fall away, people become unsure that they are dealing with the same phenomena and unsure whether to apply the concept.

Although ecological concepts of emotion are very broad, they are not as broad as vernacular emotion concepts. The ecological approach will not count disclaimed action emotions as genuine instances of the emotion concepts that are commonly applied to them. In disclaimed actions an individual produces a set of behaviors that fits local cultural expectations in order to obtain some social benefit (see chapter 6). Sometimes these "strategic" behaviors take the form of an emotion. Disclaimed action emotions are distinguished from simple pretenses by the subject's lack of conscious access to their etiology. The ecological approach will not encompass these emotions because it conceives of an emotion as a response to a class of situations with a particular significance for the organism. In the production of a disclaimed action emotion the environment does not have this significance, nor does the person take it to have that significance. A good example is the display of anger as an unconsciously implemented "strategic behavior" in a marital quarrel. The agent has reasoned that they can improve their position by adopting the role of someone who believes themselves wronged. The agent is not simply acting, because although they are motivated by these considerations they are not aware of this motivation. In such a case the agent will behave *as if* they had judged themselves to be wronged. There is all the difference in the world between this and actually believing oneself to have been wronged. So the disclaimed action anger is not a response whose function is to occur to a situation with the ecological significance appropriate to anger. Its function is to convey the false impression that the agent takes the situation to have that significance. The ecological approach will not count this response as an instance of anger.

9.3 The Weakness of the Ecological Approach

My aim in this chapter is to find categories that can be used to answer the question "What *are* emotions?" The ecological approach to emotion seems to have the resources to capture the extension of certain vernacular emotion concepts in the way that the affect program approach does not. But to be a good answer to my question, ecological categories must figure in sound explanations of emotional phenomena. The cladistic affect program approach does much better than the ecological approach in this respect. There are two reasons for this. The first is that the ecological approach can explain psychological facts only at the level of task description. The second is that these explanations have not yet been constructed and there is reason to think they may never be constructed. Furthermore, although ecological categories *might* coincide closely with vernacular categories in the way just described, there is no evidence that they actually will.

The ecological approach can explain psychological properties only at the level of task description because the causal homeostatic mechanism of each ecological category is a particular set of adaptive forces. We can use the ecological category of disgust for explanation and induction because natural selection has imposed the same requirements on all responses designed to prevent the ingestion of noxious substances. But adaptive forces are sensitive only to properties at the level of task description, so properties at the computational and implementation levels are not projectable in psychological categories derived from the ecological level (level of task description). Disgust may be a good category in cognitive ecology, but computational and neurological knowledge about disgust in rats cannot be extrapolated to birds (Garcia and Rusiniak 1980) let alone to octopuses or martians. The same task can be performed in many ways at lower levels of description.

This limitation on the explanatory potential of the ecological approach is a serious one. One of the main objects of psychology is to get behind the behavior of humans and other organisms and discover how this behavior is produced. Many psychological studies are specifically designed to make observations about behavior that cannot be explained by the ecological task description. These observations help determine the possible underlying mechanisms. Typical examples are the relative speed with which different tasks are performed and the characteristic errors made in performing a task. Cladistic emotion categories are ideally suited to psychology's interest in underlying mechanism. If an emotion is narrowly homologous in two organisms, then whatever problem it solves will be solved in the same way in both organisms, by using the computational methods and neural implementation that evolved in their common ancestor. If the two organisms use the homologue for different adaptive purposes, as appears to happen with the "square-mouthed" anger display in humans and chimpanzees, discoveries about the underlying mechanism in the one will still be projectable to the underlying mechanism in the other. If an emotion represents the same adaptive-historical trait in two organisms (so that they evolved it by parallel modifications of shared traits inherited from a common ancestor), then the additional constraints imposed by this common starting point make it more likely that they will solve the same problem in the same way.

The considerations I have outlined suggest a division of labor between the two classifications of emotion. A cladistic classification, like that of the affect program theory, will allow the explanation of the computational and implementation levels of emotion. An ecological classification will allow explanations at the level of task description. If this vision were correct, then vernacular emotion concepts would be essentially ambiguous between two theoretical emotion concepts—the concept of the task that the emotion performs and the concept of the mechanism that performs the task (the ambiguity in psychological concepts familiar to functionalists as the role/occupant distinction). The right answer to the question "What is fear?" would be that in some cases it is a response to danger implemented by an affect program, while in others it is a response to danger implemented we know not how. In the next section I suggest that the prospects for functional classifications of emotion are somewhat worse than this. Not only do they provide no explanation below the level of task description, but their pretensions to provide explanation at that level may be spurious.

9.4 Adaptive and Adaptive-Historical Explanations of Emotion

In chapter 8, I introduced the idea of ecological (adaptive, functional) classification using the idea that evolution is a matter of "genealogical actors in ecological roles" (Hull 1987). Different species may find themselves under similar adaptive pressures and respond by modifying their structures to meet those pressures. The resultant structures are not members of the same cladistic category, but they are members of the same functional category. This suggests that there is a realm of purely functional categories that enter into generalizations about adaptation. These generalizations make up "general ecology"—a theory of organism-environment interaction that applies to a wide range of taxa. I now want to throw doubt on this picture. The functional-ecological categories found in progressive research programs in biology are typically historically constrained, and sound functional explanations are typically also historical ones. This suggests that the general ecological approach to emotion may be a chimera and that any features of emotion which *are* best explained in terms of adaptive convergence should be studied as an extension of the natural historical approach which treats emotions as evolutionary homologies.

One source for the belief that there are purely functional classifications of organisms and traits are the famous cases of "parallel evolution." Mammalian and cephalopod eyes are strikingly similar. These eyes and those of arthropods also have certain analogies. Such striking similarities between parts of organisms in very different lineages can be explained, it is argued, by similarities in the adaptive pressures which produce them.[2] This suggests that eyes, a general category containing all mechanisms for gathering visual information, is a useful ecological category. There is something to this argument, but it falls far short of showing that there is a role in ecology for the pretheoretic concept of eyes. It is hard to believe that mammalian and cephalopod eyes do not perform similar functions (although some authors have suggested that the ciliary muscles of the cephalopod eye, so strikingly similar to those of vertebrates, are not employed for true focusing but to compensate for changes in pressure on the eye at different depths). Even if the cephalopod eye is functionally as well as physically parallel to the vertebrate eye, the same is not true of all eyes. The complex eyes of insects differ substantially in function. They are better at detecting movement and worse at resolving images. Perhaps in ecological terms they play a role closer to the ears of some vertebrates. So the folk category

2. Doubt has recently been thrown on this interpretation by the discovery that both vertebrates and invertebrates construct their eyes using the same ancient genetic modules (Quiring et al 1994).

"eyes" may be too large to correspond to any real ecological category. It may also be too small. A microchiropteran bat's sonar might turn out to have more in common adaptively with a human eye than the bat's eye! What emerges from this example is that parallels like that between mammalian and cephalopod eyes will remain little more than intriguing observations until they are incorporated into a methodologically rigorous scientific ecology. Natural history turns out to resemble human history. It is easy enough to draw striking comparisons between social processes in different periods, in the manner of the great narrative historians like Gibbon and Macaulay. However, few people would be rash enough to infer from this alone that there are robust generalizations to be found concerning social and cultural processes throughout history.

Developments in ecology in the 1950s and 1960s held out the promise of rigorous general ecological principles, but this promise has not been borne out. A gap has consistently existed between the abstract models developed as the basis of a general ecology and knowledge about actual ecological systems. The abstract models do not adequately characterize the dynamics of actual systems.[3] A parallel with the study of human societies is again illuminating. Philosophers have become highly skeptical of the existence of laws governing social processes. They no longer expect history to unfold in a predictable manner. The phase in ecology which has been called "the eclipse of history" offered this sort of law-governed vision of *natural* history (Kingsland 1985; Brooks and MacLennan 1991). There is just as much reason to be skeptical. Recent work in ecology has paid much greater attention to the history of particular ecological communities and its influence of their fate.

I am skeptical that substantial ecological generalizations ranging across widely different taxa will be forthcoming. This does not mean abandoning the idea that similar adaptive pressures sometimes give rise to similar traits. Whales have flukes, penguins have flippers, and fishes have forked tails because of the need for an extended surface to impinge on a

---

3. Connor and Simberloff 1979; Simberloff and Connor 1981; Simberloff 1980a and 1980b, 1983. The fact that the difficult stage in developing a biological theory is usually in establishing a correspondence between the dynamics of a model system and that of an actual system is one reason why the "semantic view" of theories seems particularly applicable to biology (Lloyd 1988). On the semantic view, theories are primarily definitions of a class of abstract models and only secondarily about actual systems in nature.

liquid medium. But the parallel response is not explained by the ecological pressures alone. It is not true that "locomotion in water requires a certain structure" (Lewontin 1978, 124). The cephalopods—the many species of squid, octopuses, and nautiluses—manage quite happily with jet propulsion. An alternative generalization that finds real support from the data is that *vertebrate* locomotion in water produces a certain structure. This is a historically constrained generalization, because it applies only within one clade. Opting for a historically constrained ecology does not collapse ecological categories into cladistic ones; it creates adaptive-historical categories. These historically constrained ecological categories are paraphyletic, containing some but not all tokens of a homologous trait. This is because membership in the relevant cladistic category is a necessary but not a sufficient condition for membership of the ecological category.

I argued for the need to "historicize" adaptive explanations in chapter 3 and again in chapter 5. I showed that the fundamental flaw of adaptive or ecological theories of emotion is that they assume the existence of adaptive generalizations which are insensitive to local conditions. These ecological generalizations state that any trait which can perform some function F will enhance an organism's fitness. This allows the ecological theorist to predict which traits will be found in nature merely by reflecting on which would be the most fit. But there are unlikely to be many of these generalizations. One of the arguments I used to support this claim in chapter 3 was that the outcomes of selection processes are affected by the availability and order of occurrence of variant forms and by purely stochastic factors. This militates against the idea that a set of alternative traits isolated from any particular historical process of competition can be ordered in terms of their fitness. This argument can be enriched by the insight that the sorts of variants that are thrown up in the face of an adaptive problem will be systematically related to the lineage of the species that faces the problem. The solution that finally emerges is a function of the resources the lineage brings with it, as well as the situation in which the lineage finds itself.

The ecological approach suggests that organisms face certain general adaptive problems. Emotions should be classified by which of these problems they solve. Fear solves the problem of confronting dangers. Anger solves the problem of conspecific threat. The causal homeostatic mechanism of each emotion category is the set of adaptive forces which have shaped that emotion. We can use fear as a category for explanation and induction, at least at the level of task description, because natural selection has made all fear responses similar. The considerations reviewed in the this section and the more general discussions of adaptationism in chapters 3 and 5 make this seem like a very optimistic research program. The proposed causal homeostatic mechanism is unlikely to explain the properties of emotions even at the level of task description.

It seems particularly unlikely that general ecological principles will explain anything about the expressions of emotion. Darwin established a characteristic pattern of explanation for emotional expressions which is clearly adaptive-historical in form. Many of the communicative elements of emotional responses are arbitrary. Their form is not intrinsically suited to their function. There is no reason why a human being should use one facial expression to convey a particular signal rather than another. They can be understood only as the result of successive modifications of a single structure through a number of different adaptive phases. The response of the lineage to each phase was not predictable unless the particular resources it brought to the problem were taken into consideration. Tooth baring and piloerection would not have their current communicative function if it had not been for the earlier agonistic functions of which they are vestiges. The details of the emotional expressions make sense only in the light of their history.

The role of history is also apparent in current hypotheses about the evolution of the general properties of emotions. The affect program theory explained the "passivity" of emotions in terms of modular information processing. The existence of these information processing arrangements is hypothesized to be the result of incorporating into a highly flexible and intelligent cognitive mechanism an existing, less intelligent apparatus for responding to certain critical classes of event. A purely ecological approach cannot appeal to history in this way, since it classifies emotions in terms of the adaptive forces that would operate on any lineage of organisms. A purely ecological explanation of passivity would have to take the form of an optimality model suggesting that there is a general selective pressure for responses to critical classes of ecological stimuli to become isolated from long-term, planned action. The passivity of emotion could then be explained as a response to this adaptive pressure. The reflections on adaptationism in chapters 3 and 5 show where such an approach would lead. An optimality argument of the kind just outlined could undoubtedly be constructed. Robert Frank's work is an attempt to construct just such an optimality model for certain social emotions. But it would be equally possible to construct a model favoring the opposite conclusion. The two models would differ in their assumptions about the historical conditions in which the emotions evolved and about the sorts of alternatives available at various points in evolution. To test either story it would be necessary to independently confirm these historical assumptions by the use of the comparative method. The resulting adaptive-historical explanation would be restricted in its application to the clade whose history was used to construct it. In order to become testable the purely ecological explanation would have been transformed into an adaptive-historical one.

We do not yet have a general theory of the relationship between organism and environment ("general" meaning that it applies to diverse lineages of organisms). The historical nature of the evolutionary process may mean that no such theory is possible. We do, however, have a sophisticated practice for determining evolutionary relationships (homologies). We know that this system of classification reflects the actual process which accounts for the diversity of life and the clustering of individuals into groups with shared features. This is as true of features at the level of task description as of features at the computational or implementation levels. To attempt to develop a science of emotion using general ecological categories instead of categories of homology would be to choose a set of categories with a poorly understood and possibly very weak causal homeostatic mechanism over a set of categories whose causal homeostatic mechanism approaches the traditional ideal of a natural kind. I showed in chapter 3 that in practice the ecological approach to emotion simply accepts the vernacular emotion categories we have and constructs speculative evolutionary scenarios on the assumption that each category has a specific ecological function. The affect program theory and some of the best work in evolutionary psychology show that we can do better than this by taking a historical, phylogenetic perspective on emotion.

I set out to answer the question of what surprise, anger, fear, joy, sadness, and disgust really are. We know that some instances of these emotions are the affect programs. This explains the properties of those instances at all three levels of psychological explanation. It may be that there is a general ecological theory which explains certain properties at the level of task description which are common to all instances of these vernacular emotion concepts. Such a theory would create an emotion category which would apply equally to the affect program instances of these emotions, to higher cognitive instances, and to instances of these emotions in minds that evolved independently of ours. However, we do not yet have such a theory, and the assumption that it would back up our current folk-psychological scheme of classification is entirely speculative. At present we should say that we do not know what the other instances of these emotions are, nor if they are in any real sense the same emotions as those instances that we do understand. If this situation continues for a long period of time psychologists may come to accept the identification of these vernacular emotions with the affect programs.

9.5 Eliminating "Emotion"

Although I have argued that some emotions are affect programs, I do not believe that the category of emotion in general should be identified with the category of affect program phenomena. Some of the work of affect program theorists shows what it would be like to make such an identification. Ekman, Friesen, and Simons (1985) ask whether the well-known startle reaction is an emotional response. They argue that it is not, because various aspects of its performance are too reflexlike. This suggests that the information-processing arrangements underlying startle are not of the same sort as those underlying the affect programs. This discussion can be understood on the causal homeostatic model. Startle does not have the same underlying nature as the other affect programs. Extending the concept of an affect program state to cover it would not be a positive step in theory construction since findings about startle may not be true of the affect program states and vice versa. So if the category of emotion is to be identified with the category of the affect programs, startle is not an emotion. The identification of emotion in general with affect program states would exclude a lot of what is currently regarded as emotion from the revised category. Many vernacular emotions would be excluded for reasons very much like those which caused Ekman and his collaborators to exclude startle. Rather than arguing that responses are too reflexlike, it would be argued that they are too flexible, too well integrated with long-term, planned action, and so forth. The extension of the emotion concept would be restricted to short-term, stereotyped responses, triggered by modular subsystems operating on a limited database.

I do not believe that we should identify emotion in general with the affect programs and make the subsequent conceptual revisions. This would not be an adequate answer to the question "What *is* emotion in general?" What is to be explained about emotional phenomena in general is the way in which they contrast to other cognitive processes. The phenomena referred to as the "passivity" of emotion are central to this contrast. I am not convinced that all instances of the passivity phenomena can be explained by the modularity of affect programs. I suggested in chapter 5 that a form of passivity may characterize some emotional responses controlled by higher cognition. These responses are *irruptive* motivations: motivations not derived from more general goals by means-end reasoning. This class of states has as good a claim to be the referent of the general concept of emotion as the class of affect program states.

The refusal to identify emotion in general with affect program phenomena leads to a form of elimination of the general concept of emotion. I argue in the next section that the vernacular concept of emotion was introduced because certain mental states appeared to have a cluster of features (passivity playing a central role in defining this cluster). The introduction of a kind term means the postulation of a causal homeostatic mechanism underlying the cluster of observed features. But it turns out that this feature cluster is explained by a different causal homeostatic mechanism in different instances. This produces a situation of "partial reference." Identifying either of the two new theoretical categories as the referent of the vernacular concept is equally justified and equally unjustified. Retaining the vernacular concept is not an option, at least for the purposes of induction and explanation, because there is now no epistemic warrant for supposing that discoveries about some emotions will extend to all other emotions. That is why no one expects discoveries about the fear affect program to apply to responses to danger mediated by higher cognition. In the light of these findings, the category of emotion will have to be replaced by at least two more specific categories.

9.6 Origins of the Vernacular Concept of Emotion

One of the problems of the old propositional attitude theory of emotion was that it made a mystery of the fact that ordinary people draw a strong distinction between the emotions and propositional attitudes like belief, desire, and intention (Schaffer 1983). The contrast between emotion and the thoughts that motivate our "cool" actions is a central element in the vernacular conception of emotion. Emotions are conceived as relatively unintegrated, irruptive sources of motivation. The existence of the affect programs goes some way towards explaining the presence of this element in our attempts at self-understanding. The affect program phenomena are a standing example of the emotional or passionate. They are sources of motivation not integrated into the system of beliefs and desires. The characteristic properties of the affect program states, their informational encapsulation and their involuntary triggering, necessitate the introduction of a concept of mental state separate from the concepts of belief and desire. If some of the work reviewed in chapter 5 is correct, there is another class of psychological states that constitutes a standing example of the emotional or passionate. These are the higher cognitive emotions. Frank's work suggests that these take the form of irruptive motivations. These motivations are not derived from standing general goals by means-end reasoning. They occur in response to certain immediate circumstances. Because they occur independently of the general derivation of means to ends, they frequently disrupt longer-term plans. Loyalty leads people to keep an agreement at great cost. People are driven to revenge themselves even when it is disastrous for them to do so. Frank argues that these emotions help to solve the "commitment problem." They allow people to adopt strategies that require them to be committed to act against their own interests should certain circumstances arise. If correct, Frank's ideas would help to explain the traditionally negative image of many emotions. The advantages of these dispositions come from being conditionally committed to them, not from their actual implementation. Actually *having* such an emotion can be disastrous! The anecdotal evidence for these sorts of motivations is presumably what caused philosophers like Nash (1989) to propose that emotions are irruptive motivational complexes. Frank has added to this anecdotal evidence some game-theoretic models of the commitment problem and some psychological experiments confirming (to a certain extent) the existence of the irruptive motivations predicted by these models.

The vernacular concept of emotion is an attempt to mark out a category of psychological states which produce behavior not integrated into long-term, planned action. The paradigm instances of this concept are the affect programs and the higher cognitive emotions. This emotion concept is constructed within the framework of folk psychology. Because of the basic structure of folk psychology, emotions are conceptualized in representational terms. There has been much discussion of the structure of folk psychology, but it is widely agreed that folk psychology explains actions in terms of the interaction of beliefs and desires. It ascribes these representational states to people and uses something akin to decision theory to derive predictions about how people will act. The fact that the vernacular emotion concept uses folk-psychological notions of representation explains some of the problems of the propositional attitude theory. The ordinary folk think of affect program responses as directed onto states of affairs in the world. This leads the conceptual analyst to claim that in order to have an emotion one must have thoughts about the object of the emotion. But in their everyday dealings with one another, the ordinary folk cope readily enough with the idea of inconsistent thoughts. They may even use something like Stocker's (1987) notion of an "emotionally held thought"—a representation available for one purpose rather than another. Ordinary folk have no difficulty thinking about situations where a person's cool evaluation of a situation differs from their emotional response. The philosophical propositional attitude theory, however, has lost this flexibility and finds these phenomena hard to cope with.

Many problems in the philosophy of mind have been occasioned by the loss of this flexibility in our thought about mental contents. It has been lost during the process of formalizing the pretheoretic practice of explaining actions by citing representational states into "belief-desire action rationalization." According to this picture of mental causation, a single stock of beliefs combines with a single stock of goals in accordance with a set of logical principles modeled on formal decision theory. Classical logic makes it natural to impose consistency under at least simple deductive operations on both the beliefs and the goals. After this process of idealization it becomes much harder to handle inconsistent thoughts or the use of different information to control different processes. The earliest example of this loss of flexibility in our thought about mental causation may well be Aristotle! His theory of "practical reasoning" was a formalized model of action explanation in which the "practical syllogism" played the role now assigned to decision theory. This model created a philosophical problem from the everyday phenomena of "weakness of will" in which a person is unable to act on their moral or prudential beliefs. The notion of modularity allows us to reintroduce the explanatory resources we have lost. It allows representations to be stored in different parts of the mind for different purposes and specialized principles of reasoning to be used for particular problem domains.

I have argued that the vernacular concept of emotion groups together all states which produce passivity. Affect programs and the less well understood higher cognitive emotions are grouped together under the concept of emotion simply because both produce a form of passivity. Folk psychology models both types of emotion as representational states, but it retains the necessary flexibility to cope with the conflicts that can arise between one of these representational states and the other. The fact that disclaimed action emotions are also grouped under the same heading of "emotion" is easily explained. These responses are socially constructed *emotions* for the same reason that "the vapors" was a socially constructed *illness*. The constructed state is an imitation of the original. Disclaimed action emotions are modeled on the local cultures' conception of emotions. They aim to take advantage of the special status that emotions are accorded because of their passivity. Like socially constructed illnesses, disclaimed action emotions are actually very different from the phenomena on which they are modeled. At a psychological level, far from being disruptive of longer-term goals, they are "strategic" devices for the achievement of those goals. Rather than involving isolated modules, or special adaptations of higher-level cognition, they are manifestations of the central purpose of higher cognitive activity—the understanding and manipulation of social relations.

9.7 Why Not Define Emotion as "Irruptive Motivational State"?

The general category of emotion subsumes three different kinds of psychological state. The best understood of these are the affect programs. The second, more speculative kind are irruptive motivational complexes in higher cognition. The third kind are disclaimed actions modeled on emotion. The disclaimed action emotions cannot be placed in a single category with the other emotions because they are essentially pretenses. It would be like putting ghost possession in the category of parasitic diseases. Averill and Boothroyd (1977) suggest that "falling in love" is the adoption of a social role which licenses the performance of certain behaviors. If so, then just as there are no ghosts to explain ghost possession, there is no state of love to explain love behavior. This would account for the particularly unsatisfactory nature of conceptual analyses of love (e.g., Newton-Smith 1973).

Excluding disclaimed action emotions from the category of emotion is no threat to the retention of that category as a natural kind. A normal first reaction to the social constructionist approach is that it reveals that people are often only pretending to have emotions. This sort of conceptual revision seems quite congenial. We normally exclude "fakes" from the extension of our concepts even when the fakes are in a majority (as with the concept "paintings by Vermeer"). If disclaimed action emotions can be excluded from the extension of the vernacular emotion concept, then perhaps that concept can be saved. The obvious way to do this is by defining emotions in terms of the common properties of affect programs and the postulated higher cognitive emotions. This suggests that emotion might be defined in terms of the phenomena of passivity. Emotions are irruptive motivational states of whatever kind. They are states which interfere with the smooth unfolding of plans designed to secure our long-term goals.

But this proposal is inconsistent with the fundamental theoretical perspective that I have adopted in this book. I have argued that emotion is a putative psychological category of motivational states that exhibit passivity. The extension of a concept is determined by our best current theory of the causal homeostatic mechanism that guarantees the projectability of the category to which it refers. Concepts behave like this, at least in the sciences, because they are tools to further explanation and induction. If there is no such mechanism, then the concept fails to refer to a natural kind and should be discarded for the purposes of explanation and induction. Ekman excludes startle from the category of affect programs because he believes that the psychological mechanisms underlying it are not of the same kind as those underlying the affect programs. The same reasoning would lead us to refuse to put the higher cognitive emotions in the same category as the affect programs. Whatever psychological mechanism underlies the irruption of these clusters of desires into belief-desire causation, it is not the same mechanism that allows the affect programs to rapidly engage various effector systems without reference to consciously accessible beliefs and desires. It might be suggested that there is some common ecological function served by all passive mental states, so that emotion is a natural kind at the ecological level, but this is not plausible. Current hypotheses about the functions of different emotions point in exactly the opposite direction. The affect program emotions are passive to provide rapid, fail-safe responses to stimuli correlated with basic survival needs. The higher cognitive emotions are hypothesized to be passive as a solution to the commitment problem. So the two do not serve the same functions. It is even arguable that the two are not "passive" or "irruptive" in the same sense.

The research surveyed in this book suggests that the general concept of emotion has no role in any future psychology. It needs to be replaced by at least two more specific concepts. This does not necessarily imply that the emotion concept will disappear from everyday thought. Vernacular concepts are involved in a whole range of nonepistemic projects. Concepts like "spirituality" have no role in psychology but play an important role in other human social activities. But as far as understanding ourselves is concerned the concept of emotion, like the concept of spirituality, can only be a hindrance.

10

Coda—Mood and Emotion

10.1 Moods and Higher-Order Dispositions

My aim in this chapter is to construct a theory of moods to complement the account of emotions developed above. Prototypical moods include depression, elation, and anxiety. In accordance with the overall aims of the book I seek a theoretical concept which explains enough about the prototypical moods to be identified with the concept of mood. My approach will be very general, and I will say little about individual moods. I make some suggestions about the vernacular conception of mood and outline a theoretical conception of mood that preserves much of this vernacular conception. The theoretical concept I outline characterizes moods at the computational level. I argue that it is consistent with and suggestive of the neuroscience of mood. This allows me to argue for the superiority of this account to other computational level accounts of mood on the grounds that it is more likely to be psychologically realistic. However, it also creates a rival kind of phenomenon at a lower explanatory level with which mood might be identified. Mood turns out to partially refer to both these theoretical categories.

Moods are needed in folk-psychological explanation because the basic explanatory schemes of folk theories of mind don't always apply straightforwardly. People have a general conception of the behavior that should result when someone fulfills an important goal. A student who wins a prestigious scholarship to graduate school should experience positive emotions. But sometimes these expectations are not fulfilled. Such variations in response between persons, or between the same person at different times, can be explained piecemeal by changing attributions of mental state. The student's failure to experience positive emotions could be explained by changing the claim that they desired the scholarship. But the requisite changes are often implausible. Furthermore, these deviations from the expected outcome occur not haphazardly, but in broad patterns which can be incorporated into the folk theory of mind. So instead of altering individual mental states, the folk psychologist responds to the discrepancy by attributing a new, more general kind of mental state. The successful person did not enjoy their success because they were *depressed*. In folk psychology, ascribing moods serves to account for systematic deviations from a central model of mental activity. Mood attributions systematically alter the transition probabilities between stimuli and mental states, and between one mental state and another (Adam Morton's 1980 analysis of mood concepts reaches similar conclusions).

The concept of a higher-order disposition was introduced by C. D. Broad (1933). Familiar dispositions like a magnet's disposition to attract iron are first-order dispositions. Second-order dispositions are properties like magnetizability—the disposition to acquire the first-order disposition of being magnetic. There is no reason to stop at two levels. Broad himself proposed that the upper limit on hierarchies of dispositions comes with a "supreme disposition." This is a property of a substance which it could not lose without ceasing to be that substance.

Broad's ideas were noticed by the psychologist Vincent Nowlis (1963), who suggested that moods are higher-order dispositions and emotions lower-order dispositions. Moods are dispositions to have emotions. He also suggested that a third order of dispositions in the same hierarchy might be called states of temperament. A temperamental trait like irascibility is the state of being markedly disposed to be in an angry mood. An angry mood is a disposition to get angry easily. Anger itself is a disposition to all sorts of behaviors and mental state changes. To take another example, being a depressive is possessing a marked disposition to become depressed. Becoming depressed would be an alteration in dispositions to have such emotions as joy and sadness. Although I think Nowlis's approach is promising, the theory that emotions, moods, and traits form a hierarchy of dispositions is inadequate in at least four ways:

1. It fails to allow for the direct influence of moods on behavior. There seems to be no prima facie reason to deny that a person's mood can affect the aggressiveness with which they perform mundane tasks, or their facial expression, without the interposition of some occurrent emotional state

such as anger. An adequate model should allow direct connections from moods to behavior.

2. Moods don't just dispose to emotions which are somehow conceptually appropriate, as when depression disposes to sadness. The known consequences of depression are wide ranging and include states such as anger and abnormal sexual excitation. An adequate model should allow for these connections.

3. There is little reason to suppose that all emotions, moods, and traits come neatly packaged in matching sets of three. This assumption should be avoided.

4. It is at least plausible that emotions may be the causes of moods. A person may be put into a bad mood by having been angry or into a good mood by a pleasant surprise. This is not possible on the traditional model of higher-order dispositions. On that model it is a necessary condition of possessing any contingent, n-order disposition D_n that the bearer already possess $D_n + 1$ (the disposition to have D_n). Lower-order dispositions cannot be involved in the production of higher-order dispositions, since those higher-order dispositions must already be in existence.

A first step to resolving these problems is to recognize that moods are complex functional states, not simple dispositions like fragility. The idea of a higher-order disposition must be replaced by the idea of a higher-order functional state.[1] Suppose a single system can realize any of a number of functional descriptions $F_1, \ldots, F_n$ at different times. Its response to a given input depends on which description it is currently realizing. Suppose further that the system realizes another functional description which relates certain prior inputs to which of $F_1, \ldots, Fn$ the system realizes at any one time. This situation provides the basis for a hierarchy of functional states (although I show below that more is required to justify using the notion of a hierarchy). Consider by way of example the computer on which I'm writing this passage. When I set up for the day, the computer realizes a functional description. When I provide a certain input, the output is the computer realizing one of a range of functional description—a word processor, a spreadsheet, or a database. In other words, one of the most convenient ways to describe the overall system is as a hierarchy of smaller sys

---

1. *Orders* of functional states should not be confused with the *levels* of functional state that I have discussed throughout the book.

tems. Similarly, a person is capable of realizing a number of functional descriptions. One such description, or more likely a set of them, is the normal functional model of persons. The normal character of an individual is an approximation to one of these descriptions. The alternative model of a person who is known to be depressed is a significant deviation from the normal model(s). An overall understanding of persons involves a number of functional models nested within a higher level model. That higher level model is the theory of moods. This theory relates various kinds of inputs to outputs consisting of the person's fulfilling one of the various first level functional descriptions within their overall capacity. This conception of moods avoids some of the problems just enumerated:

1. Moods can now cause new patterns of behavior immediately, as well as via the mediation of emotions. A change of mood alters the overall functional description of a person and as part of this it may directly bring it about that under certain circumstances patterns of behavior characteristic of that mood will arise.

2. Higher-order states don't cause a single "conceptually appropriate" lower-order state, as when depression causes sadness. The model will allow a diverse range of effects to follow from someone becoming depressed. It might cause anger as well as sadness.

3. There is no need to conceive of the emotion-mood-trait system as consisting of discrete hierarchies with an appropriate state at each level. The notion of a discrete hierarchy of states has no place in the model, which consists of a single hierarchy of overall functional descriptions.[2]

The fourth objection still seems pressing, although in a slightly altered way. The new model does not exclude the possibility that lower-order states could be involved in the production of higher-order states. Take the simple computer analogy. There is an input to the word-processing program that takes the machine back to the original operating system state. But if this is the case, what are the criteria for higher-orderedness? Why are mood states of a higher order than emotions? This problem should not be tackled by trying to introduce something to prevent lower-order states

---

2. The model I shall discuss here uses overall functional descriptions of the person for simplicity's sake. If the mind is modular in character, a more correct picture may confine the hierarchical structure to a model of certain subsystems.

from being involved in the production of higher-order states. The original idea that lower-order dispositions can't be involved in producing higher-order dispositions was itself simply confused. Broad failed to distinguish dispositions from mere *abilities*. An ability is a vague dispositional state where the eliciting conditions are left unspecified. Broad can be sure that a disposition bearer which bears D_n also bears $D_n + 1$ because his $D_n + 1$ is the property of being *able* to bear D_n. Real higher-order *dispositions* to have D_n, as opposed to mere abilities, are dispositions to produce D_n under some specific eliciting condition C. There may be many of these corresponding to a given D_n, each relating Dn to a different condition C. It follows from this that a lower-order disposition *can* be involved in producing a higher-order disposition to have that lower-order disposition. A simple distinction between type and token identity for instances of dispositions shows that a lower-order disposition can even produce the exact higher-order disposition which was involved in its own production. All that is required for this to occur is that the higher-order disposition go out of existence after producing the lower-order one and be brought back into existence by the lower-order disposition in association with some eliciting condition.

This clarification of the relationship between dispositions of different orders might seem to suggest that the whole idea of orders of dispositions or functional states is a mistake. It seems that there is simply a network of related dispositional properties. The correct conclusion, however, is that classifying states as higher- or lower-order is a pragmatic device for theory construction, rather than reflecting a genuine ontological asymmetry between different dispositional states. A dispositional or functional property D^* is one order higher than property D if two conditions hold. First, D^* must be a disposition to have D under some eliciting conditions C. There is nothing to prevent this situation obtaining symmetrically between D and D^*. Second, the relationships between these and other dispositions can be conveniently represented by a hierarchical structure in which D^* stands above a range of states including D. It is this pragmatic element that gives the direction of the hierarchy. Returning to the computer analogy, the machine's capacities could be represented by a nonhierarchical functional description like a Turing machine table. However, the fact that there is a state S from which the machine can easily be put into a number of states suited to the performance of particular tasks makes it convenient to use a hierarchical description of its functional capacities.

I suggest that moods are states with certain highly salient properties for the purposes of psychological theory at the computational level. They cause global changes in propensities to occupy other states and to respond to stimuli. The salience of these effects gives utility to a model in which moods are higher-order states which determine which of a range of lower-order functional descriptions the person occupies. This theoretical conception of moods is quite close to the vernacular conception. So if it turns out to be a useful psychological theory, its concept of a higher-order functional state may serve to clarify the vernacular concept of mood.

10.2 Implementing the Hierarchical Model

As well as being close to the pretheoretic conception of mood the hierarchical concept mirrors the neural realization of mood phenomena. While it would be possible to construct computational models of the mood system that use only a single functional level, the hierarchical theory is more psychologically realistic. I take this to be a matter of some importance. Although philosophical psychology may sometimes be interested in a maximally general characterization of the mental, scientific psychology aims to describe the minds of human beings and other particular organisms. It is this goal that rules out, for example, theories of the mind that call for more computational steps than a biological system could carry out in real time. Knowledge of the physical implementation of the system constrains the computational theory of the system. These constraints on theories at the computational level can be expressed in terms of a distinction between "weak" and "strong" realization at the implementation level. A computational model is weakly realized in a particular system if it gives an adequate input-output description of that system. Any adequate functional description of a system is weakly realized by that system. A computational model is *strongly* realized in a particular system at some lower level L_n if there is an independently motivated taxonomy of that system at level L_n which maps the structure of the functional model. It is necessary that the taxonomy at L_n be independently motivated, as it will always be possible to gerrymander a taxonomy at L_n that allows such a mapping to be constructed. An independently motivated taxonomy is one that is constructed without the guidance of the higher level model that we are seeking to map. Instead, it should emerge naturally from a search for explanatory categories at level L_n. A neurological account of the brain is presumably independently motivated. If such an account produces a taxonomy which is isomorphic to the internal structure of a computational model, then that computational model is strongly realized at the neural level. Most scientific psychology is interested in computational-level models which are strongly realized in actual organisms.

There are a number of pieces of research which suggest that moods are chemical states of the central nervous system which affect the probability that neural state transitions will take place. The hierarchical models of mood that I have described would thus be strongly realized at the neural level. This evidence fits especially neatly with the localization of the affect programs in the limbic system. Although I take the coincidence of these two groups of results to be a point in favor of a hierarchical theory of moods, I don't want to suggest that the theory is restricted to the sort of emotional phenomena covered by the affect program account. The affect program states are better understood than other affective phenomena. This makes it possible to relate them to other areas of neural research in a way which, though speculative, is reasonably well grounded. The fact that other emotional phenomena can't be related as closely reflects ignorance about their implementation rather than any lack of connection.

The classic work on the neurological basis of mood phenomena has concentrated on depression, since this is a state of particular clinical interest. Much of this research has been a result of the famous "catecholamine hypothesis" (Schildkraut 1965, 1970, 1974). The catecholamine hypothesis concerns the neurotransmitters norepinephrine, dopamine, and serotonin. The connection with the work on emotion reviewed in chapter 4 is that neurons in the limbic system are specialized to these transmitters, concentrations of norepinephrine being at their highest in hypothalamus. Under certain circumstances, drugs which decrease levels of these neurotransmitters, thus reducing the facility of synaptic transmission in the neurons that utilize them, appear to induce depression. Others, including cocaine, which inhibit the removal of these transmitters after their release, appear to produce euphoria or to relieve depression. The catecholamine hypothesis suggests that depression is produced by neurotransmitter deficit and, more tentatively, that mania is produced by oversupply. Although this simple hypothesis has led to a large body of interesting results, it is now generally recognized to be inadequate to the data available (Baldessarini 1975). Even workers most skeptical of the simple hypothesis, however, maintain that changes involving these neurotransmitters play a key role in mood phenomena. A direct connection between work on the affect programs and these neurotransmitters is proposed by Panksepp (1982). As discussed in chapter 4, Panksepp has tried to map the circuits responsible for affect program responses in the limbic system. He proposes that "biogenic amines that are widely dispersed throughout the brain may provide nonspecific excitatory and inhibitory control over emotive command circuits" (419). Panksepp is thinking in particular of serotonin and norepinephrine. Increased availability of these transmitters may, he thinks, have a respectively inhibitory and excitatory effect on the whole affect program system. Other neurotransmitters, acetylcholine and dopamine, are linked to particular affect programs in Panksepp's list. Another aspect of neurochemical research on depression is work on neural electrolytes. Sodium ions play a central role in neural functioning, and depression is associated with the importation of sodium into cells throughout the body. Lithium, an ion importantly similar to sodium, has long been recognized as an effective therapeutic tool in treating affective disorders. Moods are thus once again linked to broadly diffused effects on synaptic transmission. Finally, there is a body of work on the endocrine system. Suggestive results were obtained by E. J. Sachar (1970, 1975). He replicated the well known result that certain groups of depressives hypersecrete cortisol and suggested that this may be linked to the neurotransmitter effects just cited. Neural tracts dependent on those transmitters are known to be involved in cortisol production, and depletion of the transmitter norepinephrine in animals can stimulate the endocrine pathway involved in cortisol production. These links to the endocrine system are particularly interesting because of the importance of endocrine gland malfunction in long-term personality disorders.

Results such as these make it plausible to suggest that moods are neurochemical states, which act to modify the activity of broad areas of the central nervous system. If this is how the neuroscientific picture turns out, then their action would be precisely to modify the probability of transitions between a given input, internal states, and output. Very simply, suppose that under certain conditions, the presentation of a spider has a high probability of triggering the fear affect program. The effect of depression would be to inhibit the depolarization of neurons in the pathway subserving that response and thus to alter the transition probability between the presentation and the fear response.

The implementation level description of moods explains why moods function like higher-order states. Emotions are implemented by neural states. A mood state is a neurochemical condition which modifies the propensities of one neural event to bring about another. It thus alters the functional description realized by the affect-program system. Its effects may be diffuse, affecting the whole system, or specific, affecting the various emotional responses differently. In addition to its effects on the affect program system in the limbic brain, the same chemical condition may affect higher areas of the brain and thus affect emotional phenomena involving higher cognition and higher cognitive phenomena generally. It may also have direct physiological and behavioral effects. Given this physiological picture, the sort of hierarchical model I have suggested at the computational level will directly mirror the causal structure of the brain.

I have suggested that mood phenomena correspond to genuine explanatory kinds at two levels. At the computational level, they can be identified with higher-order functional states. At the implementation level they can be identified with global neurochemical conditions. Either theoretical concept might be identified with the general vernacular concept of mood. Particular vernacular moods might be identified either with particular higher-order functional states or with particular neurochemical conditions. Different theoretical interests pull in different directions, as they did with the emotions in chapter 9. In the case of the affect program emotions I was able to appeal to theoretical considerations to choose between two candidate identities. The cladistic concepts were embedded in a sounder inductive and explanatory project than the ecological concepts. They also explained more of the relevant features of those emotions. So I was able to reject the ecological concepts because of doubts about the soundness and richness of the explanatory project in which they are embedded. But those putative ecological kinds were located at the level of task description (ecological level). The two competing kinds in this case are located at the computational level and the implementation level. Both will correspond to cladistic categories in psychobiology. Both should have adaptive historical explanations. I suspect that mood closely resembles pain in the respects discussed by Daniel Dennett (1978). The vernacular concept postulates a single causal homeostatic mechanism underlying a cluster of features including both behavioral profile and introspective quality. In humans and their close relatives the entire feature set is highly correlated. However, the behavioral profile is explained by a computational-level category while the introspective quality is explained by an implementational-level category. There is no reason to suppose that the two categories need be coextensive in every system that fulfills the same task description as a member of *Homo sapiens*. In other living organisms higher-order functional states will probably also be realized by neurochemical states, but the same states need not be realized by the same neurochemistry. Artificial intelligence may suggest quite other realizations for higher-order functional states, bringing to our attention the independence of the two levels of description. Mood is another case of "partial reference" caused by the multiplicity of explanatory levels in the life sciences.

References

Amundson, R., and G. V. Lauder. 1994. Function without purpose: The uses of causal role function in evolutionary biology. *Biology and Philosophy* 9(4):443–70.

Armon-Jones, C. 1986a. The thesis of constructionism. In Harré 1986.

———. 1986b. The social functions of emotion. In Harré 1986.

Armstrong, D. M. 1980. *The Nature of Mind and Other Essays*. Queensland: University of Queensland Press.

Armstrong, S., L. Gleitman, and H. Gleitman. 1983. What some concepts might not be. *Cognition* 13:263–308.

Atran, S. 1990. *Cognitive Foundations of Natural History*. Cambridge: Cambridge University Press.

Averill, J. R. 1980a. A constructivist view of emotion. In Plutchik and Kellerman 1980.

———. 1980b. Emotion and anxiety: sociocultural, biological, and psychological determinants. In Rorty 1980.

Averill, J. R., and R. Boothroyd. 1977. On falling in love in conformance with the romantic ideal. *Motivation and Emotion* 1:235–47.

Averill, J. R., E. M. Opton, and R. S. Lazarus. 1969. Cross-cultural studies of psychophysiological responses during stress and emotion. *International Journal of Psychology* 4:88–102.

Ax, A. F. 1953. The physiological differentiation between fear and anger in humans. *Psychosomatic Medicine* 15(5):433–42.

Baldessarini, R. J. 1975. An overview of the basis for the amine hypothesis in affective illness. In Mendels 1975.

Barkow, J. H., L. Cosmides, and J. Tooby, eds. 1992. *The Adapted Mind: Evolutionary Psychology and the Generation of Culture*. Oxford: Oxford University Press.

Basolo, A. L. 1990. Female preference predates the evolution of the sword in sword-tailed fish. *Science* 250:808–10.

Bateson, P. 1991. Are there principles of behavioural development? In *The Development and Integration of Behaviour*, ed. P. Bateson. Cambridge: Cambridge University Press.

References

————. 1994. The dynamics of parent-offspring relationships in mammals. *TREE* 9(10):399–402.

Bekoff, M., and D. Jamieson. 1990. Cognitive ethology and applied philosophy. *TREE* 5:156–59.

Ben-Zeev, A. 1987. The nature of emotions. *Philosophical Studies* 52:393–409.

————. 1990. Envy and jealousy. *Canadian Journal of Philosophy* 20(4): 487–516.

————. 1992. Anger and hate. *Journal of Social Philosophy* 23.

Berlin, B. 1992. *Ethnobiological Classification.* Princeton, N. J.: Princeton University Press.

Birdwhistell, R. L. 1963. Kinesic level in investigations of the emotions. In *Expression of the Emotions in Man,* ed. P. H. Knapp. New York: International Universities Press.

Boyd, R. 1989. What realism implies and what it does not. *Dialectica* 43(1–2):5–29.

————. 1991. Realism, anti-foundationalism, and the enthusiasm for natural kinds. *Philosophical Studies* 61:127–48.

Brandon, R., and J. Beatty. 1984. The propensity interpretation of "fitness": No interpretation is no substitute. *Philosophy of Science.* 51: 342–47.

Broad, C. D. 1933. *Examination of McTaggart's Philosophy.* Cambridge: Cambridge University Press.

Brooks, D. R., and D. A. McLennan. 1991. *Phylogeny, Ecology, and Behavior.* Chicago: University of Chicago Press.

Cannon, W. D. 1927. The James-Lange theory of emotions: A critical examination and an alternative theory. *American Journal of Psychology* 39:106–24.

————. 1931. Again the James-Lange and the thalamic theories of emotion. *Psychological Review* 38:281–95.

Carey, S. 1985. *Conceptual Change in Childhood.* Cambridge: MIT Press.

Cavalli-Sforza, L. L., P. Menozzi, and A. Piazza. 1994. *The History and Geography of Human Genes.* Princeton, N. J.: Princeton University Press.

Chevalier-Skolnikoff, S. 1973. Facial expression of emotion in non-human primates. In Ekman 1973.

Churchland, P. M. 1979. *Scientific Realism and the Plasticity of Mind.* Cambridge: Cambridge University Press.

Clarke, S. G. 1986. Emotions: Rationality without cognitivism. *Dialogue* 25:663–74.

Clutton-Brock, T. H., and G. A. Harvey. 1995. Punishment in animal societies. *Nature* 373:209–16.

Coddington, J. A. 1988. Cladistic tests of adaptational hypotheses. *Cladistics* 4:3–22.

Connor, E. F., and D. Simberloff. 1979. The assembly of species communities: chance or competition? *Ecology* 60(6):1132–40.

Cosmides, L., and J. Tooby. 1992. Cognitive adaptations for social exchange. In Barkow, Cosmides, and Tooby 1992.

Craw, R. 1992. Margins of cladistics: Identity, space, and difference in the emergence of phylogenetic systematics 1864–1975. In Griffiths 1992.

Cummins, R. 1983. *The Nature of Psychological Explanation*. Cambridge: MIT Press.

Damasio, A. R. 1994. *Descartes' Error: Emotion, Reason, and the Human Brain*. New York: Grosset/Putnam.

Darwin, C. [1859] 1964, *On The Origin of Species: A Facsimile of the First Edition*. Cambridge: Harvard University Press.

———. [1872] 1965. *The Expression of the Emotions in Man and Animals*. Reprint, Chicago: University of Chicago Press.

Davis, W. C. 1981. Pleasure and happiness. *Philosophical Studies* 39:305–17.

———. 1988. A causal theory of experiential fear. *Canadian Journal of Philosophy* 18:459–83.

Dawes, R. M., and E. Kramer. 1966. A proximity analysis of vocally expressed emotions. *Perceptual and Motor Skills* 22:571–74.

Deigh, J. 1994. Cognitivism in the theory of emotions. *Ethics* 104:824–54.

Dennett, D. C. 1978. Why you can't make a computer that feels pain. In *Brainstorms*, ed. D. C. Dennett. Montgomery, Vt.: Bradford Books.

———. 1982. How to study human consciousness empirically. *Synthese* 53:159–80.

de Queiroz, K., and D. A. Goode. n.d. Phenetic clustering in biology: A critique. *Quarterly Review of Biology* (in press).

De Sousa, R. 1991. *The Rationality of Emotion*. Cambridge: MIT Press.

Devitt, M., and K. Sterelny. 1987. *Language and Reality*. Oxford: Blackwells.

DSM III R. 1987. *Diagnostic and Statistical Manual of Mental Disorders*. 3d ed. Revised. Washington, D.C.: American Psychological Association.

Dupré, J. 1981. Natural kinds and biological taxa. *Philosophical Review* 90:66–90.

———. 1993. *The Disorder of Things: Metaphysical Foundations of the Disunity of Science*. Cambridge: Harvard University Press.

Eibl-Eibesfeldt, I. 1973. Expressive behaviour of the deaf and blind born. In *Social Communication and Movement*, ed. M. von Cranach and I. Vine. New York: Academic Press.

Ekman, P. 1971. Universals and cultural differences in facial expressions of emotion. In *Nebraska Symposium on Motivation* 4, ed. J. K. Cole. Lincoln: University of Nebraska Press.

————. 1972. *Emotions in the Human Face.* New York: Pergamon Press.

————. 1980. *The Face of Man.* New York: Garland.

————. 1992. Are there basic emotions? *Psychological Review* 99(3):550–53.

————, ed. 1973. *Darwin and Facial Expression: A Century of Research in Review.* New York: Academic Press.

Ekman, P., and W. V. Friesen. 1971. Constants across cultures in the face and emotion. *Journal of Personality and Social Psychology* 17(2):124–29.

————. 1975. *Unmasking the Face: A Guide to Recognizing Emotions from Facial Expressions.* Englewood Cliffs, N. J.: Prentice Hall.

————. 1986. A new pan-cultural facial expression of emotion. *Motivation and Emotion* 10(2):159–68.

Ekman, P., W. V. Friesen, and R. C. Simons. 1985. Is the startle reaction an emotion? *Journal of Personality and Social Psychology* 49(5):1416–26.

Ekman, P., R. W. Levenson, and W. V. Friesen. 1983. Autonomic nervous system activity distinguishes among emotions. *Science* 221:1208–10.

Ekman, P., E. R. Sorensen, and W. V. Friesen. 1969. Pan-cultural elements in facial displays of emotion. *Science* 164:86–88.

Eldredge, N., and S. J. Gould. 1972. Punctuated equilibria: An alternative to phyletic gradualism. In *Models in Paleobiology,* ed. T. J. M. Schopf. San Francisco: Freeman, Cooper.

Ellstrand, N. 1980. Why are juveniles smaller than their parents? *Evolution* 13:1091–94.

Felsenstein, J. 1985. Phylogenies and the comparative method. *American Naturalist* 125:1–15.

Fine, A. 1984. The natural ontological attitude. In *The Shaky Game: Einstein, Realism, and the Quantum Theory,* ed. G. Leplin. Chicago: University of Chicago Press.

Fink, W. L. 1979. Optimal classifications. *Systematic Zoology* 28(3):371–74.

Flynn, J. P. 1967. The neural basis of aggression in cats. In *Neurophysiology and Emotion,* ed. C. Glass. New York: Rockefeller University Press.

————. 1969. Neural aspects of attack behavior in cats. *Annals of the New York Academy of Sciences* 159:1008–12.

Fodor, J. A. 1974. Special sciences. *Synthese* 28:77–115.

————. 1983. *The Modularity of Mind: An Essay in Faculty Psychology.* Cambridge: MIT Press.

Frank, R. H. 1988. *Passions within Reason: The Strategic Role of the Emotions.* New York: Norton.

Fulcher, J. S. 1942. "Voluntary" facial expressions in blind and seeing. *Archives of Psychology* 38(272).

Garcia, J., and K. W. Rusiniak. 1980. What the nose learns from the mouth. In *Symposium on Chemical Signals in Vertebrates and Aquatic Invertebrates,* ed. D. Muller-Schwarze and R. M. Silverstein. New York: Plenum Press.

Gazzaniga, M. S., and C. S. Smylie. 1984. What does language do for a right hemisphere? In *Handbook of Cognitive Neuroscience,* ed. M. S. Gazzaniga. New York: Plenum Press.

Ghiselin, M. T. 1973. Darwin and evolutionary psychology. *Science* 179: 964–68.

———. 1974. A radical solution to the species problem. *Systematic Zoology* 23:536–44.

Godfrey-Smith, P. 1991. Signal, decision, action. *Journal of Philosophy* 88:709–22.

Goldberg, S. 1973. *Male Dominance: The Inevitability of Patriarchy.* New York: Morrow.

Goode, R., and P. E. Griffiths. 1995. The misuse of Sober's selection of/ delection for distinction. *Biology and Philosophy* 10:99–108.

Goodman, N. 1972. Seven strictures on similarity. In *Problems and Projects,* ed. N. Goodman. Indianapolis: Bobbs-Merrill.

Goodwin, B. C. 1994. *How the Leopard Changed Its Spots: The Evolution of Complexity.* New York: Charles Scribner and Sons.

Goodwin, B. C., S. A. Kauffman, and J. D. Murray. 1993. Is morphogenesis an intrinsically robust process? *Journal of Theoretical Biology* 163: 135–44.

Goodwin, B. C., and P. Saunders. 1989. *Theoretical Biology: Epigenetic and Evolutionary Order from Complex Systems.* Edinburgh: Edinburgh University Press.

Goodwin, B. C., and G. Webster. n.d. *Form and Transformation: Generative and Relational Principles in Biology.* Forthcoming.

Gottlieb, G. 1981. Roles of early experience in species-specific perceptual development. In *Development of Perception,* ed. R. N. Aslin, J. R. Alberts, and M. P. Petersen. New York: Academic Press.

Gould, S. J. 1977. *Ontogeny and Phylogeny.* Cambridge: Harvard University Press.

———. 1978. Sociobiology: The art of storytelling. *New Scientist* 80:530–33.

———. 1985. *The Flamingo's Smile.* London: Penguin Books.

———. 1989. *Wonderful Life: The Burgess Shale and the Nature of History.* London: Century Hutchison.

———. 1994. Common pathways of illumination. *Natural History,* December, 10–20.

Gould, S. J., and R. Lewontin. 1979. The spandrels of San Marco and the Panglossian paradigm: A critique of the adaptationist programme. *Proceedings of the Royal Society of London* 205:581–98.

Gray, R. D. 1987. Faith and foraging: A critique of the "paradigm argument from design." In *Foraging Behaviour*, ed. A. C. Kamil, J. R. Krebs, and H. R. Pulliam. New York: Plenum Press.

———. 1992. Death of the gene: Developmental systems strike back. In Griffiths 1992.

Gray, R. D., and J. L. Craig. 1991. Theory really matters: Hidden assumptions in the concept of habitat requirements. *Acta XX Congressus Internationalis Ornithologici.* 20:2553–60.

Greenspan, P. 1988. *Emotions and Reasons*. New York: Routledge.

Griffiths, G. 1995. 'The myth of authenticity', in *The Post-Colonial Studies Reader,* ed. B. Ashcroft, G. Griffiths, and H. Tiffin. London: Routledge.

Griffiths, P. E. 1989. The degeneration of the cognitive theory of emotion. *Philosophical Psychology* 2(3):297–313.

———. 1990. Modularity and the psychoevolutionary theory of emotion. *Biology and Philosophy* 5:175–96.

———. 1992. Adaptive explanation and the concept of a vestige. In Griffiths, ed., 1992.

———. 1993. Functional analysis and proper function. *British Journal for Philosophy of Science* 44:409–22.

———. 1994. Cladistic classification and functional explanation. *Philosophy of Science* 61(2):206–27.

———. 1995. The Cronin controversy. *British Journal for the Philosophy of Science* 46:122–38.

———. 1996. Darwinism, process structuralism and natural kinds. *Philosophy of Science* 63(3) Supplement: PSA 1996, Part 1:1–9.

———. n.d. The historical turn in the study of adaptation. *British Journal for the Philosophy of Science.* Forthcoming.

Griffiths, P. E., ed. 1992. *Trees of Life: Essays in the Philosophy of Biology*. Dordrecht: Kluwer.

Griffiths, P. E., and R. D. Gray. 1994. Developmental systems and evolutionary explanation. *Journal of Philosophy* 91(6):277–304.

Guth, W., R. Schmittberger, and B. Schwarze. 1982. An experimental analysis of ultimatum bargaining. *Journal of Economic Behavior and Organization* 3:367–88.

Hacking, I. 1983. *Representing and Intervening*. Cambridge: Cambridge University Press.

———. 1991a. A tradition of natural kinds. *Philosophical Studies.* 61: 109–26.

———. 1991b. On Boyd. *Philosophical Studies* 61:149–54.

———. 1991c. The making and moulding of child abuse. *Critical Inquiry* 17:243–88.

———. 1995. *Rewriting the Soul: Multiple Personality and the Sciences of Memory*. Princeton, N. J.: Princeton University Press.

Hampton, J. 1993. Prototype models of concept representation. In Van Mechelen et al. 1993.

Harlow, H. F. 1961. The development of affectional patterns in infant monkeys. In *Determinants of Infant Behaviour*, ed. B. M. Foss. New York: Wiley.

———. 1963. The maternal affectional system. In *Determinants of Infant Behaviour II*, ed., B. M. Foss. New York: Wiley.

Harlow, H. F., R. O. Dodsworth, and M. K. Harlow. 1965. Total isolation in monkeys. *Proceedings of the National Academy of Sciences* 54:90–97.

Harlow, H. F., and M. K. Harlow. 1962. Social deprivation in monkeys. *Scientific American* 207(5):136–46.

———. 1969. Effects of various mother-infant relationships on rhesus monkey behaviours. In *Determinants of Infant Behaviour IV*, ed. B. M. Foss. New York: Wiley.

Harlow, H. F., M. K. Harlow, and E. W. Hansen. 1963. The maternal affectional system of rhesus monkeys. In *Maternal Behaviour in Mammals*, ed. H. L. Rheingold. New York: Wiley.

Harlow, H. F., and R. R. Zimmermann. 1959. Affectional responses in infant monkeys. *Science* 130:421–32.

Harré, R., ed. 1986. *The Social Construction of the Emotions*. London: Oxford University Press.

———. 1988. The social context of self-deception. In Rorty 1988.

Harré, R., and R. Finlay-Jones. 1986. Emotion talk across times. In Harré 1986.

Harvey, P. H., and M. D. Pagel. 1991. *The Comparative Method in Evolutionary Biology*. Oxford: Oxford University Press.

Heelas, P. 1984/1986. Emotions across cultures. In Harré 1986.

Hennig, W. 1966, *Phylogenetic Systematics*. Urbana: University of Illinois Press.

Hinde, R. A. 1966. Ritualisation and communication in rhesus monkeys. *Philosophical Transactions of the Royal Society* 251:285–94.

Hofer, M. A. 1972. Physiological and behavioural processes in early maternal deprivation. *Physiology, Emotion, and Psychosomatic Illnesses CIBA Symposium* 8:199–219.

Hull, D. L. 1976. Are species really individuals? *Systematic Zoology* 25:174–91.

———. 1978. A matter of individuality. *Philosophy of Science* 45:335–60.

References

———. 1984. Historical entities and historical narratives. In *Minds, Machines, and Evolution*, ed. C. Hookway. Cambridge: Cambridge University Press.

———. 1986. On Human Nature. *Proceedings of the Philosophy of Science Association* 2:3–13.

———. 1987. Genealogical actors in ecological roles. *Biology and Philosophy* 2:168–84.

———. 1988. *Science as a Process*. Chicago: University of Chicago Press.

Hunt, M. 1959. *The Natural History of Love*. New York: Alfred A. Knopf.

Immelmann, K. 1975. Ecological significance of imprinting and early learning. *Annual Review of Ecology and Systematics* 6:15–37.

Izard, C. E. 1969. The emotions and emotions constructs in personality and culture. In *Handbook of Modern Personality Theory*, ed. R. B. Cattell and R. M. Dreger, eds. Washington, D.C.: Hemisphere Publishing Corp.

———. 1971. *The Face of Emotion*. New York: Appleton, Century, Crofts.

———. 1978. On the development of emotions and emotion-cognition relationship in infancy. In *The Development of Affect*, ed. M. Lewis and L. Rosenblum. New York: Plenum Press.

———. 1980. Cross-cultural perspectives on emotion and emotion communication. In *Handbook of Cross-Cultural Psychology*, vol. 3, ed. H. Triandis and W. Lonner. Boston: Allyn and Bacon.

———. 1992. Basic emotions, relations amongst emotions, and emotion-cognition relations. *Psychological Review* 99(3):561–65.

Izard, C. E., and O. M. Haynes. 1988. On the form and universality of the contempt expression: a challenge to Ekman and Friesen's claim of discovery. *Motivation and Emotion* 12(1):1–16.

Jablonka, E., and M. J. Lamb. 1995. *Epigenetic Inheritance and Evolution: The Lamarckian Dimension*. New York: Oxford University Press.

Jablonka, E., and E. Szathmáry. 1995. The evolution of information storage and heredity. *TREE* 10(5): 206–11.

James, W. 1884. What is an emotion? *Mind* 9:188–205.

———. 1893. *The Principles of Psychology*. New York: Holt.

Jeyifous, S. 1986. *Atimodemo: Semantic conceptual development amongst the Yoruba*, Ph.D. diss., Cornell University.

Johnston, T. D. 1987. The persistence of dichotomies in the study of behavioural development. *Developmental Review* 7:149–82.

Kahnemann, D., J. Knetsch, and R. Thaler. 1986. Fairness and the assumptions of economics. *Journal of Business* 59:S285–S300.

Kauffman, S. A. 1993. *The Origins of Order: Self-Organisation and Selection in Evolution*. New York: Oxford University Press.

Keil, F. C. 1981. Natural categories and natural concepts. *Behavioural and Brain Sciences* 4:293–94.

———. 1989. *Concepts, Kinds and Cognitive Development.* Cambridge: MIT Press.

Keil, F. C., and N. Batterman. 1984. A characteristic-to-defining shift in the development of word meaning. *Journal of Verbal Learning and Verbal Behavior* 23:221–36.

Keller, L., and K. G. Ross. 1993. Phenotypic plasticity and "cultural transmission" in the fire ant *Solenopsis invicta. Behavioral Ecology and Sociobiology* 33:121–29.

Kelly, M., and F. C. Keil. 1987. Conceptual domains and the comprehension of metaphor. *Metaphor and Symbolic Activity* 2:33–51.

Kenny, A. 1963. *Action, Emotion, and Will.* London: Routledge and Kegan Paul.

Kingsland, S. 1985. *Modeling Nature.* Chicago: University of Chicago Press.

Kitcher, P. 1985. *Vaulting Ambition.* Cambridge: MIT Press.

———. 1993. *The Advancement of Science.* Oxford: Oxford University Press.

Kitts, D. B., and D. J. Kitts. 1979. Biological species as natural kinds. *Philosophy of Science* 46:613–22.

Klinnert, M. D., J. J. Campos, J. F. Sorce, R. N. Emde, and M. Svejda. 1983. Emotions as behavior regulators. In Plutchik and Kellerman 1980.

Konner, M. 1982. *The Tangled Wing: Biological Constraints on the Human Spirit.* London: William Heinemann.

Kripke, S. 1980, *Naming and Necessity.* Cambridge: Harvard University Press.

Kroon, F. W. 1985. Theoretical terms and the causal view of reference. *Australasian Journal of Philosophy* 63(2):143–66.

Kuhn, T. 1970. The *Structure of Scientific Revolutions.* Chicago: University of Chicago Press.

Kunst-Wilson, W. R., and R. B. Zajonc. 1980. Affective discrimination of stimuli that cannot be recognised. *Science* 207:557–58.

La Barre, W. 1947. The cultural basis of emotions and gestures. *Journal of Personality* 16:49–68.

Lauder, G. V. 1981. Form and function: Structural analysis in evolutionary morphology. *Paleobiology* 7(4):430–42.

———. 1982. Historical biology and the problem of design. *Journal of Theoretical Biology* 97:57–67.

———. 1990. Functional morphology: Studying functional patterns in an historical context. *Annual Review of Ecology and Systematics* 21: 317–40.

References

Lauder, G. V., M. L. Armand, and M. R. Rose. 1993. Adaptations and history. *TREE* 8(8):294–97.

Lazarus, R. S. 1982. Thoughts on the relations between emotion and cognition. *American Psychologist* 37:1019–24.

Lazarus, R. S., J. C. Coyne, and S. Folkman. 1984. Cognition, emotion, and motivation: Doctoring Humpty Dumpty. In Scherer and Ekman 1984.

Lazarus, R. S., E. Opton Jr., M. Tomita, and M. Kodama. 1966. A cross-cultural study of stress-reaction patterns in Japan. *Journal of Personality and Social Psychology* 4(6):622–33.

Lehrman, D. S. 1953. Critique of Konrad Lorenz's theory of instinctive behaviour. *Quarterly Review of Biology* 28(4):337–63.

———. 1970. Semantic and conceptual issues in the nature-nurture problem, in *Development and Evolution of Behaviour*, D. S. Lehrman (ed.), W. H. Freeman and co., San Francisco S., pp. 17–52.

Lenton, G. 1983. Wise owls flourish among the oil palms. *New Scientist* (17 February):436–37.

Lettvin, J. Y., H. R. Maturana, W. S. McCulloch, and W. H. Pitts. 1959. What the frog's eye tells the frog's brain. *Proceedings of Institute of Radio Engineers* 11:230–55.

Levenson, R. W., P. Ekman, and W. V. Friesen. 1990. Voluntary facial expression generates emotion-specific nervous system activity. *Psychophysiology* 27:363–84.

Leventhal, H. 1984. A perceptual motor theory of emotion. In Scherer and Ekman 1984.

Levins, R., and R. Lewontin. 1980. Dialectics and reductionism in ecology. *Synthese* 43:47–78.

Lewis, D. K. 1980. Psychophysical and theoretical identifications. In *Readings in the Philosophy of Psychology*, ed. N. Block. London: Methuen.

Lewontin, R. C. 1972. The apportionment of human diversity. In *Evolutionary Biology*, vol. 6, ed. T. Dobzhansky, M. K. Hecht, and W. C. Steere. New York: Appleton, Century, Crofts.

———. 1974. The analysis of variance and the analysis of causes. *American Journal of Human Genetics* 26:400–11.

———. 1978. Adaptation. *Scientific American* 239:212–30.

Lloyd, E. A. 1988, *The Structure and Confirmation of Evolutionary Theory*. Westport, Conn.: Greenwood Press.

Logue, A. W., I. Ophir, and K. E. Strauss. 1986. Acquisition of taste aversions in humans. *Behavioural Research and Therapy* 19:319–33.

Lorenz, K. 1965. Preface to *The Expression of the Emotions in Man and Animals*, by Charles Darwin. Chicago: University of Chicago Press.

———. 1966. Evolution of ritualisation in the biological and cultural spheres. *Philosophical Transactions of the Royal Society of London* 251:273–84.

Lormand, E. 1985. Towards a theory of moods. *Philosophical Studies* 47: 385–407.

Lovejoy, A. O. 1936. *The Great Chain of Being.* Cambridge: Harvard University Press.

Lutz, C. 1986. The domains of emotion words on Ifaluk. In Harré 1986.

Lycan, W. G. 1987. *Consciousness.* Cambridge: MIT Press.

———. 1990. The continuity of levels of nature. In *Mind and Cognition,* ed. W. G. Lycan. Oxford: Blackwells.

Lyell, C. [1830–33] 1990. *Principles of Geology, Being an Attempt to Explain the Former Changes in the Earth's Surface by Reference to Causes Now in Operation,* vol. 1–3. Reprint, Chicago: University of Chicago Press.

Lyons, W. 1980. *Emotion.* Cambridge: Cambridge University Press.

MacLean, P. D. 1980. Sensory and perceptive factors in emotional functions in the triune brain. In Rorty 1980.

Maranon, G., 1924. Contribution a l'étude de l'action émotive de l'adrenalin . . . *Revue française endocrinal* 2:301–5.

Markman, E. M. 1992. Constraints on word learning: Speculations about their nature, origins, and domain specificity. In *Modularity and Constraints in Language and Cognition,* ed. M. R. Gunnar and M. Maratsos. Hillsdale, N. J.: Erlbaum.

Marks, J. 1982. A theory of emotions. *Philosophical Studies* 42:227–42.

———. 1984. *Ways of Desire: New Essays in Philosophical Psychology on the Concept of Wanting.* Chicago: Precedent Publishing.

Marr, D. 1982. *Vision.* New York: W. H. Freeman.

Mason, W. A., 1960. The effects of social restriction on the behaviour of rhesus monkeys: I. Free social behaviour. *Journal of Comparative and Physiological Psychology* 53:582–89.

———. 1961. The effects of social restriction on the behaviour of rhesus monkeys: II. Tests of gregariousness. *Journal of Comparative and Physiological Psychology* 54:287–90.

———. 1963. Social development of rhesus monkeys with restricted social experience. *Perception and Motor Skills* 16:263–70.

———. 1965. The social development of monkeys and apes. In *Primate Behaviour,* ed. I. DeVore. New York: Holt.

Mathews, C., ed. 1989. *New Zealand Journal of Zoology. Panbiogeography Special Issue.*

Maynard Smith, J. 1982. *Evolution and the Theory of Games.* Cambridge: Cambridge University Press.

———. 1990. The evolution of prokaryotes: Does sex matter? *Annual Review of Ecology and Systematics* 21:1–12.

McKitrick, M. 1993. Phylogenetic constraint in evolutionary theory: Has it any explanatory power? *Annual Review of Ecology and Systematics* 24:307–30.

References

McNaughton, N. 1989. *Biology and Emotion*. Cambridge: Cambridge University Press.

Medin, D. L. 1989. Concepts and conceptual structure. *American Psychologist* 44(12):1469–81.

Mellor, D. H. 1977. Natural kinds. *British Journal of Philosophy and Science* 28:299–312.

Meltzoff, A. N., and M. K. Moore. 1977. Imitation of facial and manual gestures by neonates. *Science* 198:75–78.

Melzack, R. 1973. *The Puzzle of Pain*. Harmondsworth: Penguin.

Mendels, J., ed. 1975. *The Psychobiology of Depression*. New York: Spectrum.

Miles, D. B., and A. E. Dunham. 1993. Historical perspectives in ecology and evolutionary biology: The use of phylogenetic comparative methods. *Annual Review of Ecology and Systematics* 24:587–619.

Miller, R. E., W. F. Caul, and I. A. Mirsky. 1967. The communication of affects between feral and socially isolated monkeys. *Journal of Personality and Social Psychology* 7:231–39.

Millikan, R. G. 1984. *Language, Thought, and Other Biological Categories*. Cambridge: MIT Press.

———. 1986. Thoughts without laws, cognitive science with content. *Philosophical Review* 95:47–80.

Mills, S., and J. Beatty. 1979. The propensity interpretation of fitness. *Philosophy of Science* 46:263–86.

Mishler, B. D., and R. N. Brandon. 1987. Individuality, pluralism, and the phylogenetic species concept. *Biology and Philosophy* 2:397–414.

Mishler, B. D., and M. J. Donaghue. 1982. Species concepts: A case for pluralism. *Systematic Zoology* 31:491–503

Morgan, E. 1973. *The Descent of Woman*. New York: Bantam Books.

———. 1982. *The Aquatic Ape*. London: Souvenir Press.

Morsbach, H., and W. J. Tyler. 1986. A Japanese emotion: *amae*. In Harré 1986.

Morton, A. 1980. *Frames of Mind*. Oxford: Clarendon Press.

Moss, L. 1992. A kernel of truth? On the reality of the genetic program. *Philosophy of Science Association Proceedings 1992* 1:335–48.

Murphy, G. L. 1993. A rational theory of concepts. *Psychology of Learning and Motivation* 29:327–59.

Nash, R. A. 1989. Cognitive theories of emotion. *Nous* 23:481–504.

Neander, K. 1991a. Functions as selected effects: The conceptual analyst's defense. *Philosophy of Science* 58:168–84.

———. 1991b. The teleological notion of "function." *Australasian Journal of Philosophy* 69(4):454–68.

Nelson, G. 1979. Cladistic analysis and synthesis: Principles and definitions, with a historical note on Adanson's *Familles des Plantes* (1763–1764). *Systematic Zoology* 28:1–21.

Nelson, G. J., and N. I. Platnick. 1981. *Systematics and Biogeography: Cladistics and Vicariance.* New York: Columbia University Press.

Nesse, R. M., and A. T. Lloyd. 1992. The evolution of psychodynamic mechanisms. In Barkow, Cosmides, and Tooby 1992.

Newman, P. L. 1964. "Wild man" behavior in a New Guinea Highlands community. *American Anthropologist* 66:1–19.

Newton-Smith, W. 1973. A conceptual investigation of love. In *Philosophy and Personal Relations,* ed. H. Montefiore. London: Routledge and Kegan Paul.

Nisbett, R. E., and T. Wilson. 1977. On saying more than we can know: Verbal reports on mental processes. *Psychological Review* 84:231–59.

Nowlis, V. 1963. The concept of mood. In *Conflict and Creativity,* ed. S. M. Farber and R. H. L. Wilson. New York: McGraw-Hill.

O'Hara, R. J. 1988. Homage to Clio, or towards an historical philosophy for evolutionary biology. *Systematic Zoology* 37(2):142–55.

Ohman, A., M. Fredrikson, and K. Hugdahl. 1976. Premiss of equipotentiality in human classical conditioning. *Journal of Experimental Psychology* 105:313–37.

Oppenheim, P., and H. Putnam. 1958. The unity of science as a working hypothesis. In *Minnesota Studies in the Philosophy of Science,* vol. 2, ed. G. Feigl, M. Scriven, and G. Maxwell. Minneapolis: University of Minnesota Press.

Orians, G. H., and J. H. Heerwagen. 1992. Evolved responses to landscape. In Barkow, Cosmides, and Tooby 1992.

Ortony, A., and T. J. Turner. 1990. What's basic about basic emotions? *Psychological Review* 97(3):315–31.

Orzack, S. H., and E. Sober. 1994. Optimality models and the test of adaptationism. *American Naturalist* 143:361–80.

Oyama, S. 1985, *The Ontogeny of Information.* Cambridge: Cambridge University Press.

Panksepp, J. 1982. Towards a general psychobiological theory of emotion. *Behavioural and Brain Sciences* 5:407–67.

Papez, J. W. 1937. A proposed mechanism of emotion. *Archives of Neurology and Psychiatry* 38:725–43.

Patterson, C. 1977. The contribution of paleontology to telostean phylogeny. In *Major Patterns in Vertebrate Evolution,* ed. M. K. Hecht, P. C. Goody, and B. M. Hecht. New York: Plenum Press; London: NATO Scientific Affairs Division.

Penny, D., E. E. Watson, and M. A. Steel. 1993. Trees from languages and genes are very similar. *Systematic Zoology* 42:382–85.

Peters, R. S. 1962. Emotions and the category of passivity. *Proceedings of the Aristotelian Society* 62:117–42.

Pinker, S., and P. Bloom. 1992. Natural language and natural selection. In Barkow, Cosmides, and Tooby 1992.

Plutchik, R. 1962. *The Emotions: Facts, Theories, and a New Model.* New York: Random House.

———. 1970. Emotions, evolution, and adaptative processes. In *Feelings and Emotions,* ed. M. Arnold. New York: Academic Press.

———. 1980a. A general psychoevolutionary theory of emotion. In Plutchik and Kellerman 1980.

———. 1980b. *Emotion: A Psychoevolutionary Synthesis.* New York: Harper and Row.

———. 1984. Emotions: A general psychoevolutionary theory. In Scherer and Ekman 1984.

Plutchik, R., and A. F. Ax. 1967. A critique of "Determinants of emotional state" by Schachter and Singer. *Psychophysiology* 4(1):79–82.

Plutchik, R., and H. Kellerman, eds. 1980. *Emotion: Theory, Research and Experience,* vol. 1: *Theories of Emotion.* New York: Academic Press.

———. 1983. *Emotion: Theory, Research and Experience,* vol. 2: *Emotions in Early Development.* New York: Academic Press.

Putnam, H. 1967. Psychological predicates. In *Art, Mind, and Religion,* ed. W. H. Capitan and D. D. Merrill. Pittsburgh: University of Pittsburgh Press.

———. 1975. The meaning of "meaning." In *Mind, Language and Real-ity,* Philosophical Papers, vol. 2. Cambridge: Cambridge University Press.

———. 1994. The Dewey lectures: Sense, nonsense, and the senses: An inquiry into the power of the human mind. *Journal of Philosophy* 91(9):445–517.

Quine, W. V. 1977. Natural kinds. In *Naming, Necessity, and Natural Kinds,* ed. P. Schwartz. Ithaca, N.Y.: Cornell University Press.

Quiring, R., U. Walldorf, U. Kloter, and W. J. Gehring. 1994. Homology of the eyeless gene of drosophila to the small eye gene in mice and aniridia in humans. *Science* 265(August):785–89.

Ratner, C. 1989. A social constructionist critique of the naturalistic theory of emotion. *Journal of Mind and Behaviour* 10(3):211–30.

Rey, G. 1988. Towards a computational account of akrasia and self-deception. In Rorty 1988.

Richards, R. J. 1987. *Darwin and the Emergence of Evolutionary Theories of Mind and Behavior.* Chicago: University of Chicago Press.

Ridley, M. 1989. The cladistic solution to the species problem. *Biology and Philosophy* 4:1–16.

Robinson, J. 1983. Emotion, judgement, and desire. *Journal of Philosophy* 11:731–40.

Rorty, A. O., ed. 1980. *Explaining Emotions.* Berkeley: University of California Press.

————. 1988. *Perspectives on Self-Deception.* Berkeley: University of California Press.

Rosch, E. 1975. Cognitive representations of semantic categories. *Journal of Experimental Psychology: General* 104:192–233.

————. 1978. Principles of categorisation. In *Cognition and Categorisation,* ed. E. H. Rosch and B. B. Lloyd. Hillsdale, N. J.: Erlbaum.

Rosch, E., and C. B. Mervis. 1975. Family resemblances: Studies in the internal structure of categories. *Cognitive Psychology* 7:573–605.

Rosen, D. E. 1978. Vicariant patterns and historical explanations in biogeography. *Systematic Zoology* 27:159–88.

————. 1979. Fishes from the uplands and intermontane basin of Guatemala: Revisionary studies and comparative geography. *Bulletin of the American Museum of Natural History* 162:267–376.

————. 1982. Telostean interrelationships, morphological function and evolutionary inference. *American Zoologist* 22:261–73.

Rosenberg, A. 1978. The supervenience of biological concepts. *Philosophy of Science* 45:368–86.

————. 1982. On the propensity definition of fitness. *Philosophy of Science* 49:268–73.

————. 1983. Fitness. *Journal of Philosophy* 80:457–73.

Rosenberg, A., and M. B. Williams. 1985. Fitness in fact and fiction: A rejoinder to Sober. *Journal of Philosophy* 82:738–49.

Rozin, P. 1976. The evolution of intelligence and access to the cognitive unconscious. In *Progress in Psychobiology and Physiological Psychology,* vol. 6, ed. J. M. Sprague and A. N. Epstein. New York: Academic Press.

Rozin, P., and J. W. Kalat. 1971. Specific hungers and poison avoidance as adaptive specialisations of learning. *Psychological Review* 78:459–86.

Russell, J. A. 1991. Negative results on a reported facial expression of contempt. *Motivations and Emotion* 15(4):281–91.

Russell, J. A., and B. Fehr. 1987. Relativity in the perception of emotion in facial expressions. *Journal of Experimental Psychology (General)* 116:223–37.

Sachar, E. J. 1975. Neuroendocrine strategy in psychobiologic study. In Mendels 1975.

Sartre, J. P. 1962. *Sketch for a Theory of the Emotions.* New York: Methuen.

Schachter, J. 1957. Pain, fear, and anger in hypertensives and normotensives. *Psychosomatic Medicine* 19(1):17–29.

Schachter, S., and J. E. Singer. 1962. Cognitive, social, and physiological determinants of emotional state. *Psychological Review* 69:379–99.

References

Schaffer, J. A. 1983. An assessment of emotion. *American Philosophical Quarterly* 20:161–73.

Scherer, K. R., R. Banse, H. G. Wallbott, and T. Goldbeck. 1991. Vocal cues in emotion encoding and decoding. *Motivation and Emotion* 15(2):123–48.

Scherer, K. R., and P. Ekman, eds. 1984. *Approaches to Emotion*. Hillsdale, N. J.: Erlbaum.

Scherer, K. R., J. Koivumaki, and R. Rosenthal. 1972. Minimal cues in the vocal communication of affect: Judging emotion from content masked speech. *Journal of Psycholinguistic Research* 1:269–85.

Schildkraut, J. J. 1965. Catecholamine hypothesis of affective disorders: A review of supporting evidence. *American Journal of Psychiatry* 122: 509–22.

————. 1970. *Neuropsychopharmacology and the Affective Disorders*. Boston: Little, Brown, and Co.

————. 1974. Effects of lithium on norepinephrine turnover and metabolism: Basis and clinical studies. *Journal of Nervous and Mental Disease*, 158:348–60.

Schwartz, G. E., D. A. Weinberger, and J. A. Singer. 1981. Cardiovascular differentiation of happiness, anger, sadness, and fear following imagery and exercise. *Psychosomatic Medicine* 43(4):343–64.

Seligman, M. E. P. 1970. On the generality of the laws of learning. *Psychological Review* 77:406–18.

————. 1971. Phobias and preparedness. *Behaviour Therapy* 2(3):307–20.

Shepard, R. N. 1992. The perception of colours: An adaptation to regularities of the terrestrial world? In Barkow, Cosmides, and Tooby 1992.

Shettleworth, S. 1971. Constraints on learning. In *Advances in the Study of Behaviour*, ed. D. S. Lehrman, R. A. Hinde and E. Shaw. New York: Academic Press.

Simberloff, D. 1980a. A succession of paradigms in ecology: Essentialism to materialism and probablism. *Synthese* 43:3–39.

————. 1980b. Reply. *Synthese* 43:79–93.

————. 1983. Competition theory, hypothesis testing, and other community ecological buzzwords. *American Naturalist* 122:626–35.

Simberloff, D., and E. F. Connor. 1981. Missing species combinations. *American Naturalist* 118(2):215–39.

Smith, K. C. 1992. Neo-rationalism versus neo-Darwinism: Integrating development and evolution. *Biology and Philosophy* 7:431–52.

Sober, E. 1984a. *The Nature of Selection*. Cambridge: MIT Press.

————. 1984b. Fact, fiction and fitness: A reply to Rosenberg. *Journal of Philosophy* 81:372–83.

————. 1987. What is adaptationism? In *The Latest on the Best,* ed. J. Dupre. Cambridge: MIT Press.

————. 1988a. The conceptual relationship of cladistic phylogenetics and vicariance biogeography. *Systematic Zoology* 37(3):245–53.

————. 1988b. *Reconstructing the Past: Parsimony, Evolution, and Inference.* Cambridge: MIT Press.

Solomon, R. 1977. *The Passions.* New York: Anchor.

————. 1984. Getting angry: The Jamesian theory of emotion in anthropology. In *Culture Theory: Essays on Mind, Self, and Emotion,* ed. R. A. Schweder and R. A. LeVine. Cambridge: Cambridge University Press.

Sterelny, K. 1990. *The Representational Theory of Mind: An Introduction.* Oxford: Blackwells.

————. 1992. Evolutionary explanations of human behaviour. *Australasian Journal of Philosophy* 70(2):156–72.

Stich, S. 1983. *From Folk Psychology to Cognitive Science.* Cambridge: MIT Press.

Stocker, M. 1983. Psychic feelings, their importance and irreducibility. *American Journal of Philosophy* 61:5–26.

————. 1987. Emotional thoughts. *American Philosophical Quarterly* 24(1):59–69 .

Sutcliffe, J. P. 1993. Concept, class, and category in the tradition of Aristotle. In Van Mechelen et al. 1993.

Symons, D. 1992. On the use and misuse of Darwinism in the study of human behavior. In Barkow, Cosmides, and Tooby 1992.

Taylor, C. C. W. 1984. Emotions and wants. In *Ways of Desire,* ed. J. Marks. Chicago: Precedent Publishing.

Taylor, P. J. 1987. Historical versus selectionist explanations in evolutionary biology. *Cladistics* 3:1–13.

Thompson, J. 1941. Development of facial expressions of emotion. *Archives of Psychology* 37(264):1–47.

Tinbergen, N. 1952. Derived activities: Their causation, biological significance, origin, and emancipation during evolution. *Quarterly Review of Biology* 27:1–32.

————. 1964. The evolution of signaling devices. In *Social Behavior and Organization among Vertebrates,* ed. W. Etkin. Chicago: University of Chicago Press.

Tomkins, S. S. 1962, *Affect, Imagery, and Consciousness.* New York: Springer.

————. 1980. Affect as amplification: Some modifications in theory. In Plutchik and Kellerman 1980.

Tooby, J., and L. Cosmides. 1990a. On the universality of human nature

References

and the uniqueness of the individual: The role of genetics and adaptation. *Journal of Personality* 58(1):17–67.

———. 1990b. The past explains the present: Emotional adaptations and the structure of ancestral environments. *Ethology and Sociobiology* 11:375–424.

———. 1992. The Psychological Foundations of Culture. In Barkow, Cosmides, and Tooby 1992.

Trevarthen, C. 1984. Emotions in infancy: Regulators of contact and relationship with persons. In Scherer and Ekman 1984.

Trivers, R. L. 1971. The evolution of reciprocal altruism. *Quarterly Review of Biology* 46(4):35–57.

———. 1974. Parent-offspring conflict. *American Zoologist* 14:249–64.

van der Weele, C. 1995. *Images of Development: Environmental Causes in Ontogeny.* Ph.D. diss., Vrije Universiteit te Amsterdam, Amsterdam.

Van Mechelen, I., J. Hampton, R. S. Michalski, and P. Theuns, eds. 1993. *Categories and Concepts.* London: Academic Press.

Waddington, C. H. 1959. Canalisation of development and the inheritance of acquired characteristics. *Nature* 183:1654–55.

Warner, C. T. 1986. Anger and similar delusions. In Harré 1986.

Watson, J. B. 1930. *Behaviorism,* rev. ed. New York: W. W. Norton.

Weinrich, J. D. 1977. Human sociobiology: Pair bonding and resource predictability. *Behavioural Ecology and Sociobiology* 2:91–118.

———. 1980. Towards a sociobiological theory of emotions. In Plutchik and Kellerman 1980.

Williams, G. C. 1992. *Natural Selection: Domains, Levels, and Challenges.* New York: Oxford University Press.

Wilson, E. O. 1992. *The Diversity of Life.* Cambridge: Harvard University Press.

Wilson, W. R. 1975. Unobtrusive induction of positive attitudes. Ph.D. diss., University of Michigan.

———. 1979. Feeling more than we can know: Exposure effects without learning. *Journal of Personality and Social Psychology* 37:811–21.

Wouters, A. 1995. Viability explanation. *Biology and Philosophy* 10(4):435–57.

Zajonc, R. B. 1980. Feeling and thinking: Preferences need no inferences. *American Psychologist* 35:151–75.

———. 1984a. On the primacy of affect. In Scherer and Ekman 1984.

———. 1984b. The interaction of affect and cognition. In Scherer and Ekman 1984.

Index

accidie, 161
acetylcholine, 255
adaptation (evolutionary psychology), defined, 107
adaptationism, 71–74, 76, 107–112, 115
adaptive-historical approach: in evolutionary psychology, 45, 71–72, 76, 112–115; in proposed scientific psychology of emotion, 236, 238–240
adaptiveness (evolutionary psychology), defined, 107
affective primacy, 27
affect program, defined, 77
affect program theory, 3, 15, 77–99; and adaptive-historical approach, 239; on control mechanisms, 88–91; criticism of, 78–79; defined and described, 8, 13, 77–78; versus dialectical interaction model, 86–87; and ecological approach, 232, 235; evidence for, 79–84, 87–88; evolutionary psychology on, 116–117; and higher cognitive emotions, 91–97, 100–103, 104, 120–122; literal neural programs in, 84–88, 96, 255; modular systems in, 91–98; and mood, 255, 256; in proposed scientific psychology of emotion, 16, 17, 97–99, 228–231, 235, 239–242, 246–247; and propositional attitude theory, 98, 243; versus separate systems view, 84–86; on species other than humans, 58–59, 232–233; and vernacular emotion concepts, 228–231, 235, 240, 241–242, 245
Africans, facial expression of emotion among, 50
Agassiz, Louis, 196
amae, 101, 137, 138
amok, 141

Amundson, R., 219
amygdala, 96
anagenesis (anagetic speciation), 208
analogy, classification by, 12, 13. *See also* functional classification
anatomical level, 219, 221, 224
anger: as affect program, 81, 97, 100–101, 230, 231; autonomic nervous system response, 81; disclaimed action anger, 233–234; ecological approach on, 231, 232; ethological theory on, 49; evolutionary psychology on, 44, 49, 52, 65, 70; facial expression, 49, 52, 54, 65; Frank's commitment model on, 118; in hierarchy of dispositions, 250; higher cognitive processes in, 100–101; musculoskeletal expression, 49, 156; proposed scientific psychology of emotion on, 17; propositional attitude theory on, 23, 27; social construction of, 139, 140, 148, 152; and vengefulness, 121–122; vernacular concept of, 231
antithesis, principle of, 66–67, 69
anxiety, propositional attitude theory on, 28, 34
appetitive emotions, 31
arbitrariness, of emotional expressions, 58–59
Aristotle, 1–2, 23, 203, 244
Armand, M. L., 72n, 111n
Armon-Jones, Claire, 3, 8, 56, 137, 138, 161–167
Armstrong, David M., 151
Armstrong, S., 176n
artifact kinds, 189–190, 226–227
Atran, Scott, 186, 192
automatic appraisal mechanism (AAM), 92–93

Pure (New) Cognitive Theory (Nash), 23, 37–38
Putnam, Hilary, 4, 172, 174, 213, 220

Quine, W. V., 5, 180, 185
Quiring, R., 236n

racism, 125
rage, 48, 49, 87
"Rambo" behavior syndrome, 141, 155
rational decision theory, versus Frank's commitment model, 117–118
Ratner, Carl: on affect program research, 78; on innateness, 62, 164; on social construction of emotion, 103, 133, 139, 161, 164, 165, 167
realism, and natural kinds, 6, 173–175, 188
reflex emotions: affect program theory on, 92, 94, 98; propositional attitude theory on, 28, 30, 98
reinforcement, in social role model, 142–143, 155–157, 158
resentment, 70
response-dependent properties, 41
Rey, Georges, 153
Richards, R. J., 44
Ridley, M., 208
ritualization (ethology), 45, 66, 68
Robinson, J., 30
Rosch, Eleanor, 176
Rose, M. R., 72n, 111n
Rosen, D. E., 71
Rosenberg, A., 217n
Ross, K. G., 60, 131
Rozin, P., 89, 94
Rusiniak, K. W., 26, 89, 115, 234
Russell, J. A., 67, 78

Sachar, E. J., 255
sadness/grief: as affect program, 97, 230, 231; autonomic nervous system response, 81; evolutionary psychology on, 49–50, 51, 52; facial expression, 49–50, 51, 52, 54
Sartre, Jean-Paul, 28, 150–152, 154
Saunders, P., 204n
Schachter, Joseph, 81, 83
Schachter, Stanley, 24–25, 81–83
Schaffer, J. A., 242
Scherer, K. R., 84
Schildkraut, J. J., 254
Schmittberger, R., 118

Schwartz, G. E., 81
Schwarze, B., 118
secondary adaptation (exadaptation), 65–66, 69. *See also* ritualization
secondary emotions, 102–104
self-deceit, 150–154, 158
Seligman, M. E. P., 88
semantic view of theories, 237n
separate systems view, 84–86
separation reaction, 85
serotonin, 255
serviceable associated habits, principle of, 64–66, 69
shame, 118
Shepard, R. N., 223
signal detection theory, 218
Simberloff, D., 237n
similarity, of concepts, 177–178, 179–180, 185–186
Simons, R. C., 241
sincerity of emotion, 149–155, 158
Singer, Jefferson A., 81
Singer, Jerome E., 24–25, 81–83
Smiley, C. S., 83
Smith, K. C., 204n
Smith, Maynard, 217
Sober, E., 90, 200, 209, 210, 217, 217n, 218
social constructionism, 3, 8, 10–11, 15, 137–167; and causal homeostasis, 196–201; Damasio's secondary emotions compared to, 103; defined, 137–143, 149; and developmental theory, 135–136, 165; and evolutionary psychology, 159–160, 161–162, 164–165; future research recommendations, 157; and heterogeneous construction, 10, 15, 132–133, 156–158, 159, 165; on higher cognitive emotions, 11, 132–133, 157; limits of, 10, 159–167; and proposed scientific psychology of emotion, 17, 245–246; and propositional attitude theory, 27–28, 42–43, 138, 149, 163–164, 166; social concept model, 138–139, 143–149; substantial construction, 145–147, 197–198; three kinds of construction, 145–148; trivial construction, 145, 146, 198. *See also* social role model
social determinism, 132–133
social psychology, 57
social role, defined, 143